REGINALD "DUTCH" THOMPSON

BYGONE DAYS

Folklore, Traditions & Toenails

T0007086

The Acorn Press

Charlottetown

2019

Text © Reginald Thompson 2019

All rights reserved. No part of this publication may be reproduced, stored in a retrieval system, or transmitted, in any form or by any means, without the prior written permission of the publisher or, in case of photocopying or other reprographic copying, a licence from the Canadian Copyright Licensing Agency.

P.O. Box 22024
Charlottetown, Prince Edward Island
C1A 9J2
acornpresscanada.com

Edited by Lee Ellen Pottie
Designed by Matt Reid
Printed in Canada

Library and Archives Canada Cataloguing in Publication

Title: Bygone days : folklore, traditions
and toenails / Reginald Thompson.

Names: Thompson, Reginald, author.

Identifiers: Canadiana (print) 20190158034 | Canadiana (ebook)
20190158042 | ISBN 9781773660370

(softcover) | ISBN 9781773660387 (HTML)

Subjects: LCSH: Prince Edward Island—Anecdotes. | LCSH:
Prince Edward Island—History—Anecdotes.

Classification: LCC FC2611.8 .T46 2019 | DDC 971.7—dc23

 Canada Council Conseil des Arts
for the Arts du Canada

The publisher acknowledges the support of the
Government of Canada through the Canada Book Fund of the
Department of Canadian Heritage for our publishing activities.
We also acknowledge the support of the Canada Council
for the Arts for our publishing program.

Dedicated to the women of my life:

My mum Mercie Thompson and her mum Annie Hilda Cunningham from whom I inherited a memory almost as sharp as theirs and my red-headed firecracker wife Jill Birtwistle, my precious sounding-board and partner, miraculously still hanging in even after 44 years of tumultuous me.

Acknowledgements and Thanks

To the hundreds of people from the isolated Orkney Islands to the lonely East Point lighthouse who trusted me with their memories. Never a day goes by when I don't think of their courage and kindness for opening up their souls to me.

Terrilee Bulger, Jill Birtwistle, and my daughter Sara Thompson for believing I had a book in me.

Lee Ellen Pottie, my favorite editor.

Sheryl Mackay, Karen Mair, Matt Rainnie, Angela Walker, and Eva O'Hanley at CBC radio for providing an outlet for the many stories collected over the years.

John MacFarlane, Maisie Lamont Adams, Reverend Bryer Jones, Donald and Lloyd MacLeod, Roy Clow, Kathryn MacQuarrie Wood, and Captain Thomas Trenholm for pointing me in the right direction.

Jumpin Jack Proud who inspired us all by writing a book in his 90s.

Boyde Beck, Dr. Ed MacDonald, and the folks at the PEI Museum and Heritage Foundation for their kind words and awards.

The "History Gang" for following me across and around the island on our story-telling tours.

Contents

For Reg 'Dutch' Thompson – A Poem

The interviewer, Reg 'Dutch' Thomson,
is always respectful of his sources,
putting his subjects to the forefront,
asking the right questions,
welcoming the answers,
recreating the past in the present.

Looking back from the Age of Progress,
the Space Age, the Age of Aquarius,
Dutch gets the story right for this Island:
all things come back ultimately to our beginnings.

A treasure trove of Island oral history
from a litany of names:
Johnny Chuck MacAdam, Herb Schurman,
Long Vincent Gallant, Ada MacKenzie,
Helen Mae Smith, Colin MacDonald,
Clive Bruce, Annie Henderson,
Maude Palmer, Grandma Creed,
and on, and on, and on.

Y'had to be rugged boy, then.
Y'had to take it.
If you were old enough to eat,
y'were old enough to work.
Hittin' the high seas with an Imperial
single-stroke Bruce Stewart
motor aboard. I'm tellin' y'
fishin' then was some friggin' hard.

I went off the Island in 1917.
I went to Boston. I was some
lonesome. I was only to Summerside
once in my life, says one woman.
Another talked of staying healthy
on cod liver oil and black current jam,
and, of course, a good dose of
sulphur and molasses every spring.
And keeping the Sabbath, not even
having a fire in the stove on Sunday.

Country people knew the seat
that went into a crop of potatoes,
a pail of milk, a churn of butter,
and bread warm from the oven.
Food was hard-earned and required
the proper degree of respect.
Grandma just wore out
making soap and cheese and clothes.

Then, Colin MacDonald recalled:
In the summer we'd swim all day
in the Bay – not a goddamn tack on us either.
When we swam like that it was all boys,
y'mind, but there'd be an odd brassy
girl around. Girls weren't that far off.
They could see our apparatus alright.

Dutch Thompson recreating the past in the present.
All things comb back ultimately to our beginnings.

Frank Ledwell,
PEI Poet Laureate
June 3, 2003

Introduction

How good has my life been? Meeting people like Robbie Robertson and Harold Gaudet and Borden Mooney and Muriel MacKay made it fantastic. Where else but in the Maritimes could a total stranger knock on someone's door, ask to hear their life story and be invited in to record it. With tea and biscuits as a bonus.

It all started many years ago when my mum was bedridden, but still, as Elsie Collier would say, as bright "as a cricket." To cheer Mum up, I took my old Sony TC 142 tape recorder around to the old folks in the district and gathered stories about my mum's parents and grandparents. I'd hear Mum laughing at the memories, and one day a merchant mentioned two things: four-foot long Atlantic salmon his general store bought and shipped to Boston on the train in the 1930s, and a woman rumrunner who packed a shotgun and drove a Mclaughlin-Buick with solid rubber tires so the cops couldn't shoot holes in her tires when the car was loaded up with five-gallon kegs of rum. All news to me. Nevertheless, my attempt to add to those two stories led to a slot on CBC radio, thanks to producer Sheryl MacKay, featuring stories from what we called the Bygone Days, still on the air almost thirty years later.

I've always admired the oral collections and books by Nova Scotia's Helen Creighton and Chicago's Studs Terkel. While not in their league – as fiddler player George MacIntosh would say, "I'm just a scratcher" – I found my niche in life, and have driven many miles and edited hours of tape to try and preserve the stories and memories of folks born between 1890 and 1925.

This book contains some of my favorites. Bear in mind, I'm just a parrot, repeating what was told to me, but note the names of the storytellers, who shall remain alive as long as we keep talking about and listening to them.

In the Run of a Day

Muriel Boulter MacKay asked me if her story was going to be on *Compass*, the Prince Edward Island CBC TV supper-hour programme. No, I said, this is a tape recorder, and your precious memories will be on the radio.

Muriel Boulter MacKay

Muriel was 101 years old when I knocked on her door, down the road from where she grew up in Albany. She knitted and quilted non-stop while she answered my questions, everything from the sinking of the Titanic when she was 17 years old, to surviving the 1917 Halifax Explosion when she was there with her father who was training troops for the First World War. Muriel was born in the front parlour in 1895, and five years later, she marched down the road to attend the Albany one-room schoolhouse:

> The school is still up there, the same school, only someone uses it for a home now.

I don't suppose you remember your first teacher?

> Yes. Katie McCarville. She was Irish. I went to school with my next-door neighbour, Janie Malone. She was quite grown up, and she took me to school on my first day, and I was terrified of that teacher. I thought she was cross. And she was cross and cranky. I remember that.

In 1900, school started in the middle of August so the children could take time off in the fall at potato-picking time. She shared the single schoolroom with children of all ages and grades, distracting to some but to clever little Muriel, it was stimulating:

> I remember going to school and taking a little basket with my lunch in it. And my school book. I was very fond of Latin for some reason or other. They had two primers to start on: First Primer and Second Primer. I knew that First Primer before I even went to school. I knew it off by heart. I got through them pretty quick because when I was nine, I was in grade 10.

That's not a typo. If you could do the work, then you passed the grade.

> We had a very nice teacher that year, a nice-looking fella too. There were just two of us taking grade ten work, another girl and I. She was five years older than me. But anyhow, we were taking entrance work and the teacher got cross with us. He said, 'You'll never pass entrance if you won't work.' And I got mad at him, took my books, and went home. And I stayed home. My folks didn't seem to care much whether I went or stayed so I was home two years and a half.

Her parents didn't mind because, if Muriel had written and passed her entrance exams to attend Prince of Wales College (PWC), she would have been at least six years younger than her classmates there, and would have had to board in Charlottetown thirty-five miles from home. Muriel didn't even make it in to the nearby town of Summerside until she was 12. So, she spent an enjoyable sojourn from school, helping around the farm and bare-back riding her favorite horse Tom. At 13, she went back and wrote her entrance exams, passed with flying colours. and went to PWC for two years.

She became a teacher, came home to Albany to teach where some of her pupils were older than she was. She survived the Spanish Flu epidemic of 1918-19, and, in the early 1920s, packed her bags and headed west on what was known as the Harvest Excursion train, and wound up teaching German immigrant children in Saskatchewan. She met George MacKay, they married in Saskatoon, and, believe it or not, he was originally from five miles down the road, someone she hadn't seen since she was a school girl.

~~~~~

I always looked forward to a trip up to the northeastern end of PEI, because it always meant a visit to a man I grew to love. Robbie Robertson was born in 1904 on the Snake Road in Kingsboro. He was one of 14 children. His mother died when he was four, and his father, as Robbie put it, "farmed some of us out" to neighbours and relatives. Robbie was old enough to be useful around the hard-scrabble homestead. I hesitate to call it a farm – they didn't even have a cow. Robbie fished most of his life, skills he learned from his dad and five older brothers:

> One to a boat, that's all. They'd be out twice a day, out early when it was bright enough to see. They'd have their dories loaded with fish, get them in and dressed up [gutted, split and salted], perhaps have an hour's rest or so, then about two thirty go out again. Get in late in the evening, get the fish dressed up, salt at night with a lantern, and then back out again at first light the next day.

How big were the catches?

> I suppose a thousand pounds would put a dory down pretty deep... two thousand pounds each a day. There was lots of fish.

Cod mostly, some hake. Souris general stores like Matthew and McLeans Ltd. and J.J. Hughes and Co. bought the dried quintals of fish and supplied the salt. Often as not, the fishermen were paid in supplies and groceries. Like most fishermen, Robbie preferred what he called "solar salt" from a tiny Turks and Caicos island. Nova Scotian mined salt from Malagash; later Pugwash was second choice. One day while out "up country" with Robbie, I offhandedly said he must have eaten a lot of fish in his lifetime. Robbie was a big rangy guy with a quiet manner, but he shot right back, proudly:

> Caught a good many too. Well a fella would. If you worked at all, you couldn't help but catch them. Of course, some fellas there were a bit lazy. Wasn't our crowd. We had to work. But some fellas didn't catch too many. Nobody to push them.

Not a problem in the Robertson house. Robbie's father was nicknamed Johnny Jim the Bear Killer. He shot at least fourteen bears over the years with his musket and home-made lead balls. No bears on PEI now.

> You never went out and didn't get a load of fish. During the First War, the prices were pretty good, right up to three cents a pound for fresh codfish. Hake wouldn't be that much, probably two and a half. But that was the first time they got any money, cash, for fish. McLeans used to put the fish in barrels and ship them to the warm countries. Haiti. Lots of salt down there. That'd be the solar salt, made from salt water, coarse salt. McLeans would get it in by the vessel loads; ship saltfish by vessels and come home with lots of salt, yeah.

How big were the cod?

> A lot of them would weigh seventy-five or eighty

pounds. That'd be split fish you know. Head off and guts out.

So, they'd weigh a hundred pounds with everything?

Oh yes, they would alright, yeah. Used to get a lot of them in the run of a day.

Hard to believe so many big fish. Hard to believe so many fish period. Harder to believe they're gone. Half-a-cent-a-pound fish obviously didn't get much respect.

There was enough fish around to feed even a railwayman. Engineers or drivers, firemen, brakemen, conductors – all had a reputation for huge appetites, maybe unfairly because of their big lunchboxes. The lunch pails were big because the trainmen running the afternoon train down to Murray Harbour knew that they were spending the night there. And that spare loaf of bread and pound of bologna came in handy when stuck on the Souris run in a blizzard at Betsy's Cutting near St Peters.

Harold Gaudet was born in 1914 in the days of steam engines and big appetites. Harold lived in the east end of Charlottetown where many of the railwaymen lived, close to the train station and engine yard. East-enders couldn't hang their laundry outside on days the wind was blowing the wrong way because of the coal soot from the steam engines. Harold's Dad was a railwayman before him, and Harold inherited another railwayman's lunch box – Paddy Smith's big red lunchbox:

The box was a foot wide, bigger than a tool box because they carried everything: salt, pepper, tea, coffee, eggs. Some of them carried what they called pannikins [small metal pans]; pannikins, you put your meat and potatoes in. If they were going out on 'extras' like snow-fighting, they didn't know when they were going to get back so they'd make sure they had enough grub to do them.

Paddy Smith was my wife's grandfather, and when he left the railroad, he ran a grocery store on the corner of Prince and King Street. That's where my wife grew up. That's how I come to use his box. It was painted railroad red, boxcar red.

The King Edward Hotel was on Kent Street in Charlottetown where a Tim Hortons is now. A waitress named Maude Later worked in the restaurant and, when a CNR trainman came in for a meal, she'd shout out to the cook "Dinner for a railwayman," and a super-sized meal would follow.

Harold Gaudet wrote *Remembering Railroading on Prince Edward Island* about his years working on the railway. He tells about one boiler-maker who was notorious for being cranky and for always bringing in fresh eggs to fry up for lunch on the coal stove in the engine house. Harold and some pals snuck the eggs out of his locker one day and hard-boiled every one of them, and then sat back and waited for the boiler-maker to try and to crack hard-boiled eggs into the frying pan. Stubborn, he went through the whole dozen, and then chased Harold and his cohorts around the yard with the frying pan.

Every summer, I bike through Peakes on the old rail line now converted to the Confederation Trail. You can see Borden Mooney's little bungalow in downtown Peakes from the tracks. Borden was born in 1910 when Peakes had two blacksmiths, two doctors, a shoemaker, a dance-hall, a sawmill, and three general stores. You could get your grain ground into flour down the road at Leard's mill, sell your milk at the cheese factory, or catch a train at the station.

Borden's dad Peter was a "gandy dancer," a section man

in charge of keeping the railbed and bridges in top order. They were called gandy dancers because they used pry bars and mauls manufactured by the Gandy Corporation of Chicago. On Sundays, the Mooney children borrowed their dad's pump car and headed for the Church of St Cuthbert down the road in St Teresa:

> We used to go to church here on the old pump car. My father, that was his only means of travelling. He'd park it over there at the crossroads and, when there were bad roads in the spring of the year, like Holy Week, you could always take the pump car to church. Well, there were two cars; there was also a flat car they'd haul their tools and stuff on. So, we'd put that fella on the rails and then put the pump car behind, and the most able fellas would do the pumping – it took four to pump it – and the smaller ones would get on the flat car. Probably get twelve or fifteen on the flat car.

> It wasn't very good going up because it was all up grade, but I'm gonna tell you, coming down she was worth talking about. It was down grade from the time we started home. I'm telling you there were places we were probably going forty miles an hour. It's a wonder we weren't killed. It might jump the rails you know. Yessir. My father done away with it at the last of it. Oh, it was all good fun.

On a wing and a prayer. Borden was a bachelor with a famously salty tongue. He wore denim overalls and acted in plays put on by the local drama club. He loved the musicals because he loved to sing, and was a member of the church choir for 76 years. On the Sunday morning he was honoured with a Papal Blessing from the Pope for his dedication to the church, I dropped by before the church service. He was in his Sunday best, pacing, nervous as a cat. To calm him down, I asked him to sing a couple of songs for me, which might not have been a good idea. He sang "Whispering Hope," which reduced both of us to tears. He said he couldn't sing sitting down.

The pump car was long gone, so we drove to the church, and when he entered, the congregation jumped to their feet and gave him a standing ovation. He cried all over again. So did I.

Lighthouse Keepers, Bootleggers, and Other Jobs of the Past

Spurgeon "Friday" Walker

The last train left PEI on a cold December day in 1989. Two locomotives boarded M.V. *John Hamilton Gray*. Locomotive #1762 was left behind in Charlottetown, and now resides near the stone railway station in Kensington, one of the few reminders of the Island's one-time largest employer, the railway. One of the best-known railway conductors was George Hibbet from Georgetown. His best friend and younger colleague was Spurgeon Walker, nicknamed "Friday" by Conductor Hibbet, also from Georgetown:

> He was quite a horseman in his day. He was married three times. He always had horses and buggies, liked to go to town to the races. I was beginning to drive a car then, and he had an old Dodge car and his wife was doing the driving. He never drove a car. I would drive and we'd be going to town, and he'd see dust away ahead and he'd say, 'Friday, we'll have to catch up to that fella.' That old Dodge – it was pretty rough, just like a truck wagon. He had five hundred pounds of lead underneath the back seat of the Dodge to make her ride good. He used to take some of the old women out for a drive.

But anyway, after he retired, we used to go for a ride, he and I. He wasn't supposed to drive. He had a very big stomach on him, and we'd be getting along pretty good and he'd say, 'Friday, I think I can take her in tonight. I think I can handle her.' So, one day we were coming in, and he got around the first corner in Georgetown alright and when we got to the bridge where his house is, he give her a whirl over the bridge. He didn't straighten her up at all, he kept wheeling through the fence, lovely fence, and knocked the flagpole down. That was the end of us getting out on the road after that.

That'll teach a railwayman to fool around with a car. Friday was a character in his own right. Once, he was riding the rails on a pump car and flushed a silver fox out of the bushes beside the tracks. The fox had escaped from a pen, and live or dead, it would add a few extra dollars to Friday's weekly wages as a section man. Friday pumped hard and managed to grab the fox by the tail. He sold it to a silver fox breeder in Vernon River for ten dollars.

In his capacity as section man, Friday was able to confirm a story about disappearing coal that had circulated for years in Georgetown. Early one particularly cold winter, freezing rain followed a big snowfall and covered two piles of coal next to the railway station in Georgetown. Friday said the peaked piles looked like igloos. A few weeks later, there was a thaw and when the snow and ice melted, one of the igloos collapsed. The coal was gone. It seems enterprising coal-burning thieves had taken advantage of the rigid icy roof and made off with their black booty. Pretty hard to take anyone to court when the evidence is burned.

The railway's gone except for a few stations and ancillary buildings scattered across the Island. Luckily, we've managed to hang on to the iconic lighthouses that dot our coastline, albeit in some cases with scant regard for their maintenance. Nevertheless, some of the lighthouses have been sold and opened to the public as museums and cultural centres, so that has solved part of the up-keep issue. Private ownership, on the other hand, means that public access for some lighthouses is restricted, except for publicly-owned lighthouses such as Wood Islands, Panmure Island, and others. The job of lighthouse keeper is long gone, supplanted by automation and redundancy.

Born in the lighthouse in Souris, Francis MacIntosh was one of our last lighthouse keepers, the last of three generations of keepers at the lighthouse sitting high on a cliff at Knight Point overlooking the town of Souris:

> The base of that light is still there from the time of my grandfather was there, floating in mercury. Way back in his day and up until the first few years I was there, you had to wind that light every three hours. It was on a clock gear; you wound the weights up, 175 pounds. It took about three hours and fifteen minutes from the time it was up on the top block, and when it got down to the floor, you had fifteen minutes to wind it back up because if you didn't, it would be on the base of the light and you'd have a fixed light instead of a revolving light. So, every three hours and fifteen minutes, we used to wind those weights back up. Start just before sundown and you continued that until sunup in the morning.
>
> When I started there, there was two of us and we worked sixteen and eight, seven days a week. Sixteen hours one day and eight the next. Seven days a week. We had to because of the fog station and the light. Somebody had to be there, and that was the schedule. I did that up until 1972, and then

automation came into being. Then in '75, I moved down to the light station and we lived right on the station from '75 until it was phased out in 1990. But I was there fourteen years before that as the assistant. We had four girls and a boy, and we raised them all right there. Yeah.

~~~~~

Sheen Street
Summerside, PEI

Dear Mr. Thompson,

I really want to thank you for all the attention and kindness, you have shown my mother, Maisie Adams. You have made her feel very special, and also very popular and important to the people of PEI. I am also very proud of her, and always knew she should have been honoured for all the hard work and the hard life she had, and never once complained, or asked for help. Mom has always appreciated everything anyone has done for her. However, I could never have done for her what you have. I think it's wonderful you have made her golden years very special.

...I am also sure you don't realize just how hard Mom's life as been. She only tells people the good parts. I've never heard her mention on any interviews that she used to keep us kids entertained at nighttime by singing, playing the organ, and dancing some very fancy dances, I may add. Ask her about it sometime. Just don't let on where you got your information. She's very modest and possibly wouldn't tell you anything as I have asked her if I could put some stories in my Lighthouse story or history, whatever I [am] doing – I think it's more a listing of Mom's life – and she comes back with "don't you dare." But I really want you to know how much I appreciate all you've done for her.

Thanks again,
Mary

In 1941, Mary Adams Ramsay was born in the New London Lighthouse, just before her dad died, and her mum, Maisie Adams, Canada's first female lighthouse keeper, took over the light. When Mary was born, some of PEI's most interesting people were in attendance: Elton Woodside, the Flying Farmer from Clinton, had flown out Dr. Beer from Summerside. He landed the Fleet Canuck airplane, nicknamed the Flying Stork, on the beach. It turned out Dr. Beer's services weren't required because local midwife and RN Peach Duggan from French River had already delivered Mary. Add Maisie to the mix and that's a pretty elite group of Islanders.

Meanwhile, back in Souris, Francis was appropriately named for his grandfather, who was the keeper of the light in Souris for twenty-two years:

> I think he started off with forty dollars, and I think top dollar he got was close to sixty dollars a month. Bought his own food, and they supplied the house, but you had to buy your own fuel, and in them days, it took a lot of coal to keep warm.

Was there room for a garden?

> Yeah. And he had a cow, and he had a horse because he used to haul some hardwood too. The lighthouse itself would rock with the heavy winds, and there were lots of times at the breakwater, where they had diamond-shaped rocks for protection for the break-water, the seas would pick the rocks up like rubber balls and push them right across into the docks. Oh

yeah, those big gray granite rocks, and then in the spring the divers would have to go down and hook onto that rock and a crane would lift it back up again. The ships, when they came in alongside, would hit them, you see. Lots of times those rocks went right over. Some force from that water.

When I was visiting my ancestral home on the remote island of Westray in the Orkney Islands, my 64th cousin Brown took me up to the Noup Head Lighthouse on the back of his tractor. The lighthouse caretaker just happened to be there and he took us on a tour of the 75-foot-tall lighthouse, which is perched on cliffs another 230 feet above the Atlantic Ocean.

The keeper was repairing a broken window at the top, where the light and big Fresnel lens were positioned. On the floor, was the two-pound rock that, believe it or not, had been flung up and smashed through the window by the force of the waves over three hundred feet below. Fine. Don't believe me. Read the book *The Lighthouse Stevensons* by Bella Bathurst, about author Robert Louis Stevenson's amazing family of engineers. In fact, RLS's cousin David Stevenson built the Noup Head Light in 1898. One of many incredible stories in the book about the power of the sea describes another broken lighthouse window just as I described. So there.

The MacIntoshes saw more than high winds and fog. Rumrunning schooners hovered offshore with loads of Demerara rum and cases of scotch whisky and gin, $15.00 for a case of twelve quarts. Pure grain alcohol in two-gallon cans wasn't labelled except for the imprint of a black hand. Bootleggers like Souris' famous Old Red Fox received a steady supply of rum, gin, and scotch from local fishermen. Of course, the Prohibition officers on steamers like the S.S. *Ulna* regularly patrolled the area, hoping to make an arrest. One problem was the black smoke pouring out of the coal-burning *Ulna's* smokestack, giving the rumrunners plenty of time to nip safely out beyond the three-mile limit, later extended to twelve miles.

Some of that illegal liquor made its way to bootleggers in the Big Smoke, Charlottetown. Tom Hunter was one of hundreds of British airmen to pass through the RAF's pilot and navigational school, the site of the present-day Charlottetown airport. Locals nicknamed the airmen pigeons, and, like Tom Hunter from Fifeshire, Scotland, the airmen were birds of a feather in that they sorely missed the coziness of their local pubs. It was bad enough being 2,000 miles from home where the German Blitz and, later the Battle of Britain, were raging, and the only way to contact family and loved ones in the British Isles was by mail. However, Prohibition was in force on PEI throughout the Second World War.

The airmen's frustration at not being allowed even a legal glass of beer nearly boiled over into a riot during their first year on the Island. Luckily, in 1940, Charlottetown was rife with bootleggers, and, ironically, in an effort to warn the airmen where not to go, a list of all sixty-five bootleggers – and one whorehouse – was passed out to the airmen. Tom and his future wife Eileen Curley met one day while strolling around Victoria Park, and seventy-four years later Tom showed me the list:

It showed us where to go. It was a road map.

In bold lettering at the top the paper read:

The following places are
out of bounds to all ranks.

Whole blocks were out of bounds, like Richmond and King Streets, from Queen to Pownal Street. To keep the men out of these dens of temptation, the RAF assigned their own military policemen (MPs) to patrol the streets alongside regular Charlottetown policemen. Naturally it didn't work.

Quite a few of the airmen, sixty at least, married Island women. I dubbed them War Grooms. They came back after the war to live here, and several told me they'd call Ed's taxi to come out to the airbase, five of them would pile into the car, pay a quarter fare each, and get dropped off at one of the bootleggers. No doubt the taxi drivers had an idea where to find a bootlegger, or two. In fact, the Prince Grill, opposite Ed's Taxi, was on the no-go list.

> Tom laughed, "The Prince Grill served beer in a teapot."

> Eileen added, "We used to go in and ask for 'cold tea,' and that's what we got – beer in a teapot.

As I scanned the list, I was surprised by the number of female bootleggers. Tom said one of the airmen fell in love with one of the women bootlegger's daughter, and married her. Add a travelling salesman to that story and there's a joke in there somewhere. With the draconian fines made law a few years ago, bootlegging is now an obsolete occupation in Charlottetown, officially at least. But ask pretty well any Island male and you'll get a bootlegger story.

Here's mine: Back in the 1980s, I played baseball on the Island's provincial senior team and, to raise money to go to the nationals in Ontario one year, we invited the Moncton Mets over to play a couple of week-end exhibition games. The Mets were guaranteed to draw a crowd because ex-Montreal Expo ace pitcher and all-around bad-boy Bill "Spaceman" Lee was on their roster. He'd been kicked off the Expos team, even though he was their best left-handed pitcher, because he'd encouraged another player, disgruntled with his contract, to burn his Expos uniform. Bill was immediately *persona non grata*, and was blackballed out of the Majors. So, he landed in Moncton, with a rumoured thousand-dollar-a-week deal, a red convertible, and a cottage in Shediac at his disposal. He was still in the prime of his career, and his pitching mowed us down like tenpins. But he drew the crowds, and we made some travelling money. Since the games were all in good fun, after second game at Memorial Field in Victoria Park on Sunday afternoon, our team, the Charlottetown Regal Oilers, coached by Forbie Kennedy, decided to treat the Mets to a couple of cold ones.

Even in the 1980s, I think the only way you could get a drink at a restaurant in Charlottetown, especially on Sunday, was to go to the Canton Cafe and order two eggrolls and a dozen Tenpenny. So, still wearing our sweaty uniforms, we all trooped down to Georgie Reid's, the bootlegger. Bill Lee and the other Mets players were in awe: Great service, cheap beer, comfortable chairs spread out in the shade, and several of Charlottetown's finest plus a City councillor sitting at tables, enjoying Georgie's famed ambience. We couldn't beat them on the field, but we had it all over them when it came to illegal drinking.

One more story about obsolete occupations. Jimmy Doyle was one of those people you never forget. His daughter, the singer/songwriter Teresa has his wit and *joie de vivre*. Jimmy lived in Alberry Plains, half-way between Charlottetown and Poole's Corner, and the grandfather he was named for combined teaching school with a job rarely seen any more – shoemaking. First a word of warning: if you're a dog, stop reading right now. Jimmy told me:

James Doyle, he taught school in Summerville for fourteen years, and when he wasn't teaching school, he was making boots. Shoemaker. I have his boot jack. He came from Earnscliffe. He was a nice man, a smart man. He used to draw up wills for everybody around the country. He didn't do any farming; my father did the farming. He had enough to do making the boots.

Where did he get the hides?

A man named Alec MacNeill had a dog, and he killed the dog, and my grandfather got the hide off the dog and he made boots out of it, do ya see. After that, any old dogs that were around, he'd catch them and skin them and make boots. That's what he done.

It's a cheap shot but I'm going to say it anyway: hush puppies. And no, you can't get your money back.

Islanders Go to War: The War Years

Lester MacLeod

In 1933, an unusual sight caught the eye of 20-year-old Lester MacLeod heading for school in Victoria-by-the-Sea.

The plane landed out in the Strait just off Victoria, and the crew came in and stayed in Victoria. There was a bunch of them, but this fella dropped down and the rest of them kept on going. Mr. Ceretti from Borden came down and talked to them. He could talk to them.

The aircraft was an impressive sight, the Savoia-Marchetti S.55A Flying Boat, the pride of the Italian Air Force and record-holder for fastest Atlantic crossing. A squadron of 24 S.55As, known as the Italian Armada, was on its way back to Italy after attending the 1933 Chicago World's Fair, stopping to refuel in front of a crowd of 10,000 in Shediac, N.B. After giving the assembled crowd the Fascist salute, the Armada flew off. One aircraft developed engine trouble and was forced to land in Victoria's harbour. Mr. Ceretti was originally from Italy, and did the translating to order engine parts, and may have helped repair the aircraft. His family runs a garage in Borden to this day.

Some people were a bit suspicious of the Italians. This was 1933, and Fascists like Hitler and Mussolini were in power, so conspiracy theories, even in remote PEI, abounded. Margaret Crozier was seventeen the day she saw the Italian air armada.

> Four planes came over and one came down with pretend motor trouble. I was in Long River visiting my cousin and the four of them flew over. People said it was just an excuse for them to come down so they could take the soundings of all the harbours so if a war came, they would know where they could bring their fleet.

But instead of Victoria-by-the-Sea, the Italians invaded Ethiopia. Not everyone was suspicious of the Italians – someone suggested naming the nearby shore *Novis Beach* after the Italian pilot. It was a flight of fancy. Didn't get off the ground.

~~~~~

I've gone to interview many folks about a variety of subjects and had them casually mention being war veterans. Charles Gallant is a perfect example. Ostensibly, he was going to show me where a tunnel went from a cellar, under three Charlottetown streets, down to the harbour. Different people had told me that during the Prohibition years, the rumrunning vessels rarely entered the harbour because it was too easy to get trapped by the narrow entrance framed by Seatrout and Blockhouse points once the vessel was in. Many shipments of rum were off-loaded at Seatrout Point in Keppoch and hidden in the ruins of the old Marine Quarantine Hospital. Cars from town slipped out at night and picked up the kegs of rum and cases of liquor.

Anyway, Charles Gallant, born in Charlottetown in 1922, was raised by his mum. By 1938, he was alone in the world: Mum and sisters were dead and his father's whereabouts were unknown. So, 17-year old Charles rode the rails, hoboed around for two years, and finally came home to join the army when the Second World War broke out:

1939. Second Battalion Artillery, RCA [Royal Canadian Artillery]. They were from here, but when we got to England, we joined up with a regiment. The First Medium Regiment, RCA. Yeah. I got into the artillery by mistake. I met a fella uptown and he was going to the doctor to get a paper to see a dentist. There was a big line up at the drill shed to sign up in different outfits, and he said, 'Come on, follow me.' So, when he came out, he gave me a shove. I went in and it was old Dr. Jack Jenkins. He said, 'Strip off.' So, I stripped off. He said, 'Get on the scales.' I got on the scales. You're supposed to weigh at least a hundred and forty-five pounds to get into the artillery. Dr. Jack drank quite a bit. 'Yup,' he said, 'A hundred and forty-five.' I weighed a hundred and thirty.

So, I got in the artillery that way. We went out to the Exhibition Grounds first, for about a month, drilling; then we moved out to Beach Grove. We landed in England for Christmas 1940. We trained in England and we worked for farmers, too, helped them take in the hay and all odd jobs. We went for a shoot up in Scotland, training. And every time we fired the big artillery guns, we'd kill a sheep. The boys would lug the sheep back and skin him, and we'd have mutton stew. We got so sick of it, we couldn't eat any more.

So, Charles Gallant and his sheep-killing artillery mates trained and trained, and finally in May 1944, just before D-Day, they were moved to a small wood near Portsmouth.

Barbed wire all around it. You couldn't get out. I knew there was something up. We took off from Portsmouth across the Channel. When we got halfway across, I knew what was going on. I had a quart of rum with me. I was into that. I said if I'm going to die, I'll die happy.

The Normandy Invasion. Tens of thousands of Canadians, British and American troops, and their tanks, and artillery all landing at once. Chaos on the wide beaches of northern France. Allied bombers had pounded the German fortifications the night before, but the Germans were well-dug in.

Thousands of men, bullets flying everywhere. It was pretty scary. For a day, it was scary.

A 130-pound Charles didn't see much artillery duty on the big guns, and instead was reassigned to the Royal Montreal Regiment as the Allies began the slow march across France and Holland, and finally into Germany.

I still wore my artillery hat badge, but I was driving a three-ton truck, delivering ammo and food to the front. Sometimes I'd take officers up to the front in a jeep.

Pretty dangerous work.

I guess it was. Pretty scary sometimes. Just about the end of the war, I was taking the boys to a show one night in Holland, and on the way back a German plane came over and fired at us on the highway. We got out and jumped in the ditch. I figured he was drunk; just doing it because he knew they'd lost the war.

Troopships leaving Halifax and other eastern seaboard ports headed for England zig zagged across the north Atlantic to avoid the lurking German U-Boats. Roland

Pickering grew up on a farm in Seaview, working in fields that rolled down to the Gulf of St. Lawrence. He joined the Merchant Navy, often sailing in convoys out of Halifax Harbour:

> I seen lots of ships going down, yeah. You don't cross there in wartime without seeing a few ships going down. You're lucky you're not going down on one. Lots of times, you'd lose the convoy in a big storm. One of them big storms lasting three or four days. You couldn't see nothing and when it fined up perhaps you wouldn't see a ship. No radios. No wireless, no nothing. But every captain had a plan, and every day at a certain time you were supposed to be in a certain spot at a certain time. So, if you lost the convoy you made for that particular place and you'd very likely pick up the convoy. Miss the convoy there, you kept going to the next place, and that's the way it was worked.

What were the storms like?

> It wouldn't be any good me telling you; nobody would believe me anyway. Ha! I'm telling you, there's some sea running in the North Atlantic, and it would get so bad, you couldn't see nothing only just white, like a big snowstorm. You couldn't see nothing. You didn't dare go out on deck or you'd get washed over.

Did you ever get sick?

> No. Got pretty scared sometimes but never seasick. The most scary thing that I ever saw was air raids at sea. We were on a convoy one time coming out of Northern Ireland and we had thirty ships. When we got out two hundred miles, we had nineteen left.

What kind of pay were you getting for all these risks? Big dollars?

Twenty-seven dollars a month was our wages for an ordinary seaman.

Less than a dollar a day. On the 19th of February 1941, the Luftwaffe bombers targeted the Welsh seaport of Swansea. Roland's merchant ship had just docked:

> I never thought I'd see the morning. Cripes. They missed us but hit the city and the docks were tore to pieces. Everything alongside us was blown to pieces. Our ship was afire twice that night, but we didn't get any heavy bombs. We just got the incendiary bombs. They come down from a mile up. When they land, they're just like a bucket full of hot coals. They go right down through the roof of a building, right down two or three storeys. We had a load of lumber and by gosh one of the incendiary bombs went down in the hold. By God, we had a devil of a job to get it out. The big sheds on that dock were blown to pieces.

I guess people were killed.

> Huh. Heavens, I would imagine. Well I would imagine. A lot of stevedores you knew from being around the ship. I never saw any of them anymore. They were all killed that night.

Known as the "Three Nights' Blitz," German bombs killed 230 citizens of Swansea, 400 more were injured, and 7,000 houses were destroyed, as well as many downtown commercial businesses. It's estimated 56,000 incendiary bombs alone were dropped. The King and Queen and Winston Churchill visited Swansea to survey the destruction and to boost morale. Roland's ship was long gone, the load of lumber they left behind more valuable than ever.

After the war, you'd think Roland would have gone home to the farm and forgot about boats of any kind, but he landed a job on the CN ferries running between Borden and Cape Tormentine. There, he reconnected with an old Merchant Navy pal Ernest "Ben" Pike, soon Captain Ben Pike of the MV *Abegweit*, the old Abby. For years, they rode the waves together, when the worst that could happen was getting stuck in the ice and running out of cigarettes.

~~~~~

Courtney Maynard had signed on with the PEI Light Horse Regiment. He shipped to Britain on the *Aquitania* and, like Charles Gallant, wound up in the artillery. He survived D-Day and eventually wound up helping free Holland from the Nazi occupation. Like all soldiers, he relished the day a parcel of food and other treats arrived through the Red Cross from his home in Port Hill.

> Sometimes you'd get half a dozen letters at one time, and they sent cakes and socks. They could buy a thousand cigarettes for three dollars.

But you wouldn't get a thousand at the same time, would you?

> Yeah, in one package. That was the currency in Holland, cigarettes, because the money was worthless. And they'd eaten everything. They told me the only things the Germans didn't like were turnips. So, they left them their turnips and their tulip bulbs. I was going out one day to the garbage dump and there was a big lump of porridge that I hadn't eaten. I was going past an old fella, he was thin boy, and his arm shot out like a flash and took that lump of porridge. When we came into towns, the Dutch people were overjoyed at the Canadians coming. An older couple

invited us for coffee and it was roasted barley. That's all they had. What wonderful people. My gosh.

Fred Dejonge was one of those starving Dutch war survivors. Fred was born in 1933 in western Holland near the Belgium border. He had two brothers and three sisters, and even living on a large mixed farm with plenty of food. That all changed when the German invaded the Netherlands in May 1940.

First of all, the homing pigeons had to be killed. Then the rifles and shotguns and the radios – they took all of them.

Was your father able to hide a rifle or anything?

Yes, but I never knew it, of course. He wouldn't tell me. There was a hollow log on our farm that had four shotguns in it. You were allowed one pig a year – if you killed more you had to hide him. One pig, yup. Hitler was mean enough. We all had to jump through the hoops: steal your own food back from the Germans. Going back a little further than that, Stalin managed to starve seven million people to death in the Ukraine. Farmers. I can never understand that.

Joseph Stalin was our ally for most of the Second World War, so we had to overlook his genocide, known as the "Holodomor" or artificial famine, of the Ukraine in early 1930s. Jovial Uncle Joe... right. And as Fred pointed out, it happened in an area of the Caucasus famous for its fertile soil and successful farmers. Of course, it was denied and any mention of the tragedy suppressed by Stalin, but funny how word managed to reach a farm in rural Holland. Yet even today, people claim no one knew about the Holocaust. The food produced on the DeJonge farm was confiscated and sent to Germany to feed the German troops scattered across Europe.

Here on PEI, it was a world away. We had rationing, of course, but just listening to Jim Montgomery's woes shows how different things were. Even as a boy, Jim had a sweet tooth so good karma led him to a successful career selling all types of candy and chocolate plus MacDonalds cigarettes to general stores across the Island. Everyone knew Jim as the "Candyman":

> Candy was rationed; that was quite a deal. An awful lot of headaches with that, you know, because most stores could sell all the candy they could get. And it's just like anything else, if it's hard to get, then everybody wants it. I had to set a quota: they could only get twenty per cent of their previous quota before rationing came in. The different kinds of characters you'd run into: they all come to me and say, 'The hell with the quota. How much will you give me?' I remember one fella saying, 'I'm not asking you for more candy: I'm demanding it.' All kinds of characters arguing I should be giving them more. It was an awful headache, but that's the way it was.

I'm sure the boys on Juno Beach had headaches too. Not Jim's fault. He was born in 1902, as he said, "Too young for the First World War, too old for the Second." He did his part, sending candy and cigarettes to the troops.

War and rationing were becoming a way of life for the British. One-legged veterans of the First World War were still hawking pencils and apples on the streets when the Second World War broke out. Joyce Crane was born in Croydon in South London in 1923. Croydon was devastated by the Blitz, V-1 flying bombs, and V-2 rockets, including the Croydon Airport, which was London's main airport until the Second World War broke out. Yet, Joyce and her family survived all that and powdered eggs. She met her future husband, an Island soldier named Bruce

Crane when he was stationed in England. He sealed the deal in an unusual way:

> We used to go for walks; we both liked the country. Go for long walks and sometimes we'd go down to Brighton, because that was a good place to go. Always lots going on there.

Where were you when he popped the question?

> Ohhh, one of those day trips out in the country. He had a fruitcake. His sister had sent him a fruitcake, and that was a real luxury in those days. He had picked it up at the post office, and we were going for a walk. And we thought we'd have to try this fruitcake. We didn't have a knife with us, of course. I had a nail file, so we sat on the edge of a field and cut the cake with a nail file, and ate it.

I don't think technically Joyce is classified as a war bride. In fact, she served with the Woman's Auxiliary Air Force (WAAF) in England during the war. In 1945, Joyce borrowed a dress to get married in, and neighbours chipped in with their rationed butter, flour, and sugar to make a wedding cake. In 1946, Joyce came to Hazelbrook, PEI, to live in an old farmhouse where, to her surprise, the water in the kettle regularly froze on winter nights. It was the start of a new life, indirectly perhaps, one of the good things that happened as a result of the war:

> He told me that we were going to live on a farm and there might not be any close neighbours, and I said, 'Oh, that's alright.' If I had him, I didn't care. But it was an old place. Just plain floor boards.

Were your expectations of PEI met?

> Well, he told me what the countryside was like, yeah. And I always liked the country, but I really wasn't

prepared for the horse and wagon, and the oil lamps and the water pump. No sink. Snow in the winter. I hated the cold weather. Still do. The first night I was there, the house was full of neighbours. Lots of music, and a bit of moonshine, too. I was pretty tired, and I wasn't used to those kinds of parties, so I went to bed about ten o'clock. The party kept going. I don't know what time they all went home. They were celebrating.

Can't beat a PEI house party. Coincidentally, I worked with Joyce for many years in the Confederation Centre theatre where she was an extremely valued member of the wardrobe department. Always a smile: the smile of someone who's come out the other side of a war and survived.

~~~~~

Jim MacLeod and Jim MacBeath had a pair of shoes between them. Each had the opposite leg taken off in the war. So, one fella bought a pair of shoes and the other fella paid half.

Angus Johnston and his father from Murray River peddled meat door-to-door in southeastern PEI out of the back of a horse-drawn wagon. Two customers were First World War veterans who had lost legs in France. Donald MacKay told me a similar story about two Great War veterans who used to hang their wooden legs on the Breadalbane post office door when they were playing cards with Donald's father, the postmaster.

Elizabeth MacEwan lived all her life in New Dominion on a farm that ran down to the West River. Elizabeth and her five older brothers used to skate to Charlottetown and back on the frozen river, a 26-kilometre round trip. Schooners sailed up and down the river, as did a ferry transporting everything from cattle and potatoes to Model-T Fords. Spurgeon Hickox had the ferry contract when the Liberals were in power; his neighbour had it when the Conservatives were in. No hard feelings: they sold the ferry to one another accordingly.

Elizabeth was born in 1909. She and her brothers trained a cow to pull a jaunting sleigh, and the dog to pull a toboggan. One day, she showed me photos in the family album:

> That picture is my mother and the five boys: John, David, George, Gordon, and Walter. And the dog.

Boy, your mother was a good-looking woman, wasn't she?

> Poor soul, she had lots to do with five boys. I barely remember my oldest brother. He went to World War One and was killed. That's his picture there. I just barely remember him. He was killed in 1918. He was born in 1894... twenty-four just the month before he was killed.

And the war ended a month later?

> Yeah. He was killed the twenty-eighth of September. It was terrible hard. Mother got lovely letters from his officer and from a friend named Waterman. Waterman was from Nova Scotia, and he wrote to my mother, and then he was killed a month later. Last of October. The fella who wrote the letter. He didn't come back either.

Did John write home?

> Yes, I had the prettiest cards – they were all embroidered. Oh, they always sent me a card at Christmas. I had two brothers in World War One. One came home ... one didn't.

By chance, the two brothers, John and David, met in downtown London. They were with different units, and it just happened their leaves coincided. It was the last time David was seen by anyone in his family. The story of the meeting was recounted many times.

Elizabeth and her mum, like all mums and sisters, sent parcels of food and soap and clothing overseas. Adelaide Hamm from Bunbury and her Mum sent her two brothers – Charles and Allan – care packages that always included newspapers, woollen socks, and trigger-finger mitts, plus a cake and candy for Charlie's sweet tooth. Charlie requested apples from the farm, writing home later that the PEI apples "were far superior to the French apples." I bet the French wine was better though, although knowing the little church in Bunbury the Hamm family attended, I doubt either brother touched liquor. Addie told me she used to stand at the mailbox, anxious for a letter from her brothers, at the same time dreading an official-looking letter from the war office.

John Rendall was a Black Angus cattle farmer who lived on the tiny island of Papa Westray in the Orkney Islands, off the windswept north coast of Scotland. The farm that John and his father and then John's son owned happens to be the farm my blacksmithing ancestors toiled on for generations before striking out for one of the great unknowns – Canada – 220 years ago. One of John Rendall's neighbours, Woody Groat, served in the Royal Navy and came home from the Second World War with this amazing story about June the sixth, 1944 – D-Day:

> They had huge buoys in France to tie the boats up to. His job was to sit on a buoy and get ahold of their anchor – the big boats – and get it affixed to a shackle on the buoy. There came a gale of wind and the buoy he was on drifted away and capsized,

and everybody except him drowned. A telegram was written to send home, that he was drowned, when they found him sitting on the buoy still! He sat for days on that buoy! For days! And he got very bad with the cold, the exposure, and he got T.B., Tuberculosis in the neck. He was a while in a hospital in Southampton. They got it cured and he eventually came home.

Another Second World War sailor was Captain Ernest "Ben" Pike. He sailed in convoys out of Halifax with the Merchant Navy throughout the war. Hundreds of ships carrying vital supplies for the war effort would anchor in Bedford Basin, waiting for the signal to head into the North Atlantic on their perilous voyage:

> You never delayed a sailing for bad weather. You had to sail. I often thought people used to sail along the coast near the German submarines. It was just as dangerous there as it was anywhere.

Did you see ships in the convoy go down?

> Oh yes. Oh yeah. If the ship ahead of you got torpedoed, then you would have to alter course to keep away from her, so you wouldn't run into her and damage your own. I don't like to talk about those things. Very often, you'd steam through people struggling for their lives, but you couldn't do anything about it. You couldn't stop to pick them up because other ships would run into you or then you would be a sitting duck for the subs. You just went on.

> We never looked at the danger. People ask, 'Were you scared?' Well, yes, we were scared lots of times. You were scared you might get torpedoed and have to get in a lifeboat. You'd wish sometimes if you got torpedoed, you'd die right where you were standing. That was a coward's way but...

Certainly, we never looked at the danger. Every voyage that we made was a challenge, and when we got to the other side [of the Atlantic] with our load intact, boys, whether it was machinery or ammunition, we'd rub our hands and say 'We done it again.' I sailed on ammunition ships and the most explosives that any one ship could carry in a convoy was 3,500 tons. TNT and stuff like that. To give you some idea, those two ships that exploded in Halifax in 1917 [the *SS Mont-Blanc* and *SS Imo*, Halifax Explosion, 6 December 1917] before I was born even, they had seventeen tons on board. And we used to carry 3,500 tons on one of the ships I sailed on. She got torpedoed the trip after I got transferred to another ship. They just heard an explosion about five o'clock in the morning; there was a concussion and they looked, and they saw just a cloud of smoke in the sky. There was nothing there. What was left of her was up in that cloud.

Blew up totally?

Yes, yes, yes, yes.

A ship you had just been on?

Yes.

All those mates of yours.

Oh yeah, yes.

During the war, Captain Pike met fellow Merchant mariner Roland Pickering from Seaview, PEI. Ben Pike studied all through the war, every spare minute, wrote his master's papers, and after the war, moved to PEI lured by Roland's ramblings. He went to work for CN Marine and became captain of the beloved old Abby, the ice-breaking rail and car ferry *MV Abegweit*. Talk about living the dream, and well-earned too.

The dream continued in 1983 when Captain Pike and some old shipmates sailed the Abby to her present berth, as the floating clubhouse of the Columbia Yacht Club in Chicago, Illinois. Yes, that Chicago. Captain Pike said there were some tight squeezes going through the St. Lawrence Seaway. The yacht club members had competed fiercely to crew the voyage, and Captain Pike got a kick out of ordering Chicago neurosurgeons and big-money stock brokers around like they were cabin boys. Do them good, he figured.

Babs Fitzgerald from Charlottetown was one of those guys who knew everyone and who everyone knew. Babs was curious about everything, talkative, and a walking blur. His son Rowan is a well-known Island musician, a talent that runs in the family. Babs was born in 1917, his mother Flo was a midwife, radio personality, and entrepreneur.

Babs joined the 5th Canadian Signal Corps at the outbreak of the Second World War. He and his father Geoffrey were in the same unit for a brief period. His father, who had somehow managed to wrangle his way into the army, was fifty years old, but according to Babs "a tennis champion and in great shape." When on leave, Babs was continually being mistaken for his father in various pubs around London.

Geoffrey went off to fight in the mountains and beaches of Italy, while Babs did the same, only in France, immediately after the D-Day invasion.

> I spent six years over there. I was in France, Belgium, and Holland, and I ended up in Germany. You were given points for overseas service, and when you got so many points you were given a whole month's leave back in England.

After June 6, 1944, people dared hope for an end to the war:

> I had earned my points in France and I was on my way to England, and that's where I was when the war was over. I was in London V-E night. The announcement came over the radio: 'The cessation of hostilities.' Unbelievable. Just unbelievable. We went through London and beacons were all lit up... big beacons that had been sitting there for five or six years waiting to be lit. And they were lit, set on fire! It was wild going through London on a train on V-E night, I'll tell you. They were shoving bottles of whisky through the windows of the train. Oh my God, it was fantastic. Ohh, it was wild.

The war was over. Babs and his dad went home to PEI. His brother Rowan didn't. He was killed flying a Halifax bomber over Germany.

So, let's add up the soldiers and sailors mentioned more or less in passing: Jim MacLeod, Jim MacBeath, Donald MacKay, Charles Hamm, Military Medal for Bravery; Allan Hamm fought at Vimy, John MacEwan, David MacEwan, Private Waterman, Captain Ben Pike, Roland Pickering, Babs Fitzgerald, Geoffrey Fitzgerald, Rowan Fitzgerald.

On November the 11th, think of the tens of thousands not mentioned here.

Chance is a Many-Splendored Thing

Johnny Reid

I met him at the airport with the premier and his bunch with me. I had a big trailer truck, loaded with bags of potatoes, put Tom on top of it and paraded him through town with a loudspeaker playing "Bud the Spud." I had big banners strewn across the street: 'Bud the Spud is Here – Another Big Load of Potatoes!'

Johnny Reid was a PEI legend. At the age of twelve, Johnny bought a deep fryer, two hundred pounds of potatoes, and installed a telephone in the shed in his parents' backyard. His best customers telephoned in their orders for hot French fries from the numerous bootleggers in Charlottetown's east end. A boy on a bicycle delivered the hot fries. Johnny eventually parlayed that enterprise into Johnny's Fish and Chips restaurant next to the train station, which morphed into Davy Jones Locker and the Prince Edward Lounge, later renamed JR's Bar, where he showcased PEI and Canadian talent such as Anne Murray, Gene MacLellan, John Allan Cameron, and his new pal, Stompin' Tom Connors.

He was one of the best draws I ever had. The place would be packed. They were lined up for a block every night of the week. That was his first show on the Island, and that's when he met his wife Lena, at my place. She was working for me. He said to me, 'Who's that girl?" I said, 'She works here and her name is Lena, and don't you try and steal her' So they became friends and started going out, and on his next trip, she said, 'I want to give you my notice. I'm going away.' Tom said, 'We're getting married. I want you to stand for me.?' I said, 'Jeez, Tom, I can't stand for you. I'll be at the wedding, but you can get anybody to stand for you.' I knew it was going to be on TV. Tom said, 'If you don't stand for me, I'll never set foot inside your place again.' Well since you put it that way, I said, I've not got much choice, do I?

So, I stood for him, and, Pauline, who worked for me, was matron of honour and my wife, Judy was bridesmaid at the Four Seasons Hotel up there in Toronto on the TV. So, here it was, Mutt and Jeff, great big tall Stompin' Tom and short fat Johnny Reid.

Elwood Glover's *Luncheon Date* ran on CBC television in the 1960s and '70s, and, in 1973, hosted Stompin' Tom and Lena's memorable wedding, with best man Johnny "Jeff" Reid. Tom's and Johnny's friendship began years earlier when they shared a cell in the 1911 Queens County jail, and both immediately recognized a fellow rebel and soulmate.

Ironically years later, Johnny bid and won the contract to feed the jail's inmates. One of the prisoners wrote a letter to the paper criticizing the menu: he was tired of getting lobster three times a week. When I asked Johnny, he insisted it was steak, but his wife Judy confirmed the prisoner's story. Either way it was a bizarre protest.

During the Second World War, Johnny worked in an aircraft factory in Amherst, N.S. Back on PEI, the Royal

Air Force (RAF) landed on PEI in 1940, and set up a training base where the present Charlottetown airport is. Islanders fell in love with these rather exotic airmen with their English and Scottish and Welsh accents.

Helen Cudmore's family ran a large general store in Oyster Bed Bridge and Helen kept a diary of events both mundane and unusual.

> In 1942, my sister Verna had a boyfriend named Ted Farrell from England, and he used to walk from the Charlottetown airport out here to Oyster Bed to visit her [21 kilometres/13 miles]. Dad would drive him back as far down as the Milton Road, and he'd walk the rest of the way back to the airbase [13 kilometres/8 miles].

Would you see many RAF airmen out this way?

> Quite a few, yes.

What brought them out here?

> Girls. Nice-looking girls in this area. Here's another entry: June 21st 1955. Two neighbours married, Moses and Marjorie. And the groom passed away that same day. Died the same day he was married. They lived just up the hill here. Certainly, was a shock to everyone.

Helen, her mother and her sisters all kept diaries. Thanks to Helen's diary, I learned that in 1930 it cost two dollars a day to stay in the hospital – the old Infirmary on Kensington Road – five dollars for an operation, and a dollar a day for your hospital meals. The first two were deals, but a dollar for hospital food? Better food at the 1911 jail.

On the 25th of July 1958, arguably the most influential American musician ever, not that he'd ever blow his own horn, Jazz great Louis Armstrong played a show in Charlottetown. Twenty years earlier, he was paid $5,000 to appear opposite Ronald Regan in the movie *Going Places* singing the song "Jeepers Creepers" to a race horse with the same name. Even singing to a horse, Satchmo stole the show.

I can't say for a fact, but I'd bet MacKenzie Dixon played the fiddle to his horses at one time or another. Mac was born in 1926 in South Melville where his family ran a flour and grist mill. Mac loved horses, and raised champion Clydesdales, but he bought an unusual used car to court what turned out to be the number one love in his life: his future wife Erma Ings.

> The first car that I bought was a 1937 Terraplane. They were built by the Hudson Motor Company. The day we were married, a neighbour of ours was going to stand for me, my best man, and we were heading for the church in Millview – that's where Erma came from – and down in Churchill Hollow, the front axle broke. We went right over the bank, and it was steep enough. Of course, we had no seatbelts in those days, and my head went down and I struck my nose and started bleeding all over my white shirt and tie. And believe it or not, the first car that came along was the RCMP, and I got in with them. That was a good start wasn't it?

What happened to the car?

> That was the end of that one. It served its purpose, it got me that far and that was it.

The Churchill and Strathgartney hills have claimed many cars over the decades. Model-Ts often had to back up the hill because of their gravity-fed carburetor. Johnny MacGillivray and his father before him had a blacksmith shop across from the church, and every spring, he and his team of horses would pull countless cars out of the mud. He said there was a bit of irony there.

One day, a car from Ontario coming off the Borden ferry ran into the back of Johnny's car. The Ontario driver complained to the RCMP that Johnny hadn't signalled a left turn, and this the Trans Canada Highway. Johnny protested, "Why would I signal? Everyone knows I live here."

Mac Dixon's mother was Edna Smith Dixon, one of the multi-talented Smith sisters, who grew up playing music and helping her parents run the Pleasant View Hotel in Hampton. The Pleasant View was a rambling, three-storey hotel where Upper Canadians and New Englanders came by rail, steamboat, and finally horse and coach to spend the summer months, basking on the beaches, enjoying the salt air, cool nights, and three meals a day – plus snacks – of the celebrated Smith home cooking.

When Edna was two years old, she fell from a third-storey window and landed on her back in front of the horrified guests. Not a scratch. As well as doing the high-diving act for people who had paid their two bits, Edna was a great cook. After she married Johnny Dixon, who was by that time running the mills, she'd probably fed half the countryside. She sometimes cooked for fourteen different people a day: farmers waiting for Johnny to mill their wheat and oats. As Mac said:

> We'd feed their horses, and them too. That was all free gratis. When my grandfather John Dixon was running the mill, this day, Matthew Smith, who ran the Pleasant View Hotel, [came] with a grist of wheat to get ground. His little daughter was with him, just came for the trip to the mill, you see. And John Dixon's son Johnny Dixon was there, and he was two or three

[years] older than this little girl, Edna Smith, and he came in to the mill and he thought she was going to be bored, sitting there, so he asked if she'd like him to show her around the farm. So, this was great.

And after she went home to the Pleasant View, her mother asked her how was her trip to the mill. 'Oh,' she said, 'It was a great trip, and this nice little boy Johnny Dixon took me by the hand and showed me all around the farm, the sheep, the lambs, everything.' Fifteen or sixteen years later, they were married. And became my parents. So that's got to be my favorite story, wouldn't you think, Dutch?

Edna and Johnny played concerts at the Hampton Hall, piano and violin. Mac was also a fiddle player, and once I managed to get Mac and two other millers together. Turned out, all three were fiddle players, and spent three hours talking about old fiddle tunes instead of grinding wheat. So instead of Red Fife it was "Red Wing."

From Dixon's Mills to Saskatchewan, the land of wheat, via Albany, PEI, where Muriel Boulter MacKay was born in 1895. In 1918, after surviving the Halifax Explosion a year earlier, Muriel went west on the harvest excursion train to teach school in Saskatchewan. That's where she met and married George MacKay, a farmer originally from PEI.

January 1918 in Saskatoon, Knox Presbyterian Church, and the Reverend Wylie Clark. I remember it all quite well. It was thirty below. There was no wind but the air was full of frost. He was from this area, right up opposite the school. I knew him for six years before I married him.

[He courted me with] horse and wagon. He had a lovely horse, a prize horse, it would beat any horse on the road.

Was that one of the reasons you were attracted to him?

> Oh, I don't know. I know my parents weren't attracted to him because he was a farmer and Mother said, 'Don't marry a farmer. Marry somebody else, don't marry a farmer. Too much work and too little money.'

It turned out to be a very successful marriage. When George was PEI's Lieutenant-Governor, they hosted Queen Elizabeth at Fanningbank, and Prince Philip was very curious about Island farming methods and crops. And who better to ask...

Gladys Walsh also married a farmer: Heber Bryan from the western end of the Island. Gladys was born in 1918 in Elmsdale, the same year the MacKays exchanged vows in chilly Saskatoon. She met her future husband in 1934.

> I was at my grandmother's and Heber's father had bought a house in Alberton, and they were shingling and Heber came up to help his father. I was over looking up at the men shingling the roof when someone said, 'Which one of those Bryan boys do you like?' 'Oh,' I said, 'I think I'd like the little one.' So anyway, he must have heard me. He came down the ladder and when he was leaving, he came over to say hello. He said, 'Could I come back and take you for a drive tonight?' Sure enough, he showed up. I was only sixteen then.

They courted and sparked for two years, and when Gladys turned eighteen, Heber popped the big question in a typically male roundabout way.

> Guess where he proposed to me? Underneath an apple tree. We were visiting friends in Elmsdale, they invited us for supper, and while they were washing the dishes, we went out into the orchard, and were sitting under the apple trees, and Heber

said, 'Gladys,' he said, 'Would you like a job for the rest of your life?' I said, 'What do you mean?' 'Well, we could get married.'

What was your job going to be? Looking after him for the rest of your life?

Yeah. So anyway, I said yes, and so we were married about a month after. My gosh, what a time that was.

This is where Muriel MacKay's mother's advice about not marrying a farmer might make sense.

We never got a honeymoon. They were picking potatoes at the Bryan farm when we got married. They had the great big party there that night. Oh, we danced all night. Then in the morning, they had the potato pickers coming. I spent my first married day cooking for potato pickers, at eighteen years old. Now just imagine, eh?

October 14, 1936. And the future didn't look much brighter for Gladys and Heber when they took possession of their own fifty-acre farm down the road.

Honest to heaven, a grasshopper would starve to death jumping across that farm.

The other side of marrying a farmer is, of course, the farmer's extraordinary optimism. Every time they plant a seed, a farmer takes a chance, hoping for rain and sun – and very few grasshoppers – to harvest a crop four or five months down the road. Gladys was as optimistic as Heber, a perfect match. For years, to make ends meet, they took turns delivering the mail first by horse and wagon, then in an old Model-A car Gladys hand-painted. They contributed to the school and their church, and became valued neighbours. Over the years, the Bryans added hundreds of acres to the original fifty and built their farm up into a hugely successful operation. That and their good name is their legacy.

~~~~~

Cars were banned or partially banned on Island roads from 1908-1918. Marguerite Cudmore Stewart was born in 1916. When she was growing up. there were few drivers let alone women drivers, but one day in 1934, Marguerite and my future father-in-law Ken Birtwistle went for a spin in an old Dodge coupe owned by his father, who just happened to be the chief of police in Charlottetown:

> We were the best of friends, oh yes. We were out for a drive one day and Ken was teaching me to drive. We were out on St Peters Road near Wright's Bridge. I was behind the wheel and he was watching me, you know. And when we got to the bottom of the hill on the bridge he said – he used to call me Pegs – he said, 'You better step on the gas, Pegs. Or you'll never make this hill.' So regardless of the car that was already at the bottom of the hill, I pulled out and passed, and who came over the top of the hill but the Northwest Mounted Police. And here I was in the chief of police's car. I wasn't arrested, but they charged Ken with reckless driving and driving without a licence. Anyway, Ken got that fixed up with his Dad, and somehow or other my mother and dad never knew anything about it for weeks after until it was all fixed up.

I could be talking to a felon. I'll never forget that.

Using your connections on PEI? Never. However, Marguerite was wrong about it being the Northwest Mounted Police – by then, they were the Royal Canadian Mounted Police, but it was an honest mistake because, in fact, Ken's Dad, Archie Birtwistle had joined the NWMP when he immigrated to Canada from Cheshire, England, and served with them in Saskatchewan until he moved to PEI to become the chief of police in Charlottetown.

~~~~~

George Hart was born in Charlottetown and a Second World War veteran. In 1940, George survived the London Blitz, continuous bombing raids by the German Luftwaffe. Three years later, he survived another attack by one of Hitler's secret weapons: the deadly V-1 flying bomb.

> I was transferred to London and I went to the Haymarket Theatre to see John Gielgud in *Hamlet* and these buzz bombs were coming over at the time. Suddenly, there was a huge noise and a great cloud of dust between the spectators and the stage. A sign came on for us to go to the air shelters. Nobody moved. And when the dust settled, we went on with the play. That was the old British 'stiff upper lip' business, yeah.

What was Gielgud like in *Hamlet*?

> Oh, terrific. Terrific.

But soft, what light through yonder ceiling breaks. Sorry, wrong play. That's *Romeo and Juliet*. The show went on, so all's well that end's well. George was inspired by Gielgud, and, after the war, he became an accomplished amateur actor. Odd you might think, since a lousy show is called a "bomb." Well, that's show biz.

Cream Eaters

John and Lois Campbell's wedding

They came here every summer wearing their suits and white shirts and got the best of everything; food, beds, and never lifted a finger. They were nothing but cream eaters.

Ralph Cooke from Cape Wolfe, PEI, talking about his expatriate relatives in the Boston States coming back to visit the old homestead. Cream eater isn't in the dictionary but every Maritimer knows the meaning. Ralph had ten brothers and sisters so the cream eaters literally took over the house, as if Ralph's mother Ruth didn't have enough to do with eleven kids and neighbours to feed.

She was blessed, she was the best cook. She could make a meal out of nothing. We raised our own pork and our own beef and we had our own milk too. And fish, and we grew some potatoes, the cellar would be full of all kinds of jam, wild berries, everything preserved, starting with the rhubarb in the spring. Hundreds and hundreds of bottles. Unbelievable.

Did you have a favorite meal?

They were all favorites, it seems. There were a lot of bachelors around, and they didn't cook nothing for themselves to be realistic about it. You could count on at least three of them at our place every day for one meal or two meals, sometimes three. I've seen my mother and my sister set two big batches of bread a day. Go through a big bag of flour in less than week. Hundred-pound bag of flour didn't last a week at home.

When our family's cream eaters showed up, the bottles of wild strawberry jam and mustard pickles flew off the shelf. And if you've ever picked wild strawberries then you know how many it takes just to make one bottle of jam. It took another generation – mine – for the visits to peter out, either because they weren't interested in our colonial lives anymore, or maybe because we stopped making wild strawberry jam.

Lois MacKay from Stanley Bridge married a Grahams Road farmer named Johnny Campbell in the mid-1950s. When she was a girl, her uncle Dolph, a piano salesman, and his wife visited every summer from Ontario.

He would always come home, dressed to the nines, and had these big black boots on, but he had these old shoes that he wore around the farm. My father used to take his boots and hide them on him, and my mother would say, 'Now do you have everything, Dolph? What about your boots?' And here was Dad kicking the boots under the kitchen couch.

Mother always made the best of everything when he was here, lots of baking, and would say, 'Now, that's for Dolph' and us kids had to eat the crust of the bread. We were poor and Dolph was well-off, but they never left anything. He was a cream eater.

My five brothers and I were thrilled to see the relatives show up because like Mrs. MacKay, that's when Mum and Grammie cooked special meals. Rich Uncle Tim from Boston who wintered in Fort Lauderdale and wore aftershave that smelled like what I imagined an orange tree smelled like, would always peel back the top crust of his apple pie to sprinkle on a tablespoon of sugar. He insisted down in Florida they were used to things being sweeter than what we were used to. The first time he did it, I watched, fascinated, and tried it myself. I got my arse kicked later for putting on airs.

Mum and Grammie never complained about the extra work, and were always overjoyed to see their aunts and cousins who sometimes brought a box of second-hand clothes for us kids, tee-shirts with faded yet exotic American slogans and beer ads on the front. Sometimes, as in the MacKay household, not-so exotic clothes came from relatives who'd moved to other parts of Canada.

> We never had any relatives down in Boston but my mother had a brother who was the Postmaster out in Regina, and he had two daughters around the ages of myself and my older sister. So, they sent a big box of their used clothing home. Well, it was just wonderful. We'd go through those boxes. We'd be looking for those boxes to come through the mail. Every time a box came, it was Christmas all over again.

Bertha Ross did not suffer fools, and spoke her mind. Bertha was born in the tiny hamlet of Durrell, near Little Pond, not even a dot on the map of eastern PEI anymore. Her dad died in 1923 when Bertha was twelve years old and her mum, as tough as boot leather, carried on with the farm. Bertha and her three brothers and sisters probably worked harder in the summer months when school was out, servicing the Boston cream eaters.

> Of course, we would be hard at work at everything, and then have to feed them too. Cook and bake and work work work. They'd be a whole bunch, be here a couple of weeks. We'd have to borrow beds for

them. Ohhh, it was a lot of work.

Borrow beds. They'd eat you out of house and home.

Well, practically, yes. The only thing was, we'd have our own calico potatoes and vegetables and our own milk but we had to bake all our own bread and pies and cookies and cakes and everything else. And come time for them to go back, the cousins would say, 'We have to go back to go to work.' The inference was we were having a perpetual holiday but THEY had to go back to go to WORK.

What did you think of that?

Well, if it was now, they would have gotten a strip taken off them. But back then, I didn't say anything.

Bertha's aunts and their families showed up in waves, each spending two weeks at a time, lounging in their white shirts on the front porch, smoking cigarettes, polishing their cars, and generally just watching Bertha and the gang do the chores and cook the meals. Perpetual vacation indeed.

So, what do you call someone who went to Boston and came home every summer but instead of lounging around actually pitched in, milked and made hay and cooked? A two-percenter? A skim-milker? That describes Kathleen Gillis from Indian River, born in 1914, and who followed in her father's footsteps by heading to New England looking for work. Kathleen worked as a domestic making ten dollars a week in Boston and then, for the next thirty years, waitressed at Boston's South Station, the busiest bus, tram and railroad terminal in New England.

This day, a couple sat at the counter where I happened to be working. They told me they came from North Carolina. I gave them their water and put down the menu and went on with other customers. I came back thinking they'd be ready to order and he wanted to know if I was from Maine. I said no. Now this the most amazing thing – I said I was from a little place called Prince Edward Island, you probably never heard of it. She perked up and looked me straight in the eye, 'By any chance, would you be from Indian River?' Ahhh, I could have fallen to the floor. I still get goose pimples when I think about it.

I said, 'What made you say that? I AM from Indian River.' She knew Grace Easter, Eddie's sister just down the road. She's my neighbour,' I said. Me from PEI and them from Carolina, and both of us in Boston!

They say anything can happen when there's a war on, and this was wartime Boston in the early 1940s. So, thanks to Grace Easter, Kathleen and the North Carolinians had a great chat.

The last question from him was, how do you like your boss? I made it sound really nice whether I liked it or not. It didn't bother me. Turns out it was his own brother who was my boss. He was just picking at me on purpose to see what I'd say.

Not sure I would have taken that leading question with the good humour Kathleen did.

~~~~~

Because he was good with horses, my father always took his hard-earned two-week vacation at haying time so he could mow and rake with my grandfather's and uncle's horses. Louis MacDonald from Cornwall, PEI, told me his father always cut the next year's firewood at Christmas when he was sure all his sons, some in Boston, would be home to help. Louis said even the son who was a priest pitched in.

Annie Callaghan was a century baby, born in 1900. She first worked in a mill in Maine making cardboard and then took a dip in pay to work instead as a nanny and housekeeper for the town banker and his family. One year, she brought her boss home to Lake Verde with her. He was hooked, and came back several times to pick blueberries and split wood, always in his blue suit and tie, relenting to doff the suitcoat only on the really hot days. He squired the family around to church and house parties in his big car; he drank moonshine; cleaned the kerosene lamps; didn't mind the outhouse; and pumped water every day for the cows and pigs.

Annie and her family adored the banker, and it was a tear-fest when he headed back to Maine. Every visit, he brought presents, long underwear for Annie's three brothers, and bolts of cloth for the sisters and her mum. One year, he brought shoes.

Kathleen Gillis too helped out on the farm, and always brought lots of presents.

> Oh, always. You felt that you better bring things. Clothing mostly, something useful for sure. But one of the trips I was stopped at the border. I had a false bottom in a suitcase.

What? A false bottom? Please tell me you were smuggling balls of yarn, or tea cozies.

> Cigarettes. The boys wanted cigarettes.

God love us all. We're going to jail.

> I was foolish to be bothered pleasing the boys but I got away. I acted unconcerned that the customs man was going through my stuff, and he looked at me and he said, 'You don't have any tobacco in the suitcase?' I said, 'No.' And I guess he believed me.

And you with cigarettes in the false bottom.

    Yeah. I bet he could smell it now that I'm more wise.
    I bet he just let me get away.

I wonder. What's the statute of limitations on tobacco smuggling? I will bet that after the telling of that story over tea and biscuits, those cigarettes tasted even better, smoother. Like a perpetual holiday.

If it Doesn't Cure You...

Helen Chandler

Tie a man's bootlace around a baby's neck to ward off croup. It had to be a man's bootlace. Swallowing little pieces of raw suet was a cure for consumption of the lungs. TB. For pneumonia, cut a skunk right down the middle of the belly and put on your chest.

Home remedies were not for the faint of heart as told to me by one of the smartest people I ever met—the late Helen Chandler, born in Hazelbrook in 1910. She was a teacher, a farmer, and a retainer of cures and home remedies passed down by her great-grandmother, grandmother, and mother:

> My mother saw a woman pouring warm molasses into her son's ear to cure earache. It cured it alright because he was deaf afterwards. Deaf in that ear, yep. For weak eyes, pierce the earlobe with a darning needle with a piece of yarn in it. Pull the darning needle and yarn through, tie the yarn, and leave it in the earlobe. My mother had that done and another woman told her mother had it done.

Did it work?

> No. It didn't work. Why would it?

Indeed. Helen was a straight-shooter. She worked hard all her life and survived a variety of home remedies to live to 107. In recording people like Helen, I've tried to emulate one of my heroes, the great collector of traditional songs, folklore, and home remedies, Nova Scotia's Helen Creighton. She's major league, I'm bush league, but I've still managed to record common home remedies such as boiling cherry bark with a little sugar to drink for a cold. For a "bealing," such as an infected finger or to draw out a splinter, a plantain leaf poultice was applied. Tommy Gallant's mother in Stanley Bridge made her poultices out of salt fish:

> She used salt mackerel – the skin part not the good meat – for a poultice. I took pneumonia and pleurisy an awful lot when I was young. When we were sick at night, she'd take a brick and wrap it in newspaper, one for each foot. She'd heat the bricks so hot! I have a mark on my shin yet.

Hot bricks and the darning-needle-and-yarn cures notwithstanding, people used home remedies because they believed they worked. That, and a 100 years ago, it cost money to visit a doctor. Actually, a 100 years ago, the doctor usually visited you. Tommy Gallant grew up in a family of thirteen children. His father was a fisherman and a sometime rumrunner, and his mother was an angel of mercy:

> Very seldom did we ever call the doctor. Mother used Friar's Balsam a lot for croup. [Friar's balsam is a pungent mixture of aloe and benzoin resin in an alcohol base. Still used as an expectorant and also to heal cuts and abrasions.] I had a brother, Walter, when he was a young fella, eight or nine years old, he used to take croup off-and-on all winter, and he'd near go for it. My mother saved him from dying all the time. She'd have an old milk can and a piece of cardboard that she'd fold up, and put the Friar's

Balsam in the milk can with the cardboard on top and put it on the stove. She'd put his mouth over the cardboard funnel and he'd inhale long enough to get his breath again. He'd get all better. Just Friar's Balsam.

Friar's Balsam was cheap, and cherry bark and plantain leaves were free unlike doctors like Dr. A. A. Gus MacDonald in Souris who charged $2.00. As beloved as he was, he too had to make a living. Mary Malone MacPhee from Souris Line Road was Dr. Gus' patient but her mother usually relied on home cures, some rather unappealing:

> I'll tell you the worst I ever heard was rancid goose grease with molasses in it for a sore throat. It was a cough syrup, to drink. And for a bealing finger, use a milk and bread poultice. Old Dr. Gus said you were putting more infection in than you were taking out.

Goose grease didn't have to be rancid to work, although it seemed to be the foundation of many home remedies. In 1997, on my first visit to Amy Bryanton in Spring Valley, she offered me a swig of goose grease she kept in an old wine bottle. There were rivulets of dried goose grease along the side of the bottle that looked like candle drippings. I graciously declined the invitation when I found out it was grease left over from the Christmas goose, and this was August. Amy called me a wimp, tipped the bottle back, and took a long swig. It was how she started every day. Rancid goose grease might have been Amy's secret to eternal youth: she was born in 1913, and lived to 104.

As a girl, she went the woods with her Grammie Caseley to gather barks, leaves, and spruce tips to brew up into various home remedies. Amy was also the first one to tell me about the salt-herring-on-the-soles-of-your-feet cure. We'll come to that later. She also told me about a remedy for earache: blowing tobacco smoke in the ear.

One day back in the 1920s, Mary Malone MacPhee's brother was playing in the barn and climbing down from the loft, caught his finger on a rusty old ladder:

> My mother was good. When my brother got his finger split, my mother took my grandfather's twist tobacco that he chewed [Hickey and Nicholson Black Twist – it looked like a six-inch piece of twisted rope that had been dipped in molasses, which it more or less was]. She bound the finger up with the tobacco leaves and then put a bandage over it. She'd smell it to see if everything was ok, and in a week or so she took it off, and it was all knitted together. It healed; just little ridges were left.

Nowadays, you'd get stitches in it?

> Oh, yes. It was split bad. You'd have stitches here and stitches there, and probably a little cast over it. There were some funny ideas. Every district had different cures, but see this was an old Scottish district, but my mother was Irish. She made salve out of alder bark. Alder peelings and lamb suet, and it was good for burns. Take the bark off the alder and she'd steep it. I don't know if she put water in or what. It was a brown liquid and then she'd add lamb suet from a lamb roast, nice soft clear suet. She'd put that in little cans: you'd have this off-white soft salve that was good for burns. She likely learned it from her mother. It must have been an Irish custom.

There was lanolin in the lamb fat, and interestingly the word "alder" in some Indigenous languages translates as "healing woman." Several cures are attributed to alder including toothache and headache. Bark from the willow tree is sometimes called "nature's aspirin."

Margaret Arsenault's mother had her own arsenal of home remedies:

Oh dear, dear! I used to cry my heart out with ear-aches when I was a kid. My father never smoked a pipe but he always kept a pipe in the house because if we got an earache, he would smoke the pipe and blow the smoke in our ear. And it really helped. And the earache and goose grease: Maman would take the goose grease, warm it, put it on the end of a spoon and drop it drop by drop in your ear. And that helped too.

When my father blew smoke in my ear, it came out the other side. Cold remedies were popular, especially home-made cough syrups involving lots of sugar, and, in Amy Bryanton's Grammie Caseley's recipe, a stewed mixture of cherry bark and the tips from spruce or fir boughs that bubbled on the back of the kitchen woodstove for days. But Margaret Arsenault's Maman concocted a mixture new to me:

When you'd get a cold in the winter – the cough, the cough. She used to take molasses, put it on the stove, chop up an onion, and she'd add that and ginger and a bit of soda powder. But the ginger. When you swallowed, it's a wonder we have any throats left. She'd wake you up – because you were asleep and didn't know you were coughing – sit you up and stuff this into you. That's the truth.

Did it work?

Oh yes, yes.

For chest colds, mustard plasters were liberally applied in the Arsenault home too, a mixture of mustard powder and flour that was usually wrapped in brown paper:

First rub your chest with lard because if you didn't, the mustard plaster would burn you, it was so powerful. Then Maman would lay this brown paper with this concoction of stuff in the middle on your chest and time it. After five minutes: 'Is it burning?' ' No.' After ten minutes: 'Is it burning?' 'Yes!'

Margaret's sister Florence remembers her honeymoon and one mustard plaster only too well. She needed some of Mary Malone MacPhee's alder salve for burns:

> I came home on my honeymoon because I took a bad cold. My husband and I were in bed, and Maman brought up the mustard plaster poultice. She put it on me she said, 'Now Pius,' that's my husband, 'Don't leave it on too long because it'll burn her.' I went to sleep. My God, I had blisters. On my honeymoon! My husband made fun of that for a long time.

Mustard plasters and honeymoons: one way or another, there's gonna be a hot time in the old town tonight. I think half of all home remedies were invented to cure the other half.

One of PEI's more open-minded doctors was Dr. Lester Brehaut from Murray River. He brought along a midwife for confinements back in the days when most doctors disliked midwives for their lack of formal training, plus the fact midwives rarely charged. Or were expected to work for free.

Dr. Lester chewed tobacco and had a sense of humour. One time in the 1920s, he was called to an overly-dignified lady's house in Wood Islands. He asked what the problem was and she hissed, "It's the servant girl. She says she's sick and won't get out of bed. I'm sure she's faking." Dr. Brehaut climbed the narrow back stairs to the tiny room above the kitchen where the "girl" lay with the covers up to her chin. "What's the problem," he asked. "They owe me two months' wages and won't pay me, and I'm not getting out of bed until they do," she answered. "Move over," he replied, "They owe me money too." She might have been making ten dollars a month, tops, and Dr. Brehaut two dollars a visit.

One time, Ada Baker MacKenzie was at a Beach Point house where Dr. Brehaut was attending a difficult birth. Ada said her neighbour was exceptionally poor, and the doctor knew he wasn't going to be paid. After the baby was born, he looked around for something to wrap it in. Finding nothing clean, he took off his shirt and wrapped the baby in it. When he left, there was five dollars on the kitchen table.

Dr. Brehaut brought Alvin MacSwain from Peters Road into the world in 1922. Alvin confirms Ada's story about the kind-hearted Dr. Brehaut:

> One story I liked about him was about a woman he said needed food as bad as she needed medicine. He would mail her the medicine and when she opened it, there was a five-dollar bill along with the medicine.

Dr. Lester Brehaut: legendary stories and a stash of five-dollar bills.

Alvin also had his own take on home remedies:

> Mustard plaster was a good thing but it was never a home remedy, was it? I was in the hospital one time and I had a mustard plaster put on me. But we all used old home remedies. The doctor was for them too. Dr. Brehaut told me a story one time. He had a woman come in to see him because she had bad eczema on her hands. He mixed a salve up for her – he did that a lot in those times – and sent her on her way. A few weeks later, he met her down in the village, 'So that stuff fixed your eczema did it?' She laughed, 'Oh no doctor. It was no good. I threw it away.' 'So how did you cure your hands?' 'Someone

told me to put crushed cranberries on my hands and that would cure the eczema.'

Dr. Brehaut asked for some of the cranberries, and a day later she brought him some. He sent them off to a lab to test what was in them. And the acid in his salve was exactly the same as what was in the cranberries only ten times higher. It would have burnt her. But the natural berry didn't. That's one of his stories.

Google the web and you'll find cranberries are still recommended for eczema but ironically an allergic reaction to cranberries results in hives on the neck, face, or hands.

I mentioned Amy Bryanton was the first person to tell me about using salt herring to cure a fever. When she was a girl in Spring Valley, she was seriously sick with pneumonia. In her fever, she overheard the doctor tell her mother and grandmother that there was nothing more he could do for her. Her grandmother Caseley took a salt herring, split it in half, and put the two halves on the soles of her feet. She put a pair of woollen socks on Amy's feet to hold the herring in place. Amy said, "When I woke up in the morning the fever was gone and the fish was cooked. They had to carry me downstairs to the table because I wouldn't walk on the herring."

When we put that story on the radio, you could hear the co-host and me giggling, making fun of the cure and at the same time disrespecting Amy. Well, the CBC switchboard lit up with calls from people who had had the salt-herring cure themselves. I went out and interviewed ten of those people and put their stories on the radio the next week.

Velma Ross used it and other home remedies passed down by her Grannie Gillis, who was a midwife:

In the 1940s, there was a big blizzard when we lived down at Carleton [Siding], and my little niece, four years old, had pneumonia. And we couldn't get the doctor, Dr. MacNeill down in Cape Traverse. The roads were all blocked. I put the goose grease on her chest and then a mustard plaster on her chest; she was very sick. She came out of it in a few days. Actually, putting salt herring on a person's feet would take out the fever. I've done that. I came home from the hospital one time – my son had an awful bad fever. We didn't know what to do, so I did that while we were waiting for the doctor to come. It took his temperature down.

What did the doctor say?

That doctor was from the Magdalene Islands and he was used to all those home remedies. He thought they were great.

Years later, I've collected well over a hundred similar salt-herring stories. When I asked Henry Gallant from Wellington if he ever heard of the salt-herring cure, he said, 'Sure, my mother used it all the time to cure a fever.' 'On the soles of your feet?' I said. 'What! Are you crazy?' Henry replied. 'You put it on the back of your neck.'

~~~~~

I have a collection of old magazines – *Time*, *Life*, *Saturday Evening Post*, *Liberty* – cluttering up the house, and I'm always amazed now to see the number of tobacco ads. Magazines as late as the 1960s were full of ads extolling the benefits of cigarettes as a cure for bad nerves; menthol cigarettes were recommended by doctors as a way of soothing sore throats. Sore throats probably caused by smoking cigarettes.

Go back another generation, and chewing tobacco ads were also rife in magazines such as *The Farm Journal* and *The Family Herald*. Farmers wanting a hit of nicotine chewed tobacco, especially when their chores required two free hands, like threshing grain or milking cows. The favorite chew on PEI was home-grown and manufactured in Charlottetown – Hickey and Nicholson Black Twist. The "figs of twist," as they were called, looked like a six-inch piece of twisted rope that had been dipped in molasses. Which in fact it had, a secret recipe of molasses and licorice. Sounds tasty, which is what John Moore, born in 1925, thought when he was fifteen and working on the family farm in South Milton, watching the hired hand chaw off a chew of twist:

> One chew in my life. One chew done me. We were in the field working the hay you know, a long ways away from water and the house. And the man who chewed, he'd be in his forties, the high forties, and he says, 'Take a bite of this.' I took a bite of it and boys, that was enough, it pretty near put me on the ground. By the jimminys, that was enough for me. I never tried it after. See, I was thirsty and just didn't know how to chew it right, I guess. I swallowed. Awful stuff, boys. Sickening time for a little while.

Thirty years later, I could repeat that story word for word except substituting carpenter for hired hand and Hickey and Nicholson for Pictou Twist. Sick as a parrot. I'll wager, one chew did a lot us in.

I interviewed Bob Nicholson, the last to run the family tobacco factory, which was down where the co-op apartments are now on Hensley Street. He showed me a photo dated around 1910 of his grandfather standing waist-high in a field of tobacco somewhere around North River Road. You could see the river in the background. It was all farms and orchards there at one time. Queen Square school pupils told me they used to sneak down to the Hickey and Nicholson factory and cut pieces off the big blocks of licorice. Apparently by itself it wasn't too tasty either.

Frances Clinton was born in Suffolk, PEI, in 1924. Her grammy, Loretta Court:

> Had them all. One was goose grease and turpentine. When my mother cooked a goose, she always saved the grease, and if you had a cold in your chest, you mixed it with turpentine and rubbed it on. It was a good remedy.

Grammy Court also had an unusual remedy right out of Oliver Twist: gruel.

> It was made with milk and oatmeal and brown sugar and a little bit of ginger. That was used if you were getting a cold. A cupful. It was lovely to drink.

I can't imagine.

Not every doctor was as sympathetic to the old ways, and most doctors did not condone midwifery. Of course, that didn't stop people from using both the old cures and midwives. Every community depended on midwives, the forgotten women of Island history. Make that Canadian history. Correction: world history.

Velma herself was born in the family dining room in 1926 with her Granny Gillis as the midwife. And the salt herring cure doesn't always involve the soles of the feet. The same week Amy Bryanton opened my eyes to that unusual cure, I happened to meet Henry Gallant who was living in Wellington but was born in 1909 in Urbainville:

> Well, if you had a fever or a headache, split a salt herring in two, and put a slice on your head, for a headache. And if you had a fever, split a herring and

put that in your socks on the soles of your feet. We
thought that was alright, it would work.

Did you ever do that and did it work?

Oh, yes. It was good.

Henry's Mum also used tansy as a home remedy. Tansy
grows about a metre high, bright yellow flowers and looks
something like goldenrod. Folks used the dried tansy
flowers for everything from expelling worms to treating
colds to stimulating the appetite. Henry's father was a
horse and cattle trader who used tansy tea, made from
both the flowers and the leaves, to treat a lame horse,
bathing the affected leg in the warm tansy tea.

From French River, Maisie Adams' mother was a midwife
and "country nurse." Mary Lisa Duggan put her life at
risk during the 1918-19 Spanish Influenza epidemic, going
into sick homes to clean the sick, wash bedclothes and
leave food. Maisie's brother Donald was working with
a skittish horse one day when the horse crushed him
against the barn wall. Donald's entire side bruised up
badly, and he was confined to bed for several weeks,
with daily soakings of tansy tea by his Mum. Donald
was a well-known horseman, and I've been told that
blacksmiths always kept a patch of tansy in the yard. I've
tasted tansy tea thanks to siblings Marjorie and Harry
Heffell from Travellers Rest who had a patch of tansy in
their front yard. It tasted bitter, but I've not been lame
since. However, be careful, tansy can be poisonous.

Jumpin' Jack Proud, whose father was P.J. Proud of Proud
and Moreside, Charlottetown blacksmiths, told me about
a vile-sounding home remedy that he thinks might have
saved his mother's life:

We pretty near lost her. Dad used to come home,
and he'd take liver and mix it with ginger ale, and

my mother drank it. That's what kept her going. Raw liver. Just the sight of it would make you upchuck. But that's what kept her going, and she lasted a long time.

I'm guessing she needed extra iron. Incidentally Jack's mum Winnifred was an RN, so there must have been some scientific basis for drinking a raw liver/ginger ale float. Better than chewing on a rusty horseshoe to get your iron.

Frances Clinton was born in 1924 in Bedford, PEI. Her grammie Loretta Court was a midwife and brought Frances into the world. Her grandmother made bloomers out of flour bags and was related to the Rustico Courts, famous for first catching and then peddling fish door-to-door. When cod and hake was gutted and split, the livers were tossed into an open barrel, eventually rotting down to a smoky-coloured cod liver oil.

"It tasted awful!" laughed Frances. That was just one of Grammie's home remedies.

> She had them all: mustard plasters was a big one, and another one was goose grease and turpentine. When my mother used to cook a goose, she always saved the grease and if you had a cold in your chest, you mixed it with the turpentine and rubbed it on. And she always used to make what we called gruel. It was made with milk and oatmeal and brown sugar and a little bit of ginger. That was used when you getting a cold. Take a cupful – it was lovely to drink, or eat – whatever. Gruel – that's what we called it anyway.

Gruel sounds like how it must taste. Wasn't it gruel little Oliver Twist asked of Mr Bumble, "Please Sir, I want more"?

Mustard plasters as a remedy were ubiquitous. I interviewed Margaret Shaw when she was a 101, and again when she was a 103, and she was still going strong as PEI's oldest resident at a 109. Margaret was born in her grandparents' house in Riverdale in 1908, and grew up in the era of no money, distant doctors and home remedies:

> I guess mustard plasters would be one. And my mother had a remedy called cherry bark. You go to the woods see, and there's a thin, thin layer of bark on the cherry tree. Cut off the top bark and throw it away, and you peel off thin layer underneath. If you start at the top, you might get it to go right to the bottom. Then cut that up in slices — it was kind of brownish. Put that in a pot of water and boil it and boil and boil it, and you'd have perhaps a cupful of bark water. Juice. By golly it was rank and bitter. Whew. Put some sugar in it and drink that. That was your spring remedy, like a tonic. Then there was a booster, what they'd call a booster today: sulphur and molasses. Take that for a booster to clean out your system. Oh, holy saints.

Did you ever take that?

> I had to. Whether I wanted to or not. Oh, mercy goodness, that was horrible stuff. Everybody pretty near had to live outside.

Some people thought the worse the home remedy tasted, the better it worked. The annual spring "tonics" as Margaret just mentioned are cases in point. Even the molasses couldn't disguise the metallic taste of the sulphur. It is still thought by some that eating blackstrap molasses with its high copper content reverses gray hair. Kids took the "tonic" everyday for a week, and I'm told shaking your socks over the woodstove produced a shower of sparks from the sulphur working its way down to your feet. A one-room school teacher confided she wished school was closed that week, the smell emanating from her pupils was so bad.

My Grammie was a great believer in spring tonics, and even the farm animals weren't forgotten. Cod liver oil was dosed out to one and all, and was even put in the hens' cooked mash every day along with the boiled potatoes, bran, and supper leftovers. Although, I don't recall hens' gizzards being part of her home remedy repertoire.

George Hart who grew up in the Brighton area of Charlottetown, once took a remedy using gizzards, that digestive stomach particular to fowl:

> Oh, we had mustard plasters and goose grease. Oh yes – and my grandmother one time gave me chicken's gizzard. For when you have a cold. She made a tea out of a chicken's gizzard, and, by God, it really upset my stomach.

Did it cure your cold?

> Oh, it might have.

I'm waiting to hear back from Twinings, the tea people, about my new Gizzard Brew. I love that the tea upset George's stomach. Took his mind off his cold.

That reminds me of the story about the farmer who raised a flock of turkeys to sell at Christmas. He owed a neighbour a favour and promised him a free turkey. Christmas came and went, and no turkey. Weeks later in the new year, they met in town and the neighbour exclaimed, "I thought you were going to give me a turkey for Christmas my dinner." The farmer replied, "Oh yes, I was going to, but the bird got better."

Daring Flyers and Their Machines

Alfred McGaughey

I remember seeing the first airplane. We were in school and it was Mrs. Jack Jenkins from the Upton airport. All the hens and ducks ran to hide. Thought it was a big hawk. The cattle were scared, it wasn't up that high.

Alfred McGaughey, born in 1916, lived in Bonshaw and was thrilled when he saw his first airplane, a de Havilland Puss Moth flown by PEI's first female pilot.

Mrs. Doctor Jack Jenkins, she was from England. He met her in the First World War when he was overseas. She came from millionaires. She was one of those highly-educated ladies because she married a doctor.

Alfred had most of his facts right. Louise Mitchell Jenkins, aka The Daring Lady Flyer, was married to Dr. Jack and they owned Upton Airport, PEI's first, situated on their huge farm just west of Charlottetown. She came from a moneyed family in Pennsylvania and she met Dr. Jack while both were working in an army hospital in England during the First World War. She was the first woman in Canada to own an aircraft, and she set several speed and distance records with her Puss Moth, registered CF-PEI.

When not soaring in the clouds, Louise drove around in a red Rolls Royce with a Russian wolfhound sitting in the front seat. The car had the steering wheel on the right side, so when she met another car, it looked like the dog was driving. She was an amazing woman, loved adventure, rode camels in Egypt, skied the Alps, and drove ambulances in the First World War.

Lloyd Gates certainly knew who Louise Jenkins was. Lloyd, who always wanted to be a pilot, was born in 1924 in West Royalty and grew up in the shadow of Upton Airport. Just down the road, loomed CFCY's tower, PEI's first radio tower, ideal for a young man, who wanted to fly and who wanted to prove he wasn't afraid of heights.

> I started climbing the tower one day on a dare, seventy-five feet high. I got up about half way, and Fred Large, he was the engineer then, he came roaring and yelling at me, 'Get down off that tower or it'll kill ya.' Well, there wasn't too much excitement around. You had to make your own excitement in those days.

Like all young boys, Lloyd was entranced by the aircraft and the men – and woman – who flew them.

> . I was making model airplanes when I was a kid... I watched [the pilots] flying in weather when even the birds weren't flying. You'd hear them coming but you wouldn't see them until the last second, just lifting over the trees in big heavy snowstorms. There was no radar or anything else. They just flew by the seat of their pants. Exciting days.

It was no coincidence that Lloyd and his brother Bobby wound up in the Canadian Air Force during the Second World War.

In the 1930s, Keith Pratt ran a large general store in the western end of PEI. The train went through Bloomfield Station every day, and Keith became what the English call a trainspotter. Keith became friends with the drivers, firemen, and trainmen; he and his wife Jean serving them tea and cinnamon rolls. Keith also photographed everything to do with the railway, right down to the bricks and eggs being shipped out, to the puncheons of molasses and carloads of coal coming in. Keith was an all-rounder, interested in everything. He also knew the man who owned the first airplane in West Prince County.

> Frank Doyle from out in Glengarry, Joe Doyle's son. Frank and Oscar and Mike, they all went to the States, and Frank came down with an airplane. He followed the railway track down from Boston. They had a field cleaned for him to land. He gave everybody a flight in it. I had a flight in it. Ohh, it was lovely. Lovely. And there was a young fella who sold bread — I can't think of his name now — and he had a plane and he gave us a flip around Portage. It was nice. He sold bread.

Maybe that's how he got his bread to rise.

During the Second World War, Avro Ansons and Bristol Bolingbrokes from the RCAF Mount Pleasant air base did manoeuvres over Prince County. Until the Second World War, airplanes were unusual sights over the Island. Then three Commonwealth and British pilot and navigational air bases arrived lock, stock, and barrel. Suddenly airplanes were everywhere.

Keith Pratt missed seeing Fairey Battles and single

engine Harvards in the PEI skies. He was in the army serving overseas.

~~~~~

The hangar at Upton Airport was situated where Diagnostic Chemicals' main building in the West Royalty Industrial Park is now. One of the pilots at Upton was Junior Jones, who flew around the Maritimes taking people up for a flip for $5.00, and landing in farmers' fields.

> The first time I took to the air was February 1937. I was thirteen. Bob and I would go up almost every day after school to Upton Airport. We'd beg the pilots for a ride. Canadian Airways were flying there every day with the mail from Moncton and Pictou, flying de Havilland Rapides, an eight-passenger, twin engine biplane.

> One day just after they changed an engine, the pilot and engineer said we could go with them and fly over Charlottetown to check the engine, see if it worked. So, we both got on and I sat on Bob's knee. The plane was on skis – it was wintertime – and I said if mother knew she'd probably kill us. Exciting old time.

Upton Airport was officially opened in 1931 when Doctor Jack and Louise hosted the Trans-Canada Air Pageant, attended by over 8,000 people.

> Back then, they had air pageants, and planes would come from the States and Canada. All kinds of aerobatics and they'd throw flour bombs, a bag full of flour, to try and bomb something. I saw my first autogyro there, the prototype of the helicopter. We were sure it crashed because it came straight down and we knew planes didn't do that. We ran

all the way up to the airport to see the crash. But it never happened.

Islander Harry Whitlock joined the Royal Flying Corps along with Canadian pilots Billy Bishop and Billy Barker, famous for shooting down German planes. Both were awarded the Victoria Cross among numerous other war decorations. Harry was Edith Whitlock Pryce's favorite uncle, and she and Harry's Mum decided to hop on the train and visit Harry. He'd moved to Montreal after the war and become a wealthy businessman.

> We went to Montreal to see my father's brother, our famous millionaire uncle. He was always called a millionaire. He took us to a flying show because he had been a pilot in the war. Handsome man. All the girls were crazy about him. And I was his favorite, would you believe. So, he took us to an airshow, and I was fascinated and immediately wanted to be a pilot. And it's a wonder I didn't. I guess it was not really available here on the Island. There was a little place, Upton Airport, and I think they had maybe one or two planes.

There were always at least two aircraft at Upton, flown by the airport's owners Dr. Jack and Louise. Louise would probably have been sympathetic to Edith's dream. Edith did get a chance to fly again after she came home from visiting rich Uncle Harry.

> I went up in one of those planes, only room for the pilot and myself. You sat almost on the floor. Now that pilot stayed with my grandmother. [Edith's grandmother Whitlock ran a high-end boarding house in Charlottetown.] That's how that came about, that I was able to go up in that little plane. I was crazy about flying. Just loved it. But I never did go into that.

Edith was the daughter of Edgar Whitlock, famous for running a tire and vulcanization shop on Kent Street, and for taking his wife trout fishing in Kings County for their honeymoon. Edith eventually took to the air again in a roundabout way: she married a British airman who came to PEI in 1940 when the RAF set up a pilot and navigational school on the site of the present-day Charlottetown airport.

~~~~~

Crashes were all too common. Dr. Frederick Banting and Dr. Charles Best, the two co-discoverers of insulin, which has saved millions of lives around the world, both have a PEI connection. In the 1970s, Dr. Best bought a heritage riverfront home in Cardigan, the McNichol-Best house, a unique mix of arts and crafts, shingle, and chateau styles, built partly with sandstone quarried nearby.

In the Second World War, Charlottetown pilot and businessman Carl Burke was a member of Ferry Command, flying aircraft of all types built in Canada across the Atlantic to Britain. Syd Clay was born in Nottinghamshire, England, and came to Canada in 1940 with the Royal Air Force to set up an air training base where the Charlottetown airport now sits. Syd worked with Carl Burke after the war. Syd was also an artist with an encyclopedic knowledge of the war and PEI.

> One of these Ferry Command Hudsons took off from Dorval for Scotland, and, in addition to the pilot and navigator and wireless operator, it was carrying Dr. Banting, the medical scientist who invented insulin. This plane ran into difficulties over Newfoundland because of very adverse weather. Eventually, they ran out of fuel and crashed near a small lake.

In February 1941, Dr. Banting was headed to London, England, to test a new flight suit he'd invented that would keep pilots from passing out in high altitudes when the Lockheed Hudson bomber crashed in dense woods.

> But there was no plane available there to get to it, so a call was sent out, and Carl Burke and his mechanic Ralph Yeo took off from Moncton in a de Havilland Dragon, a biplane, this was on skis, of course, in the wintertime, and they flew to Newfoundland, refueled, and went to the search site. They landed on the lake, donned snowshoes, and trekked into the wreck, and they brought out the ... bodies of Banting, and the navigator, and the wireless operator. The pilot who was an American, a civilian, J.C. Mackey, was still alive and they brought him out.

> They flew into Gander, which was a fledgling Royal Canadian Air Force base at the time. The pilot was transferred immediately to the hospital. Now there's another PEI connection there. A young man had graduated from medical school. He joined the RCAF as a medical officer and was stationed at Gander, and he happened to be Dr. J.K.L. Irwin of Charlottetown. Irwin kept the pilot alive for two weeks until he could be transferred to a major hospital. And he survived.

What a tragedy. Dr. Banting was already a First World War hero, awarded the Military Cross for bravery on the battlefield serving with the 13th Canadian Field Ambulance at Arras. At the Banting Interpretation Centre near Musgrave Harbour, the wrecked Lockheed Hudson bomber and a fully intact one sit side-by-side as a memorial to Dr. Banting, just a few miles up the rugged coast from a tiny fishing community called Deadman's Bay.

Banting died serving in the Second World War, yet miles

from the firestorm raging across Europe. A decade earlier, the scent of war was already in the air in the shape of a German zeppelin. This huge silver airship was named in honour of a First World War German Field Marshal named Ludwig Hans Anton von Beneckendorff und von Hindenburg. Try writing that on the back of your Visa card.

The Hindenburg advertised the Third Reich as it floated eerily over land and water with swastikas painted on its tailfins. En route from Germany to New Jersey carrying both passengers and freight, it was seen by hundreds of Islanders including Yvonne Gauthier:

> We were playing as children around Rustico, and noticed this in the air, and we thought we were going to be bombed. We were really, really afraid. It was fairly low to the ground and it was so huge compared to what we had ever seen in the air.

With Yvonne that day was her schoolmate Lucy LeClair.

> We were going to St Andrews School, and we were down by the brook, and we saw the zeppelin coming over and we didn't know what it was. Yvonne said she thought it was a rocket ship but I don't know what I thought it was. I knew it was German.

On the north side of central PEI is Rustico and, as the Hindenburg loomed over the hills, it and its shadow scared cattle and poultry. One man told me his hens stopped laying and his cows didn't milk for two days. Yvonne's parents also saw the zeppelin, "Our parents were afraid of it as we were and they couldn't explain why it had come over Rustico."

It must have sailed over Charlottetown as well, because Minnie Down Clay, the aforementioned Syd's wife, saw it over Esher Street. Her brother climbed a telephone pole to try and touch the zeppelin. Lucy LeClair's husband Leonard, a Second World War veteran, also saw the German dirigible the same day as Lucy and Yvonne.

> At that time, when I was a kid, we used to have rum-runners. They used to be right out past the harbour there, and that's about the same time that zeppelin came over. Fishermen used to go out there and buy the booze off the rum boats, and bring it in here. You used to find it everywhere then. Everybody had rum at that time thanks to the rumrunners. My uncle had a keg of it in the hay in his barn over there.

With all that rum and this strange airship people thought they were imagining things?

> Yeah right. It all happened about the same time, yeah.

Silver zeppelins instead of pink elephants. I must mention Leonard LeClair was one of seven brothers who fought in the Second World War, plus the baby of the family too young for the Second World War, so he enlisted and fought in the Korean War. And, coincidentally, the brothers had at one time or another all been bellhops. And the good news is, they all came home.

But bad news: the Nazis used the Hindenburg as a giant mobile advertising sign for hate. The company operating it had been established by Hermann Goering in March 1935 to ensure Nazi control, hence the swastika tailfin decorations.

In May 1937, the Hindenburg crashed while docking at Lakehurst, New Jersey, in a fiery explosion that killed thirty-six passengers and crew. After similar crashes by American and British airships, it was the end of the rigid airship era. But it was not the end of the death and destruction that even more deadly aircraft would inflict on the world just a few years down the road.

Buoys, Bombs, and Doodlebugs: D-Day Connections

Star Weekly magazine

Almost as important as the First World War's Battle of Vimy Ridge was in solidifying a Canadian identity, in the Second World War was the D-Day invasion of France. Canadians fought with the Americans, British, and other Allies on the beaches of Normandy on 6 June 1944, the beginning of the end for the Germans under Hitler's regime. Canadian soldiers, sailors, pilots, doctors, and nurses did Canada proud that day and in the subsequent push to liberate Europe.

First World War veterans were notably reluctant to talk about their experiences in the trenches of Flanders or manning mine-sweepers in the English Channel. I've found Second World War veterans to be a bit more forthcoming maybe because the reasons for the war – Hitler, in particular – were more obvious. Here are stories from some of the veterans, all with a D-Day connection.

On D-Day, Islanders fought alongside other Canadians in the Normandy invasion of France. One veteran told me he remembered the noise as much as anything else. To him it seemed all the aircraft, ships, and guns were amassed along the Normandy beaches that dawn. One of those gun-soldiers was Private Raymond Dixon with the North Nova Scotia Highlanders, better known as the

North Novies. Raymond was born in 1912, and joined the army in 1942.

> They'd never have finished the war only for me. I'd hate to tell you a lot of the stuff I saw. Went in D-Day with them. I was just glad to land. We didn't care if we got killed, we were so sick. An awful storm that morning. It's a good job I didn't swim because I'd have drowned [trying to get to shore], but he drove [the landing craft] right up pretty close. Oh, we had some hard times. Scarey. A lot of dead fellas there. The engineers went in first to clear the beach. We seen them floating in the water. But we didn't care; we figured we were going to get it. I was so seasick, I didn't care. And as far as you could see up the Channel, it was just a mass of ships. France was all smoke. You'd think she was all on fire. They'd bombed for hours there. Big ships out at sea shooting twenty miles in. Firing. The Germans had pillboxes right along there, all cement. We got quite a shelling. A lot of our fellas were taken prisoner. Only five came back that night from our platoon. I never thought much about it. Just wondering what's ahead and what you're going to do. Lots of fun. Once we struck land, we met a lot of women, lots of kisses from the villagers.

It takes a brave man to admit he's scared. Raymond and the North Novies moved on, helped in the liberation of Holland and then on to Germany. Raymond proudly wore the D-Day battle ribbon after he came home, but it took decades after the war ended for the sailors of the Merchant Navy to be recognized, and paid, for their contribution in the Second World War.

Vincente Elordieta was one of those merchant seamen. Vincente was born in 1909. He grew up surrounded by sailors and, as he put it, "was proud to be a Liverpool

Dock Road urchin." His Basque parents and grandparents moved to Liverpool, England, and recruited sailors and shepherds from the Basque country on the border of France and Spain to emigrate to North America. The shepherds continued on to the American mid-west, where they met vicious opposition from cattle ranchers. The sailors worked on White Star and Cunard luxury liners crossing the Atlantic. Even though his father, grandfather, and several uncles died at sea, Vincente became a merchant seaman in the 1930s.

In May 1942, Vincente was in the port of Hoboken, New Jersey, loading a shipload of supplies and equipment to literally build a hospital from the ground up:

> I was on the steamer *Kitty's Brook* – chief engineer – and it took us two weeks to load up everything for a hospital: operating tables, beds, linens, even pianos. On the deck, we had bulldozers and two big cranes on the foredeck to lift up the steel girders to make the building. It took over two weeks to load the ship jack-pack full. When bang. We got torpedoed. And all that stuff disappeared in ten minutes. Ship and all that cargo – everything was gone. I think we lost fourteen men.

On the tenth of May 1942 at 3:10 in the morning, the unescorted *Kitty's Brook* was hit by one torpedo fired by the German *U-Boat 588* off Cape Sable, in southwest Nova Scotia. Records show nine deaths and twenty-five survivors. Vincente ran up to the main deck as the sea poured in, and wound up in a life raft along with the captain and several other crew members. They spent five days at sea and were eventually picked up by a fisherman out of Lockeport, N.S.

Two amazing things happened: the U-Boat surfaced and the men in the rafts thought they were going to be machine-gunned. Instead, the German captain identified himself, and asked if they knew their way to land, which they did. He saluted them as the submarine disappeared beneath the icy sea. After the war, it took Vincente years to track down U-Boat captain Victor Vogel, actually, his widow because three months after sinking the *Kitty's Brook*, *U-Boat 588* was tracked and depth charged on 31 July 1942 by the Canadian corvette HMCS *Wetaskiwin* and the destroyer HMCS *Skeena* off the coast of New-foundland. All forty-six crew on U-588 were lost.

The second amazing part of this story changed Vincente's life, as if being sunk in the Atlantic by a U-boat and surviving isn't life-changing enough. Vincente had a bad head wound and his legs had developed gangrene from exposure. The survivors were ambulanced from Lockeport to Camp Hill Hospital in Halifax:

> I was pretty far gone by this time. I was flat out when we landed in Halifax at midnight. The orderlies gave us all a bath, cleaned us up, and put us into a johnny shirt, and so on. About half past one in the morning, I got wheeled up to a ward-Q ward. And the nurse in the ward said, 'I've got him.' And she said to me, 'I'll put you into this bed.' In those days there were seventy beds in every ward in Camp Hill Hospital. She put the stretcher alongside the bed and went to the other side of the bed, and she said, 'You better help me if you can.' But my feet were swollen like pumpkins because of exposure. I was pretty bad.

The nurse insisted Vincente roll off the stretcher onto the bed on his own. He, in turn, insisted she help since that was her job. She told him she knew what her job was and that was to assay his condition. Two stubborn heads knocking together. Finally:

> I got in the bed. And I married that girl. The first time
> I met my wife, it was half one in the morning, and I
> was all dressed up in a johnny shirt.

After the war, Vincente came back to Halifax and courted
Helen Soloman, an RN from Georgetown, PEI. Her family
was one of the first Lebanese immigrant families to PEI,
and her father Peter ran a grocery store and sidelined
as a photographer. After Vincente and Helen married,
he went back to school and became a marine engineer
designing ships and ice breakers. They lived in Montreal,
eventually moving to PEI where Vincente worked for
Northumberland Ferries.

However, 1942 was not the end of the war for Vincente.
After his legs healed, he was assigned to the cable ship
CS *Cyrus Field* based out of Halifax. Fittingly, the vessel
was being used in anti-submarine service, laying mines
in east coast harbours. Then in 1944 – here's the D-Day
connection – the CS *Cyrus Field* ran the undersea radio
cables that helped in the Allied victory on D-Day.

Far from the English Channel, John Rendall farmed Black
Angus cattle on the tiny Orkney island of Papa Westray
off the windswept north coast of Scotland. The Rendall
farm happens to be the where my blacksmithing ancestors toiled for generations before striking out 220 years
ago for one of the great unknowns: Canada. One of John
Rendall's neighbours, Woody Groat, served in the Royal
Navy and came home from the Second World War with
this amazing story about D-Day.

> They had huge buoys in France to tie the boats up
> to. His job was to sit on a buoy and get ahold of
> their anchor – the big boats – and get it affixed to
> a shackle on the buoy. There came a gale of wind
> and the buoy he was on drifted away and capsized,

and everybody except him drowned. A telegram was written to send home, that he was drowned, when they found him sitting on the buoy still. He was sitting for days on that buoy. For days. And he got very bad with the cold, the exposure, and he got tuberculosis in the neck. He was a while in a hospital in Southampton. They got it cured and he eventually came home.

While recuperating in the Southampton hospital, Ensign Groat met another Royal Navy sailor who asked Woody where he was from. Woody replied, "Oh I come from Orkney." "What part of Orkney?" "Papa Westray," Woody replied, thinking the man wouldn't have a clue where this isolated little island was. Turned out the other sailor had been stationed at the British naval base at Scapa Flow in Orkney and claimed Woody couldn't possibly be from Papa Westray. "No," he said, "You dinna come from Papa Westray. There's nobody alive on Papa Westray."

John Rendall knew why the sailor was skeptical:

> For a year before D-Day, the island was used for target practice for the navy. They left Scapa Flow, and they lay way out over the horizon, and shelled us for a whole year.

Everyone had been ordered to evacuate Papa Westray so the Royal Navy could use it for target practice. The order fell on deaf ears.

> We were all living here but nobody knew we were here. They thought there was nobody on the island.

Did you hear the bombs and shells?

> Oh yes. Every house shook every time a big shell landed. They fired all night as well and they put up great big flares and it was daylight night and day.

Woody was astounded to hear this news and wrote home, and in a week received a reply from his parents. Like John Rendall's family, the Groats feared if they left, they wouldn't be allowed back, so they stayed put, proving once again that islanders are a stubborn, independent breed. My Thompsons came from Papa Westray. When I visited in 1999, one man told me the island was "bombed" day and night for weeks. No one was killed, but there were still huge holes in pastures and fields.

~~~~~

Back at the Normandy invasion, another Islander, Charles Gallant from Charlottetown waded ashore with fourteen thousand other Canadians on the beach code-named Juno.

It was pretty scary. Oh jeez, there were thousands of men, bullets flying everyplace.

Were there bodies in the water?

Yeah. Fellas I was with fifteen minutes earlier... they were gone.

At the age of seventeen, Charles had signed up to fight immediately when war was declared in 1939. Underage, he forged his enlistment papers: both of his parents were dead. He was with the Second Canadian Artillery Battery and, like many Canadians, his first taste of live battle was at D-Day.

It was pretty scary. I ducked underneath a wall, and the infantry and the tanks came up, and after that is was pretty good going, we had them on the run. After we got through, I was on my own and they gave me a truck or a Jeep and a map reference. I didn't know where I was going. I'd just drive, delivering ammo, food, everything for the front lines. I'd take officers up to the front in a Jeep.

Dangerous work.

> I guess it was. Pretty scary sometimes. This German
> plane came over and started to fire on the highway.
> I stopped the truck and jumped and got in the ditch.
> He just kept on firing. I figured he was drunk. That
> was kind of hairy. I had a quart of rum with me and
> I was into that. I said if I'm going to die, I'm going
> to die happy.

Bill Price knew all about drinking on the job. Bill was born in 1910 in South Wales and, along with their "bait," the lunch served in the field, the labourers on his grandfather's farm were given a tankard of either weak cider or beer to wash down their bread and cheese. Bill served in the Second World War with the Argyle and Sutherland Highlanders who trained all over Britain before finally bivouacking on the south coast of England in May 1944. Bill and tens of thousands of other soldiers were waiting for D-Day.

> It was all kept hush-hush, wasn't it? We were down
> in Sussex and all around, there was full of soldiers.
> Canadians were down there; they used to put on
> big ice hockey matches in Brighton. Ice hockey was
> a new thing in England then, and we used to think
> it was wonderful. Clever people at it, weren't they?
> That was it, aye.

Bill had already been across the Channel fighting and stayed lucky until the German retreat after D-Day.

> After Normandy, I was wounded at the Battle of
> Falaise [12-21 August 1944]. If I told you how many
> places I was during the war, it's a list as long as your
> arm. War was organized bloody chaos. Somebody
> had the master plan, but in the army, you always
> thought how did we ever win the war.

Tank battles with a desperate retreating army, commanded by a madman named Hitler must have frustrated everyone. Ivan Connors from Charlottetown was another D-Day veteran who found that the noise of the aircraft and the constant bombardment by off-shore naval vessels, not to mention the defensive fire of German machine-guns and mortars, almost drove him mad.

> PEI was a million miles away when I was crawling on the beach of Normandy. A lot went through my mind.

Ivan was with the 22nd Field Ambulance Unit. His job was rescuing wounded Canadians at Juno Beach and delivering them to one of the mobile medical hospitals, which had been set up immediately after the invasion. Ivan said there were plenty to rescue:

> There were smashed streets, and the rubble was thirty feet high.

Ivan might had run into another Islander that day: Dr. Gordon Lea, who was frantically patching up the soldiers brought to his mobile hospital. Gordon Lea was born in 1913 on a farm in Victoria-by-the-Sea. Young Gordon attended the two-roomed school in Victoria, breezed through college and university, and by 1938, added M.D. to his name. A year later, the war started, and he enlisted. In 1938, he graduated from medical school. Six years later on D-Day 1944, Major Gordon Lea found himself with the 7th Canadian General Hospital, the first medical unit set up after the Normandy invasion.

Years ago, when I went to interview Dr. Gordon Lea, initially, it was talk about his beautiful flower gardens in the Brighton area of Charlottetown. Dr. Lea was born in 1913, and had planned to take over the family farm in Victoria-by-the-Sea. His father, Walter Lea, was a career politician and the first farmer-premier of PEI. In the 1935 election, his party won all 30 seats in the Legislature – a first in the British Commonwealth.

> We crossed the Channel in style in what had been a luxury ship for the tourist trade. When we got into that I thought, 'The war is a snap,' but first light in the morning, we could see the coast there and the shell-fire going on. We were taken off this lovely thing and put on a raft with four oil drums under each corner and an outboard motor. We invaded the damn continent in that.

Patching up the wounded is hard enough at the best of times but under continuous enemy, fire it must have seemed impossible:

> We were at one side of the landing beach, and I thought they were so busy over there I hoped maybe we could sneak in and that's literally what happened. For the first month, we were largely a casualty clearing station. We gave them first-aid treatment and got them on the first plane back to England. There was a constant shuffle of ambulance planes back and forth. I don't think anybody who was wounded wasn't in a hospital in England within three or four hours of being wounded.

Charles Gallant might have trucked medical supplies to Dr. Lea, and Ivan O'Connor might have brought him wounded soldiers, but such was the tremendous shelling and gunfire in those early days of the invasion, the three Islanders probably didn't know the others existed. The Allies kept pushing the retreating Germans further away from the coast; the three Islanders in the thick of the battles. Both sides suffered tremendous losses. Gordon continued:

> After we got into Normandy, we had all sorts of

German prisoners of war come in as patients. We just treated them exactly the same as our own.

Was there ever any fear that they might attack you?

No. They were guys doing their job and we just doing our job. We looked after all sorts of Germans who were shot down or that sort of thing. They were decent guys, same as me.

A farm boy from the German equivalent of Victoria.

That's right. What the hell am I doing here? Why am I not home picking potatoes?

He was a better person than I'll ever be, patching up the enemy. Registered Nurse Mae Ames told me a similar story. When her street in Manchester was bombed by the Luftwaffe, a neighbour she had said hello to on her way to the hospital that morning was killed by a bomb. All they found was a button from his coat. Later that day, Mae's floor at the hospital was taken over by armed soldiers who were guarding wounded German airmen who had been shot down in that air raid. Mae wound up nursing those men. The only upside to the story was Mae fell in love with one of the Canadian soldiers on guard duty. She married Frank Ames, and that's how she eventually came to PEI. Mae was full of spirit and fire.

My great uncle and my wife's grandfather both served in the medical corps in the First World War. Both men came home, became doctors. However, traumatized by what they had witnessed in France and Belgium, they moved as far away as possible from so-called civilization: one to northern Saskatchewan, the other to what is now a ghost town near Alaska in northern British Columbia.

Man's inhumanity to man countered by man's magnanimity to man. The Germans might have been in full retreat, but exactly one week after D-Day, the first so-called vengeance weapons rained down on England, the infamous V-1 rockets, nicknamed Buzz Bombs and Doodlebugs by the still-stiff-upper – lipped British. The attacks were in retaliation for D-Day, and the deadly rockets killed indiscriminately. Margaret Quinn was working as a children's nurse in southern England in June 1944, and throughout the war, had witnessed daily dogfights and bombings.

> We saw thirty-nine planes shot down, and we saw eighteen pilots bailing out of the planes. Some landed, but they used to fire at the parachutes and the pilots would come down and just be crushed. No survivors.

Then, on the thirteenth of June 1944, something new and ominous streaked across the sky.

> I was going to work at six o'clock in the morning and I was sure it was the devil I was seeing, because this thing was going in and out of the clouds with this huge red tail. This was the rocket fire, see. Unfortunately, at one of our wartime nurseries, the ack-ack [anti-aircraft] guns hit one of the Doodlebugs. The wind took it and it landed on the nursery, and it killed twenty-nine children and nineteen nurses.

If you believe in curses, maybe Margaret's village was under a spell. She lived in Hever, Kent, famous for its moated castle, the home of Anne Boleyn, Henry VIII's second wife whom he callously beheaded.

Margaret left both the old and new carnage behind in 1946 when she married an Island soldier and came to PEI as a war bride. Dr. Lea came home to PEI, ran a successful medical practice, and in his spare time, cultivated roses and other blooms that drew a stream of admirers.

War and the beaches of Normandy must have seemed a long way off.

Both Mae and Margaret would probably agree with Dr. Lea's paradoxical assessment of his experiences in the Second World War:

> I hated every minute of it and wouldn't have missed it for the world.

Amen. We never did get around to talking about his flower gardens.

Island Women (Even the Boats): Strong, Smart, Determined

Maud Prowse Thompson

Strong, smart women have been a part of my family since anyone can remember. I've lucked out for at least four generations: mother, wife, daughter, and my grandmothers, both of whom were midwives. My father's mother – Nanny Thompson – put my Dad in the warming oven to keep him alive after he was born, the smaller and weaker of twins. He was 89-years strong when he died. My Grammie Annie Hilda Cunningham, an RN trained in Newburyport, Mass., who had to quit work when she got married, once sliced off most of her big toe with the axe while splitting firewood. Both her son and husband were bedridden at the time. She was 20 miles from a doctor, so she pulled off her rubber boot, poured out the blood, and sewed her toe back on. And then probably made bread, and went out and fed the hens.

I was fortunate to have met many other strong women from that generation. Like Grammie, Ella Willis was an RN, and a strong, determined woman. Ella was born in 1910 on the family farm in Hampshire where she walked the two miles to and from school every day:

The poor teachers, they had a rough time of it. They'd have about twenty-five or thirty children, grades one to ten. There was always big, young men in school, because they stayed home in the summertime and helped on the farm, and then they went to school in the wintertime. I recall one particular gentleman – he turned out to be a lawyer – but anyway, when he was in school, he was a menace as far as the teacher was concerned. One of his tricks: at noon time when she had gone to her boarding place to eat her dinner, he got all the children – it was wintertime and we used to wear long scarves – he got those scarves and he tied them around our waist. Over the teacher's desk was a trap door going up into the attic. He got up there and opened it, and he hauled us all up there. Teacher came back, rang the bell for school to start, and no children. He waited until she was a little frustrated, then he started dropping us down one at a time. She tried to punish him by putting him out in the woodshed. He was one character.

Ella was a nurse – one of the few jobs available to working women a hundred years ago. Nurse, school teacher, shop assistant, telephone operator, domestic, farm labourer, maybe. Even then female school-teachers were usually paid less than their male counterparts. No wonder so many of that generation headed south to the Boston States where at least a domestic servant could save a few dollars to send back home to the Island.

~~~~~

When I was sixteen, I started out to teach school and I got thirty-five dollars a month. For ten months.

Born in Emyvale on the 4th of December 1904, Mary Morrissey knew a thing or two about women as second-class citizens. Women didn't have the vote and were expected to give up their job as soon as they married. If not before. There weren't many jobs open to women either: teacher, nurse, domestic, milliner, seamstress, store clerk.

> That's the reason that so many of the young girls, my sister included, went to Boston to work at housekeeping. They'd go up there and get in with a wealthy family, and they'd give them a decent wage.

In the States not only was the pay better, it was usually prompt. On PEI, Mary was supposed to receive an annual teaching supplement of $75 provided by the local school trustees. That would have bumped her pay to $425 a year, but like many rural teachers she didn't always get the supplement. Some districts didn't have the resources to pay a supplement at all.

> Anyone who was working at the five and ten or any of the stores in town made about the same wages. Just a few dollars a week.

Mary taught school for eleven years and she did not receive a raise during that time. Eventually, she went into business for herself, buying a Charlottetown corner store, the Economy Grocery, and didn't look back. She lived to be 110 years old.

Stella MacDougall was born the same year as Ella Willis: 1910. At the age of sixteen, Stella went to work down the road at Fulton Court's general store next to the train station in Bedford. That same year she saw her first automobile:

> There were three people that used to come to the store who had cars. I could almost write out their order before they gave it to me. They were the ones who could have a can of something – a can of peas. And I remember the first can of peaches that [was] on the shelf. Everything was in bulk: tea and sugar,

beans and rice, barley and whatever-name it, it was in bulk. You had to bag it up. They would give me a list.

The train came at four o'clock, and people would come and get their mail and get their groceries. And after five o'clock, everything went quiet. In those years, people were travelling the railway tracks looking for work; the men. It was nothing for someone to come into the store, 'I want a fig of twist' [chewing tobacco] or 'I want a package of tobacco. I have no money.' I told the manager, and I said if they come in asking for it, they get it. But nobody would ever lay a hand on you; I was never really scared of anybody. They'd just come in off the track: 'I have no money.' Well, give it to them, and away they'd go. They'd thank you and take off. Today, they'd be called hobos. But they weren't hobos; they were just people who were looking for a job, just like ourselves.

Riding the rails, even on PEI, and this was the 1920s before the Great Depression. Stella was making $35 a month, working 75 hours a week behind the counter at Court's Store. She told me that for some reason Tuesdays were the busiest nights in Bedford. Usually, it was Saturday night when the country stores would be packed with folks shopping, gossiping, and gawking. People have pointed out to me the tough times in the Maritimes started right after the First World War, which also coincided with the end of the wooden shipbuilding era. I'd like to know how many Boston houses were built by Maritime shipwrights and carpenters. I bet those houses don't leak and, in a pinch, will float.

~~~~~

Nellie Young was born in the Boston States in 1906 because her Dad had moved the family there looking for work. The family eventually moved back to PEI. Nellie landed her first job as head cook at Johnston's lobster factory in North Lake making "big money":

> God. Nothing. Ten dollars a month. I had two cookees. Three o'clock in the morning until ten or eleven at night. The fishermen slept upstairs where I was, some of them, and three o'clock, I'd get up and the girls would get up with me. We had a great big range-great big oven. We used to put a quarter of beef in it at a time, steak and roasts, and all that. I'd hit the stove pipe and you talk for a racket then. They'd come down the stairs for breakfast. He had eighty-four boats going out the harbour. I was there for years. We'd sell a meal for a quarter: fisherman come in with his little purse and give you a quarter, pay for his supper. Then wages started going up. Off and on, I'd get a little bit more. Ten dollars a week. Never got a helluva lot, anyway.

Nellie worked there thirty years, averaging a dollar-a-year raise. Who says women's work was undervalued? Long hours over a hot stove feeding the factory workers, the fishermen and their corks who worked for the factory plus the independent fishermen like the guy with the "little purse" digging out his quarter to pay for his supper:

> They had five meals a day. They had their breakfast, and they'd take their lunch with them. Then they'd be in at eleven for their dinner. Then they had a supper, and at seven o'clock, they all be back for the lunch. I used to make soup out of the bones and give them that for their lunch [the evening snack]. Put a big pot of beans on, stoke up the oven, go to bed. Beans would be all cooked in the morning; still be hot. Prunes. I never want to see another prune. God. Raisin bread. I used to make a hundred pounds of flour into bread every day. Hundred-pound bag.

Biscuits. Big pans filled with biscuits. Sweets: cherry pie and apple pie and raisin pie. Cut up the apples. Cinnamon rolls and donuts. That was a big job, donuts. I used to set bread twice a day. They were starved. Beans and prunes. I thought they'd blow up, but they didn't. It was a lot of fun. Nice bunch of girls, great workers. I liked it, all them years. I loved it.

After Nellie retired, she went right back to work cooking and helping run the family tourist home and motel.

If you lived in the country, one job everyone shared in the fall was potato pickin'. Girls as well as boys were welcomed across the Island to help get the crop in. It gave girls a chance to make a few dollars to spend on things their hard-working parents couldn't afford. Maude Henderson Palmer was born in 1905 in Freeland Lot 11, one of ten children.

If we ever went baby-sitting for a neighbour, we never got anything for it.

What was your first paying job?

Pickin' potatoes at George Palmers', and he gave me a dollar. I picked potatoes all day, but I got dinner and supper. And I ran all the way home, and it was a good long piece, and I said I got a dollar. I thought I was rich.

Ella Willis grew up on a farm, too, in the days even before beater diggers were used to knock the potatoes into the rows for the pickers to gather into baskets.

Potatoes were plowed out. Pick them and fill your basket. Somebody would empty your basket for you when you were a kid. I earned my first store coat picking potatoes for fifty cents a day. The coat cost twelve dollars. Twenty-four days. Saved up my money for it.

Maude Henderson Palmer was one of the thousands of Island young women who went to Boston. She worked for the telephone company there, learned to drive a car, saved up her money, moved back home, and, in her seventies, she drove around in a little yellow sports car. Good on you, Maude.

Fran Jenkins Mollison was born in Charlottetown, and started her radio career at CHGS in Summerside. The call letters stood for Call Holman's Guaranteed Satisfaction, and the studio was set up in the huge Holman's department store. Trains rumbled to the back of the studio, and the freight elevator rumbled at the front. Yet the shows always went on.

Fran went on to become one of the first female producers at the CBC, working alongside legends like Norman Defoe, Fred Davis, and another Maritimer, Max Ferguson, better known for his radio persona *Rawhide*.

But one little person didn't follow the script: Fran was overdue with her first baby, and she was growing a tad frantic.

> I was overdue and if there's anything worse for a woman, it is to be overdue. I'm about five feet one inch, and I swear I was five feet by five feet. I was a BIG girl. And I couldn't wait 'til this was over but nothing would happen.

Her brother-in-law Grant Mollison, a paratrooper, came up with a fail-safe solution.

> They took me out on old rutty gravel roads, which is the normal thing around here for people who are overdue, a rutty road. Well, we tried everything. I don't know how many rutty roads we went on.

> There was some para-jumping event outside Summerside, and Grant was jumping. We went up [to the

show]. I had never seen Grant jump before. And he kept coming down and coming down, and the damn chute didn't open, and he was practically on the ground before the chute opened. I was terrified. I was petrified. And I was in the hospital a half hour later.

It was a boy.

~~~~~

A warm December meant rumrunners might sneak in one last load to ease the long winter months ahead, their schooners tied up in an ice-free harbour like Louisbourg, the luckier ones heading south to the Caribbean with a load of pine or fish, rum and molasses back. The most famous rum vessel to service PEI, as evidenced by song and tale, was the Nova Scotia-built schooner *Nellie J. Banks*.

Wally Andrew was born next to Wrights Bridge on a farm in East Royalty in 1913. In 1930, Wally was courting a lovely young lady who lived in Dalvay-by-the-Sea, a mansion overlooking the sand dunes of PEI's north shore. Her father happened to be Edward Dicks, Captain of the *Nellie J. Banks*.

> They were having a party there to which I was invited. I was in the kitchen with the young lady, and this knock came on the door. Her father said, 'Are you alone?' And she said, 'No. Wally's with me.' And he said, 'Oh well, that's alright. No problem about him.'
>
> So, she opened the door, and the Captain came in and he had a pillow slip, an ordinary pillow slip, and it was bulging and full to the top. He just opened it enough to show me. He said, 'You may as well have a look at this,' and he opened it up and the only thing I could see was hundred-dollar bills. It was stogged full. He had just unloaded a ship off the three-

mile limit. So, there was lots of interesting things back in those days.

The end of the *Nellie J. Banks* is a sad tale. She was sold to a former Borden CN ferry boat officer who intended to restore her to former glory; ultimately, she was hauled up on the shore of Murray Harbour. But before that Captain Hubert White, born in Murray Harbour in 1916, a sea captain from a long line of schooner men, witnessed an unusual sight: the RCMP cutter S.S. *Ulna* heading for Charlottetown:

> Towing the *Nellie J. Banks* loaded with booze. Yeah. I knew those fellas [there were three Dicks brothers, all captains] and I knew the *Nellie J. Banks* really well. She was hauled up on the shore down here, and they were repairing her and never finished her. Eventually, they burnt her.

In December 1953. A sad day for old Captain Dicks, a sad day for the *Nellie J.*, and a sad day for rum running. At least she went down under a different name: the *Leona G. McGuire*. She was 43 years old, ancient by schooner standards, but long enough to win a place in so many Prince Edward Islanders' hearts.

Barnstorming

Lloyd and Donald MacLeod

December 7th is International Aviation Day. Airplanes played a significant role in the First World War and captured the imagination of old and young alike. After the war, newly-minted pilots cruised the skies across North America, landing in farmers' fields, and, for the bargain price of two dollars, would take people up for a "flip." "Flip" and "airplane" in the same sentence would be enough to scare me off. However, Lloyd MacLeod, born in 1920, and who ran a general store in Vernon River with his brother Don, had no such trepidations when one sunny day a biplane landed in the field across from his family's store.

> My first trip was with Paul Sharpe. I guess they called it barnstorming. They'd land in any field in the country and then the people out of curiosity would assemble and he'd take them up for a ten-minute trip. I remember it so well.

Usually the Murray Harbour train rolling through was the thrill of the day but one afternoon a new mode of travel, a Canuck two-seater, landed in the field across from the store.

> I guess they called it barnstorming. A crowd gathered but I was the only one who went up with him. That was, Don, in nineteen... now let me see now, remember Mrs. Herman Ings died, Don? I used to know the year... but he took me up and we circled all around, and, as soon as we left the ground, we could see Orwell Head Church, which is no longer there, and we circled around and I saw Keefe's Lake off to the north.

Were you scared?

> Not a bit. And I'm no good to climb. I was never even on the roof; you couldn't get me to climb on any roof and still I wasn't a bit scared up in that. I'll never forget that first trip. And then the joke was, someone asked, 'Where's Lloyd? He's got the keys to the store.' And someone else told my mother, 'Lloyd is up in that airplane.' My mother wasn't too happy about that, I remember.

What goes up my must come down. The airplane anyway. Years later, Lloyd was still high from his flip.

> I'll never forget that first trip. I can remember it so well! And not a bit scared. And I'm no good to climb. You couldn't get me to climb on any roof and still I wasn't a bit scared up in that plane.

Years later, Lloyd flew in another Fleet Canuck two-seater piloted by the man known as The Flying Farmer, Elton Woodside from Clinton, PEI. Elton was one of a handful of Islanders renowned for their flying skills, transporting everything from the daily newspaper and the mail, to the injured and sick to hospitals. Aviation pioneers like Elton Woodside, Reg Pope in Summerside, and Carl Burke in Charlottetown not only flew but built some of their own aircraft. Naturally, many of those barnstormers had been pilots in the First World War. Islander Harry Whitlock joined the Royal Flying Corps along with Canadian pilots Billy Bishop and Billy Barker. Bishop and Barker were famous for shooting down German planes, and both were awarded the Victoria Cross among numerous other war decorations.

Across the Northumberland Strait, Pictou County native Don MacNeill was smitten by the flying bug much the same way as Lloyd MacLeod.

> I wanted to fly desperately. I wanted to be a pilot. The first plane I remember would be about 1930 or '31. We were quite taken with Lindbergh's trip in '27, and I had my first trip when I was twelve down in Cape Breton in an airplane that was on floats at the Isle Royale Hotel [in Sydney]. Dad got hold of the pilot and he took us up the next morning. That was my first trip in an airplane. Well, I fell in love with flying.

> I got a chance to fly from Trenton [NS] to Montreal. The flying instructor was looking for someone to go up with him to pay the gas more than anything. It was June of 1934. June the sixth, and the way I remember, it was my brother's birthday and D-Day was on June sixth, quite a famous day. I flew up to Montreal in what was called a Fleet Finch, one of the old biplanes, wide open cockpit. Nothing over you at all, pretty hairy when I think of it now.

Five years later, Don was a bomber pilot with the RCAF, flying U-Boat patrols from northern Scotland to Norway across the North Sea. He came home from the war and decided to raise money to start his own flying school by, what else:

> We did what we called barnstorming after the war. A partner and I operated a flying service in New Glasgow. We used to barnstorm when things were quiet. Get a couple of cans of gas and go out to some place outside of Pictou or Charlottetown or Summerside or New Glasgow, and drop down into a farmer's field. Take him for a flip. 'Do you mind if we use the field?' 'No.' And then we'd hawk passengers at two dollars a head. Somebody'd say, 'What are you doing?' 'Going barnstorming.' 'What do you charge?' 'Two dollars a snout.' And then we'd take then up for a flip. Yeah, it was pretty hairy.

Don did some of his RCAF training on PEI. He flew dozens of missions during the Second World War, through fog and ice and blizzards, and always brought his crew home safely for which he was awarded the Air Force Flying Cross.

After the war, one contract his Gulf Flying Service landed was flying the mail to and from Pictou Island, not nearly as exciting as chasing German U-Boats in a Flying Fortress. Or barnstorming.

Don barnstormed alongside Paul Sharpe and another pilot noted for his skill behind the joystick, Junior Jones. They were also friends of Lloyd Gates when he was a young lad growing up next to Upton Airport. Lloyd's family ran the Mayflower Mill, one of the largest – and last – flour and grist mills in the Maritimes.

> It was a huge building, forty-five feet high anyway. It was a landmark especially for the pilots. They'd come in during a bad storm and they'd see the millpond and knew they were home. Slip in over the

trees. Oh, every day after school, we'd run up to the airport to see what was going on. They weren't too happy with us sometimes, except when we took them up buttermilk. They thought that was good. It was put to good use.

Good use indeed if you happened to be a passenger flying out of Charlottetown in the 1930s. The buttermilk was a cure for hangovers.

> There was Gordie Gray and Walter Fowler and Jonsie [Junior Jones] and Carl Burke, just some of the pilots. Anderson was the chief mechanic. Frank Bell had a farm next to the airport. That's why they call it Bell's Hill. I watched Carl Burke come in one day, and he landed crossways on that little runway. I don't know how he did it, but he did.

Bell's Hill is still there, on the right heading west of the Trans-Canada Highway, more or less where the West Royalty Industrial park is. Upton Airport had two runways, north-south and east-west. Bell's Hill and the clay road into Charlottetown was a mud hole for three months every spring. A passenger once complained to Garnet Godfrey, pilot, mechanic, and manager at Upton Airport, that it took longer to go the final three miles into downtown Charlottetown by car than it did to fly from Halifax. Accordingly, master-of-all-trades Garnet also manned the bulldozer that pulled cars buried axle-deep in Island mud.

Carl Burke became the Island's and one of Canada's best-known aviators. He was an exceptional pilot and en-trepreneur, starting up Maritime Central Airways (MCA), which morphed into Eastern Provincial Airways (EPA), eventually a keystone of Air Canada. Inspired by the Carl Burkes he saw every day, Lloyd Gates and his brother Bob both joined the RCAF and fought in the Second World War.

Garnet Godfrey came from a railway family and was considered a black sheep for going off-track with his airplane fascination.

> I went from flying in an open cockpit, single engine, no brakes airplane to flying a jet with a hundred passengers.

Garnet lived to be ninety-nine, worked for Carl Burke, and proved himself to be an amazing pilot, flying everything they threw at him from First World War biplanes to the first commercial jet aircraft.

> The jets were the ultimate airplane, the 737s. You didn't have to heat up the engines to get the jets going. We flew turbo-props for a while, and then we got into the straight jets. I did the initial jet training in San Diego. We used to go out into the desert from San Diego.

Garnet flew in 100-degree heat and minus-50-degree cold, from the Anza-Borrego Desert to Baffin Island where he flew supplies for the Distant Early Warning Line (DEW). Nothing stymied him, nothing surprised him, even the "monkey flights" for Big Pharma.

> The pharmaceutical people used Rhesus monkeys to make Salk vaccine when polio was on the go. The Flying Tigers, an American outfit, used to collect the Rhesus monkeys in Africa and India. A planeload of caged monkeys, hundreds of monkeys in cages, fly them into London. And we would go over to London and pick up the cargo, and fly it to Connaught Laboratories in Toronto. Monkey flights. To this day, there's nothing smells like a planeload of live monkeys.

When Garnet and his simian passengers landed in Gander to clear customs, the agents wouldn't go near the aircraft.

These days it's nothing for a chef or restaurant to fly in fresh food from the ocean or farm assuming you have the clientele to pay the bill. Bus Gay from Tea Hill, PEI, was a man ahead of his time.

> Go out to the henhouse and get some eggs. Take them down with me.

"Down" was The Big Apple, New York City. Bus was determined to turn it into The Big Omelet one egg at a time, treating his Aunt Margaret and Uncle Harry to breakfast.

> Fly from here to Moncton, then from Moncton on Northeast Airlines right through into New York City. Take eggs down with me. Uncle Harry used to say, 'Fresh eggs?' And I'd say, 'Sure, I took the eggs out of the henhouse this morning.'

Any fresher and he would have had to bring the hen down instead. And Aunt Margaret and Uncle Harry can just be thankful their nephew wasn't Garnet Godfrey.

The Farmers' Market Unofficial Mayor: George Wotton

George Wotton

George Isaac Wotton was a friend to many, and, for years, the unofficial mayor of the Charlottetown Farmers' Market. George was the archetypal people person, glad-handing old and new friends not only at the Farmers' Market but throughout his entire ninety-three years on this earth. Every time I pick a tomato from my little garden, I think of George because for years he gave me tomato seedlings that he'd lovingly grown in his greenhouse. George was loyal if anything, and fiercely proud of his roots in Victoria-by-the-Sea where he was born in the front parlour of the family farmhouse in 1923. The railway bypassed Victoria so when he was a boy, a big day out was a trip with his dad, Fred, a rural mailman, to pick up the mail off the train in Breadalbane:

> What an excitement that was for us kids to see and hear that train coming into the station. He would always sound the whistle and to see that big, big machine come rolling in was just such a thrill. There

was Kennedys' store [both Murdoch and his son Ivan were general merchants in Breadalbane], and I can relate to that song "Downtown Heart of Breadalbane" by Allan Rankin as well as anybody who hears it. The railway was how people travelled in those days — there wasn't buses or cars. There wasn't transportation except by rail. And that was another thing my Dad did: he provided transportation to and from the station in Breadalbane.

Minor MacNevin, who ran a general store in Victoria, told a story about how one spring, when a traveller coming to his store had to use Dad's horse and sleigh. The roads were halfway between snow and mud; there were so many bare spots that my Dad and the passenger had to get out and walk beside the sleigh. When they reached the store, Minor asked what kind of a trip he'd had, and he replied, 'I walked most of it with the mailman and horse while the horse pulled the sleigh.' There was no other way to get to Victoria.

It's ironic to hear George mention his dad and Murdoch Kennedy in the same breath because Murdoch, elected five times to the PEI Legislative Assembly, famously resigned as a member of the Conservative cabinet in 1913 when the ban on automobiles, which had been introduced in 1908, was partially lifted. Ironically, 1908 was the same year the car that changed the world, the Model-T Ford, came out. Fred Wotton had one of the first Model-Ts on PEI and certainly one of the first in the district:

For fifty years, my Dad drove mail between Breadalbane and Victoria, something I sometimes wonder about because it certainly wasn't a money-making affair. Something people may not even remember today, one of the chores he was called on to do was grocery shopping for people all along the way. They'd leave grocery lists in their mailbox. This wasn't required; he just did this as a favour to these people. He would go to the grocery store in Breadalbane, get the groceries, and drop them off with the mail on the way back. It was a good neighbourly thing to do and good neighbourliness was how people lived and survived in those days. It became a matter of pride with him, I think.

There was never a day, never a storm that would stop him from starting out on the mail route. He might get a half mile before the horse bogged down in snowdrifts and not be able to get through and, very often, he would then take the horse and sleigh, go into an adjoining field, cut the barbed wire fences, and start a new route through there. If it was humanly possible, he'd make it to Breadalbane and back.

Obviously, Fred Wotton, also known as F.A., kept a stable of good horses as well as that Model-T. He was up at 4:00 every morning harnessing the horses for the 20-kilometre [14 mile] jaunt to pick up the mail. His pay worked out to about the same as a farm labourer would make, a dollar-a-day.

Fred had special permission to travel back and forth to pick up the mail. However, as George wryly noted:

My Dad pioneered the car in our area. On trips to Charlottetown, he would go by way of Bonshaw, and come home by way of Lot 65, because farmers everywhere hated the car, because it scared their horses and that's what they depended on for transportation. Even horses in the fields would take off running when they'd hear the car coming.

So, they declared two days a week, that my dad could go by car, but he had to go one way and come home another, because farmers would bury old hay mower cutting blades across the road and destroy his tires. So, my Dad sued to have to carry a complete set of spare tires with him.

The Bonshaw 500 was never this interesting.

When George was growing up, Victoria was a seaport, with a string of limekilns still in use for burning the chunks of limestone brought in from the mainland to put on crops or use in plastering walls. Limestone and coal in; potatoes, vegetables, fish, lobsters, pulp and beef cattle out.

Ahh, Victoria, my wonderful Victoria. It has a great history. It had two fully-operating lobster-packing plants. It had three wharves, and everything shipped in and out from that whole central region went through Victoria, some by small freighters, but mostly by sailing vessels.

Victoria had several general stores, a tailor, a milliner, and a two-room schoolhouse. Lester MacLeod's father Louis aka L.D. ran a butcher shop in Victoria.

He was the Meatman. He had a truck out on the road. Peddled all over. I started off with a '29 Ford truck and my father started with a Model-T.

L.D. also bought produce and cattle to ship to other parts of Canada:

He went around buying cattle all over the Island. Quite a few went to Montreal and a lot went to Newfoundland. My garsh, they were cheap. I was with my father one day going in to buy a steer and they got stuck on a dollar. My father offered twenty dollars and the other fella wanted twenty-one. And my father wouldn't give it to him. He left it at twenty dollars. A fully-grown steer. That would be in the 1930s. One year, he shipped twelve hundred and some cattle and I hauled nearly all.

George Wotton remembers those days:

Cattle were shipped on a larger vessel. It's memorable because on the day that the cattle were being shipped, the farmers in Albany, Breadalbane, Kelly's Cross, South Melville, and Bonshaw would all start their cattle early in the morning, herding them towards Victoria on the road. It was like a real cattle drive and, on the way, farmers who had cattle to go would join the cattle parade, and run ahead and block off the driveways to keep the cattle on the road.

Lester MacLeod helped his father L.D. the Meatman drive the cattle with an old Model-T truck to their slaughter-house in Victoria. "It was a sedan but he cut the back off just left the front seat and built a box on the back."

George: So, you had this cowboy outfit steering them towards the wharf in Victoria, just like a scene from the wild west during roundup days. Try as they might, teachers couldn't contain the kids at school. They had to desert school and run down to see these cattle being herded onto the wharf. On the wharf, they were put in slings and hoisted onboard the ship.

The steamship S.S. *Harland* docked in Victoria twice a week, dropping off guests for two local hotels, the Orient and the Pleasant View. People came from across North America to stay for the season. There were cake raffles at the village hall, clams and oysters to dig, and maybe a tour of Dixon's flour and gristmill in nearby South Melville. Guests played croquet on the wide lawns of the Pleasant View Hotel, ate Mrs. Smith's blueberry pie, and in the evenings, were serenaded in the parlour by her daughters, all of whom were talented musicians. Your meal, accommodations, and transport to and from the train station in Breadalbane were included all for a $1.00-a-day or $5.00 a week.

The only thing the tourists missed out on was skating in the huge barn-like Victoria rink, a covered rink but with natural ice. The rink was operated by husband and wife H.B. and Kathleen Wood, who installed electric lights and a Rink-o-Phone that played music while the skaters circled first one way and then the other. Victoria also had the Maritime champion Victoria Unions hockey team, and their equally-skilled female counterparts the Union Sisters.

As a boy, George played hockey with flattened tin cans in the rink, and he loved to climb up on the rink's high roof, with views across to the Mainland. The fun ended in 1939 when the Second World War broke out. Suddenly the Mainland – and Europe – were a lot closer. George joined the Royal Canadian Navy. He was seventeen years old, his first time away from home and Mum's cooking:

> Ah gee – the food in the navy generally was passable. But, unfortunately, we had a cook who I should forget but I remember. His name was Karlson – Cook Karlson. He would boast to us time and time again that he had the record of feeding our ship cheaper per capita than any other ship in the flotilla. So-help-my-God, he was not paying for the food. It was being supplied by the government, and he could have given us anything he wanted to, within reason. But he took pride in making himself the least expensive cook. We got a lot of macaroni, that I detested. A lot of soup. You didn't get a heck of a lot of memorable

food. I always used to take a stash of food to sea with me, chocolate bars and canned juices, for when I got really hungry.

George celebrated his eighteenth birthday at sea. Previous to joining the RCN, his only experience with the sea was in a rowboat in Victoria Harbour. Oddly, his war duty took him across the continent to the other Victoria in British Columbia. He was the lone Prince Edward Islander on HMCS *French*, a heavily-armed cruiser doing convoy patrol duty out of Halifax. One day during a hurricane, a convoy was attacked by German submarines off Nova Scotia. George was washed overboard. After that scare and rescue, he vowed to make the most of life every day.

That credo was immediately put to the test. In 1943 while at sea, George somehow contracted tuberculosis. He was shipped ashore to recover, sent back to PEI, and for months he sat on the roof of the PEI sanatorium, later the Dr. Eric Found Centre, in all weathers, wrapped in a woollen blanket. He survived TB but lost a lung.

For years, George was the PEI Provincial Photographer, but before that he was a print journalist. Even as a boy, he was interested in cameras and photography. He sold a thousand magazines to pay for his first camera and darkroom. After the Second World War, these skills led to him becoming a newspaperman and eventually City Editor in Summerside. I wonder how many people knew much about George's distant past. For someone who loved to chat and kibitz, especially when making the rounds at the Farmers' Market on Saturday morning, he managed to get people talking more about themselves than him. But if you had a chance to ask what his childhood had been like in Victoria, he'd focus his mum Ada and his dad Fred:

Oh, my mother – when I think of her, so under appreciated. Everyone came before her when meals were being served – if there was a shortage of food, she would be the one to go without or take the smallest portion. She made all of our clothes, she baby-sat us when we were growing up while she did her gardening or her housework. She cared for everybody before she cared for herself. You know I wish that I could thank her for what she's done.

And my Dad who worked so hard and so long at so many things. He was highway superintendent, God forgive him, under the Conservatives. He could give out these good government jobs to unemployed people until they earned enough to pay their taxes [i.e. school and road taxes], and then he had to fire them and hire another bunch who owed taxes. Some of these laid-off men would come to the house, and I saw men cry. Grown men, crying because they couldn't get hired back on to earn more money they needed so badly for groceries. But the government taxes, that's the thing that came first. Isn't that awful.

My Dad was so opposed to liquor. I can't believe he'd be associated or have anything to do with the handling of liquor. They all closed their eyes to others who handled it and offered it. He was a Temperance man. To my knowledge, my father only took one drink of liquor in his life. One time he was nearly dying in his bed with a severe cold. I was home from the navy and had a little bottle of navy rum. I poured a small tumbler for him and said, 'Here Dad, some medicine. Drink this. Gulp it all down.' And he did and he near died – his eyes bulged and tears flowed. He was gasping for breath. Straight navy rum for a man who never touched liquor. It was quite a shock to his system. But, he got better.

Madeline Stordy Roberts

Joe Kelly, from Kelly's Cross, he was the fiddler. We danced every Sunday night at somebody's house and he was there. Give him a little shot of beer or something, and he'd play twice as good, and he lived to be ninety-eight.

Madeline Roberts was born in 1921, and grew up in prime fiddlin' country, the rolling hills around Brookvale, PEI. Unlike many old traditions that have faded with time, singin' and dancin' to the fiddle at kitchen and house parties is a Maritime tradition that continues to this day. Entertainment back then was homemade and cheap, like listening in to other people's conversations on the telephone party line.

My favourite party line story – we'll get back to the fiddle – was the time a mother in Kings County was giving her daughter the recipe for Grammie's Red Velvet cake over the telephone. She got all the ingredients mixed together and was saying, 'Put it in a cake pan with a layer of wax paper, and then in the oven at 350 degrees. Oh wait – I have to go – the minister just arrived at the door!' The next day, she met a neighbour on the street in Montague, and the neighbour asked, 'So, put the cake in the oven at 350 degrees, but how long do you cook it?'

Back to Madeline Roberts and house parties, who said:

> Oh, there were all kinds of good times. It didn't cost anything; we went from house-to-house. Mouth-organ playing in another corner, oh yes, lots of fiddlers too: Maurice MacDonald and Maurice's wife, she was a great fiddler, and he was a step dancer. He could step dance on a dime. Maurice's sons were all fiddlers too. There were house parties there and everywhere. Kelly's Cross was known for house parties. Yeah.

Did you know Ambrose Monaghan's father?

> Yes, Jimmy Rosie – that's what they called him. Jimmy Monaghan was kind of red-complected, so they called him Rosie.

His son, Ambrose, has a different version of how his father got that nickname.

> Jimmy Rosie, they called him, but Jimmy Ronald was his proper name, but his mother was Rosie McGuigan, and he always got Jimmy Rosie. If there was a dance, it was at Jimmy Rosie's, Saturday or Sunday, it didn't matter and there was always lots of violin players. Dad played and we had a piano that we rolled up a long hall to the kitchen. My brother-in-law, Joe Kelly played, and a neighbour Levi Trainor, and a young friend of mine Stephen Smith all played. All kinds of music. I had two first cousins on my mother's side [who] played the violin and that would be the third generation... and the dances went on at Jimmy Rosie's right up after I got married.

My wife and I used to go to Saturday night dances at the Eldon Legion featuring the Elliott Wight Orchestra, and occasionally to the old Vernon River hall where the caller would fly into a rage because by the 1990s, few of us knew the steps to all the old sets, and he did. By the end of the night, we were all afraid to take to the floor, and instead watched him pace the stage, alone, purple, and apoplectic. The old dances have mostly died out, the Lancers and Quadrilles, the square dances and old time sets with my favorite, the Paul Jones. But back in the days of Jimmy Rosie's, Ambrose said everyone knew the steps.

> Six or eight or ten couples it didn't matter, you went right a round. You'd start to swing one around, then swing the next one, you swung all night, you never stopped. Sometimes the fiddler would get tired playing for to get them all around. And there were some great step dancers. Yeah.

Something I never ask about is religion, because religion is very personal and none of my business. I will point out that most, maybe not all, of the folks who hosted kitchen parties on Sunday night were Catholics. Dozens of Protestants told me they'd sneak across the field to attend a house party at a Catholic neighbour's house, even if it wasn't on the Sabbath. Harold Dunphy from Millvale told me the Protestants even put a bucket over the rooster on Sunday, so he couldn't have any fun.

When I was a kid, the Saturday night house party switched gears around eleven p.m., after the "lunch," and then the old hymns and spirituals were sung. Until midnight. On the dot. Then home to bed.

Ambrose Monaghan recalled the time the new priest showed up at Jimmy Rosie's and demanded they stop with the house parties. The fiddle was an instrument of the devil. Like that old joke about Presbyterians banning having sex standing up because it might lead to dancing. The next Sunday, Jimmy Rosie hosted a card party, which the priest considered an even worse evil. Outsmarted, he allowed houses parties back on the schedule.

Dancing makes for a dry throat, so let's head down to Murray Harbour North where the Presbyterian and moonshine-and-wine-making Ben Clow ran a big general store. One day, young Roy Clow popped in to visit his favorite uncle.

Oh God yes. Ben was a big big man, about six foot four, and he'd weigh close to three hundred pounds. And he was good on his feet, light on his feet. He used to get a barrel of whisky in every fall [the Clows had their own wharf and lobster factory] on a schooner from Barbados. If you wanted a keg of rum, he'd have the keg of rum brought in too.

The light-on-the-feet bit will be important in a minute.

He bought blueberries from all the ladies around the country and he shipped them to Charlottetown in shooks [Like eggs boxes, for some reason blueberry boxes were called shooks]. He took one of those whisky kegs, a forty-five-gallon barrel, and he'd buy thirty pounds of blueberries, and he'd dump them in the keg, and he'd put twenty pounds of sugar in on top of them, and put a box of yeast cakes in with them. He'd take his boots and socks off, and get a bucket of water, and he'd wash his feet right clean, and he'd get in the barrel. He'd walk around and around and around the barrel, smash the blueberries all to pieces with his bare feet. He'd walk around the barrel, and I'd see him doing it, and he'd be laughing to kill himself.

He'd leave that for thirty days, and then he'd take a glassful out of it. And holy old... you talk about strong blueberry wine! He gave me a glass — I was only a little fella — and he set me drunk. I was as drunk as hell when I went home.

Uncle Ben's converted nephew. I bet Roy went to Sunday school twice that week. Roy was born in Murray Harbour North 1917, a Second World War veteran who grew up farming and fishing like his father and grandfather and his father before that. Uncle Ben taught Roy the art of moonshine-making, a skill highly-prized during the long Prohibition, that lasted two generations on PEI. Nearly every farm had a still out behind the barn near a stream. According to Roy, many of those stills were compliments of an enterprising tinsmith in Montague:

> He was in behind Poole and Thompson's warehouse. Glad Hickenbottom. He made a dandy still. He was a tinsmith and he'd make them whatever size you wanted out of copper. He made a still for me one time – it was five gallons and you could put two gallons of beer [mash] in it. Raymond Ronalds and my brother Ed had the still, and I stole it. We used to dig a hole in the horse manure – the horse manure heated all winter – and we'd fill the hole with straw and we'd put the still in it and leave it for ten days. My mother was home and I didn't want her to see me, so early in the morning after I milked the cows, I took the hand sleigh and I went down to the shore. I had a two-gallon mash of beer and three coils of three-eighths copper tubing. I told Mum I was going fishing. I thought this would be a great place to set the still up. I could lay down beside the still. Which I did. I turned the propane gas stove on, pumped it up real good, and turned it right up full and lay down alongside the still. And I fell asleep. Of all the stupid things to do.

> It didn't take it long to start to boil. The first thing that woke me was this awful bang. I looked up quick, and the pipe was going round and round in the air. The plug blew out of the top of the still, the pres-

sure was so high and all the beer went out except for about two cupfuls, so I lost the first half gallon of moonshine right there. So, the last half can of beer I had to run, I got a half gallon of moonshine. Really good strong moonshine.

Across the Northumberland Strait in New Glasgow, NS, two bachelor brothers, Donald, a cobbler, and George MacIntosh, a milkman, would appreciate Ben and Roy's liquor-making talents. The tape recorder was running one night as Donald and George both played the fiddle for me, topped off with Donald's spirited rendition of "St. Anne's Reel."

> George: Here's one now: "Lord MacDonald's Reel." It's out of my class but I don't know if he [Donald] can now but he used to play it.

> Donald: Let's see the fiddle. I don't know what I can do.

> George: You see what I mean now? I'm not in his class at all. I'm just a scratcher.

> Donald: He plays tunes I don't play. I'll take a gamble on that "Lord MacDonald's Reel." Don't expect wonders now. I'll see what we can do. Carry on...

There was some fiddle playing, with Donald's right foot pounding away.

> Donald: Years ago, you weren't born, I played at open air dances at Moose River. I got thirty dollars and played for six hours. And the moonshine come over from Barneys River and I used to get into a little of that.

When the conversation turned to moonshine and liquor, they told me about two other brothers in New Glasgow who ran a local undertaking business, and used their hearse to transport the odd ten-gallon keg of Demerara rum to a church in Blue Mountain where they hid the rum in the church cellar. Three names came up: a car called a Star, manufactured by the Durant Motor Company in the 1920s; a local businessman nicknamed The Beaver who died a mysterious death; and a former boxer-turned-town cop named Spinney Wright.

> George: Do you know what, Spinney Wright, I thought of all the fellas in uniforms, he stood out. And the lovely step. Spinney. My, he had a lovely walk. He looked great in uniform.

> Donald: Listen. Do you remember a fella out the road here, he got drowned or something, the Beaver, Basil B. MacDonald? Alright. He got married. Lots of people get married, I didn't. OK. You know where the Church of England is? Right across, but not right across, diagonally, the Beaver, I played for his wedding, and do you know what time I left in the morning? God help us, five o'clock. And I had George's Star, and do you know who was sitting inside sleeping in the front seat? Spinney Wright!

> George: Different nights, Don would be out playing and he might drive one or another cop's home. In those days they did more travelling by foot.

> Donald: And they knew I was drinking and playing the fiddle.

Donald played in bootlegging joints down near the train station in what was known as The Devil's Half Acre. It's all cleaned up now, no more Beaver, Spinney, Star, or Devil. And sadly, the MacIntosh brothers are both gone. They brought more joy into people's lives than anyone I know. Right now, up in heaven, George is smoking a fat cigar, eyes closed, listening to Donald's "Lord

MacDonald's Reel," right foot pounding away. There's even a name for this magical place: "Fiddler's Green," where there is "perpetual mirth, a fiddle that never stops playing and dancers who never tire."[1] Count me in.

---

1   David Burke, *Singing Out: A Folk Narrative of Maddy Prior, June Tabor & Linda Thompson,* "Essential Listening," United Kingdom: Soundcheck Books, 2015, (143).

Folklore, Traditions & Toenails

Gus Gregory

Groundhog Day always baffles me. A weather-predicting rodent? Surely, we can do better than that. After all, our ancestors didn't have Groundhog Day, but still managed to come up with some dandy folklore.

There was a watermill in the Baltic [East Baltic near Souris], and there was a watermill in Gowan Brae, and they sawed shingles. They went to the woods in the decay of the moon in June, what they called the dark of the moon, and they cut the trees down and trimmed them up and left the limbs from about ten or fifteen feet from the top of the tree.

Gus Gregory was born in 1918 in Chepstow, northeastern PEI into a family that brought their traditions over with them from England.

That would draw all the sap out of the tree. Then cut it up into logs and haul it to the mill and block it up for shingles. The shingles would wear out before they'd rot.

The dark and the light of the moon played heavy in the old beliefs. Crops were planted and harvested according to the right phase of the full moon and, in the fall, animals were slaughtered for the winter accordingly.

> My father, when he was going to butcher a pig for our own use, would feed the pig on pretty near nothing but grain and water for about ten days before he'd butcher him. It had to be just about the time the moon was full, a few days before the full moon, because if you get the pork butchered at the wrong time, in the decay of the moon, the pan will fill with grease and the pork will shrink up to pretty near nothing. Whereas, if you butcher it in the growth of the moon just before the moon is full, the meat will stay three-quarters the size and you won't have much grease in the pan.

Gus claimed his grandfather taught him how to tell if store-bought bacon was killed in the light or dark of the moon. Problem being there was no way of knowing until the bacon was fried up for breakfast. But if the bacon shrunk, Gus always returned it, which no doubt would please his grandfather.

> My grandfather was more of a superstitious man. His father, my great-grandfather Gregory, came from England. When he sowed wheat for flour, the wind had to be southwest at a certain time of the moon, in the light of the moon the day he sowed the wheat.

The rule of thumb for planting was crops on top, like oats and barley and clover, by the light of the moon; crops below ground like turnips and potatoes and beets, by the dark of the moon, when the full moon was on the wane.

Some people believed there was a lunar effect on births since the moon's gravitational pull causes high tides. Humans are 80 percent water; therefore, the moon's pull affects us too, especially at childbirth. A baby boy was thought more likely born on a rising tide, a baby girl at ebb tide.

Tides are also associated with death. John Stow, in his 1598 *Survey of London*, wrote this about Wapping, at that time a filthy hamlet on the Thames where "at the low water mark was the usual place of execution for hanging pirates and sea rovers, and there to remain till three tides had overflowed them."[2].

Food from the sea has also figured prominently in folklore. In the Bible, Leviticus 11:9-12 dictates: "These you may eat, of all that are in the waters. Everything in the waters that has fins and scales, whether in the seas or in the rivers, you may eat. But anything in the seas or the rivers that has not fins and scales is detestable to you. You shall not eat any of their flesh, and you shall detest their carcasses."[3]

One assumes that includes lobster. Arthur Hughes was born in 1913 on a farm in Bedford, PEI, east of Charlottetown. Arthur grew up hearing the old adage "only poor people eat lobster."

> It wasn't counted much of a delicacy back them times. You could buy a pound of lobster for ten cents. There were two lobster factories in Grand Tracadie canning them when I was a youngster. They got nothing worthwhile for the lobster. They used to haul the lobster bodies from the factory and spread them on fields. You had to get them plowed down pretty quick or crows would feast on them. But the lobster backs made great fertilizer. You grew great hay with them. You could get them for nothing.

I asked if he had ever heard of anyone planting a herring with their potato sets.

---

2   John Stow, *A Survey of London*. London: Imprinted by John Windet, 1598, archive.org/details/asurveylondono6stowgoog/page/n19

3   King James Authorized Version, originally published in 1611.

Oh yeah, for fertilizer. But you didn't want any cats in the neighbourhood when you did that because they could smell the fish in the ground and scratch them out. You had to watch them pretty close or the cats would make for the field if there was fish buried there.

I met Arthur years ago at the Dundas Fair and Plowing Match, one hot August afternoon when we were both cooling off and admiring the hens and roosters on display in the poultry barn. It was a chance meeting with one of the smartest men I ever knew. Not sure what the moon or tides were doing at the time.

Another chance meeting was the day I met Leo Farrell. Leo was from Central Lot 16, but was waiting patiently in 19th century clothes at a sound stage in Summerside. He was going to play the fiddle in a scene in the TV series *Emily of New Moon*. I was working in the locations' department and helping with the historical accuracy of the scripts, and, while having a cup of tea at the craft services table, Leo and I got chatting about fiddling. He got his first fiddle when he was eight years old.

They had a fiddling contest in Summerside in the winter of 1924, so my parents went and by cripes they brought me home a fiddle and bow. Cost five dollars. So, I started going to dances and got learning, picking up music. Well, you'd sit in the corner of the room by yourself and tramp your feet and play away with the music, and people would dance away.

Our chat led to folklore and the old traditions, and what's more traditional in the Maritimes than fiddle-playing, a house party, moonshine, and a big brawl to cap off the perfect evening.

I'd play, cripes, until two o'clock in the morning. I'd be playing at parties, and there was a lot of home brew, and people would get pretty well loaded and start fighting. I'd have to get out of the way. I didn't like to have my fiddle broken. They'd fight for a while and then say, 'Come on back here, Fiddler, let's get dancing again!'

I played up in Portage for three or four years for Gabe Shabell, he had a dance hall up there. I saw them fighting out in the middle of the road in Portage, holding up the traffic.

Easy on the bragging there, Leo. I remember similar dances at the Fort Augustus Rec Centre where the combatants fought like the devil in the middle of the road, lit up by car headlights. One night, the fight lasted half an hour. Nobody was going anywhere until the fight was over. Not that anybody wanted to.

The devil. My grandfather used to modify things by saying "the deuce," as in "Alec and Effie went by here heading for town going like the deuce." Some people considered it bad luck to even say the word "devil" and substituted "deuce" instead. Like "old Nick," deuce is another term for devil, as in the Old High German "was der daus" or the Latin "deus," an association with God.

There are Devil's Punchbowls around the world. A quick Google search finds them in Oregon, Ontario, Manitoba, Wales, Scotland, and England. The Devil's Punchbowl in South Granville, PEI, has connotations with a fiery Hell thanks to a lost puncheon of the devil's drink: rum. Demon rum.

The deep hole in Granville runs along the old Princetown Road, the first road connecting Malpeque and Prince County with Charlottetown in Queens County. At a crossroads nearby, sat the South Granville school, now gone, kitty-corner to the little Presbyterian church: there still, but in sad disrepair. Dorothy MacKenzie MacLure attended both the school and church. Dorothy was born in 1912 and, as a girl, picked berries in the churchyard.

> All the school children would run over to get the blueberries in the cemetery. My gorsh, the blueberries were simply beautiful there. We picked day after day after day. Some of us were afraid to pick off the graves, that was sacred you know. But when berry picking was over, the graves were picked clean. Some of the others weren't afraid of eating off the graves. I didn't pick any. I was superstitious.

Not so superstitious that she wouldn't follow her schoolmates and climb down into the Devil's Punchbowl to get chunks of rock used to mark on the school slates.

> Going down into the Punchbowl at dinnertime. Sometimes we'd be late for school. It's quite a depth, but we'd go right to the bottom thinking nothing of it, and scramble back up, get a cool drink of water. We'd have keel, a soft clay, a red clay, and we'd sharpen that into slate pencils at school.

Dorothy grew up in South Granville, settled by Highland Scots who brought along Scottish traditions, such as Gaelic and a strict sect of Presbyterianism that lasted well into the 20th century. The little church didn't have an organ until the 1960s, and no stained glass or interior adornments whatsoever. One story tells of a little girl placing a bouquet of lilacs at the front of the church one Sunday. The minister angrily swept them to the floor. When the organ made its first appearance around 1961, one family stood up before the service commenced and marched out in protest and didn't return for over 40 years.

I take some credit for their return. We shot several episodes of *Emily of New Moon* at the church and, like everyone, the family was curious when the show biz "circus" – hair and makeup vans, lights and props trucks, zoom booms, horses and buggies – roared by, raising the dust on their quiet clay road.

Raising the dust, or raising the devil.

I asked Dorothy what she had heard about the Devil's Punchbowl when she was little.

> Well, there's a lot of stories about that. Some people say it was a cask of rum that fell in there. There were prohibitionists in those days. You weren't supposed to touch liquor, you know. And the devil was supposed to have appeared. He appeared on other occasions too. If you played cards, he was often under the table. Someone I knew wasn't used to playing cards, and he was tempted one night to play cards, and a card fell on the floor, and he looked under the table and he saw the devil. He never played cards again.

I can't imagine those Presbyterians in Granville ever playing cards.

Dorothy responded, "Oh, this fella strayed. Sometimes some of them do."

One more superstition from the sea. Jane Fraser was born in Murray Harbour in 1912. Her father Billy was a sea captain with a very odd superstition.

> For some unknown reason, his mother would never allow them to cut their toenails or fingernails on a Sunday. I'm sure he never did that ever in his lifetime. I don't know why. We always laughed about it.

From the same area in eastern PEI, my old pal Roy Clow knew a man, also a sailor, who never cut his toenails. Ever. Roy neatly combines two great Maritime traditions: gossip and nicknames.

> Jack Hicken — they called him Toenails — worked on the ferry, the first old ice-breaker [the SS *Prince Edward Island*] at Borden. He was a big tall man, big shoulders, and when he was home, he never wore boots. He went in his bare feet. He had toenails, by gee — I saw them-they were that long! He'd make a good backhoe. He could dig backwards. Why he never cut his toenails, nobody ever knew. He'd have to put his feet on a block of wood to cut the nails with an axe. Scissors would never think of cutting them.

How did he get his boots on?

> He had boots, I'd swear they were sixteen inches long. Rubber boots, up to his knees. And that's all he ever wore, bare feet and the rubber boots, summer and winter.

I wondered if he called him "Toenails" to his face.

> Oh yes, right to his face. 'How ya doing today, Toenails?'

A female friend of mine heard the story and declared Toenails couldn't have been married. He was, and had at least one child. I know because word got out that I was retelling Roy's tale, and Toenails' grandson contacted me and confirmed the story.

The deuce you say.

Sunday Rules: No Fun Allowed

Margaret Shaw (nee Matheson)

I used to spend summers with my grandparents who lived twenty miles from the nearest town. Wednesday was half day and the stores all closed at noon, and Thursday was go-to-town-day. That was it. If you forgot something that day, you waited until next Thursday. I don't know what Grammie would think of Sunday shopping. Actually, I do know: she'd be appalled. Secular Sunday: business as usual.

For folks like Margaret Shaw, born in 1908, still living in 2018, and a Presbyterian like my Grammie, two services on Sunday, and in between, quiet Sunday:

> Strict? Oh, my land, yes. You did all your cooking on Saturday, all but set the table. Sacrament Sunday in DeSable – that was the first Sunday in July – the first Sunday I went. I think we had thirty-five for dinner. The neighbours, I'll not bother mentioning the name – it was the MacKays – they used to have fifty or sixty for Sunday dinner. And a lot of them stayed overnight because they came a long way in

horse and wagon. They'd come Thursday afternoon for the evening service, and stay on 'til perhaps Monday afternoon. Monday morning was another big service. They went through quite a rigmarole.

Margaret attended the Free Church of Scotland, noted for its strict adherence to the Sabbath. On the farm, the animals were milked, fed, and watered but that was it. Period. Reverend Donald Nicholson recounted one Sacrament Sunday at their farm in Hartsville, so many people came to stay his father underestimated the drinking water. The bucket and dipper were dry, but no one could go to the well until a non-Presbyterian neighbour happened to visit, and it was deemed kosher to let him refill the bucket.

When Reverend Donald went back to the Scottish island of Raasay, he was surprised to find his Scottish cousins, strict as they were, weren't as strict as his own family who'd been on PEI for over two hundred years.

Charlie Scranton's family weren't quite as strict. Charlie was born in South Manchester, Nova Scotia, in 1916 on an isolated, hard-scrabble farm:

> It was a hard place to be brought up. I had three bosses, my father and mother, and my brother fourteen years older than me. My mother was a terrific strong person, very hard-working. She was one of the best cooks that ever lived. Corned beef and cabbage, salt pork. In the wintertime, everything was preserved by salting it. In the fall of the year, we'd kill an animal and if you hung it in the woods, it would keep all winter, almost into the first of June. It would get a little mould on the outside of it, but I've seen my mother going out to the woods with the butcher knife and slicing off some steak and it'd still be frozen that late in the year.

Charlie became a born-again-Prince Edward Islander after emigrating, as he put it, from rocky Guysboro County to rockless PEI in the 1940s. He said he thought he'd gone to heaven. Lots of farmers, good soil, and horses. And if you hung your meat up in the woods, you didn't have to worry about bears. The last bear on PEI was killed in 1927.

Charlie led an interesting life: egg grader, chicken sexer, and caponizer, and for years, raised money for needy children at the annual Easter Beef auction in Charlottetown, wearing his trademark ten-gallon Stetson hat. He was honoured with the Order of Canada and a Doctor of Laws from UPEI for all his movin' and shakin':

> I was fortunate: I married my wife Helen McKeen who was just as good a cook as my mother. I recall when we lived in Hazelbrook, we always had four desserts. Four desserts. But I went so fast in my life, I burned it all off.

Charlie wasn't much of a drinker, and Margaret never tasted alcohol in her life.

Oliver Smith in Mt. Stewart was known to have the odd taste, but Oliver was a Second World War veteran in the Merchant Navy, convoying gasoline tankers across the German-U-Boat-infested Atlantic, and a drink or two helped calm the nerves. His father Tom Smith was a fisherman and, to make ends meet, augmented his three-cents-a-pound lobster catches by running rum:

> For years, my father was one of the top fishermen over here, and always kept a good boat. At that time, back in the '30s you got along whatever way you could. So, when the rumrunning started, he did most if not all the rumrunning for this area.

The price of fish was terrible in the Depression years of

the 1930s. Tom Smith paid $5.00 a gallon to the New-foundland schooner captain, and sold the rum for ten:

> I used to be with him fishing and hauling liquor. think the most famous load, if you want to call it famous, was 1935 or '36. There was a Eucharistic Congress up here at St Andrews at the church. We came in with a hundred and ten kegs on this load and the Mounties were waiting for us. Mounties made a dive for him, but he just turned around with the dory and rowed back out. My father had taken all the oars out of the boats before we left, and we hid across the bay at what we called MacPhees Cove. We slowed the engine right down so you could hardly hear it and went up the Crick Bridge and unloaded the liquor there, threw it up on the road. There were two or three old cars there – I think they were REOs [made by Ransom E. Olds]. The fella that ordered the liquor was called Pete MacDonald who ran The Two Mac's drugstore in Charlottetown.

Until 1948 when prohibition was finally repealed, the only legal alcohol on PEI was for medicinal purposes. You went to a script doctor, pleaded bad nerves, and got a prescription to go to the drugstore for a quart of rum to soothe them. On PEI for fifty years, a lot of people had bad nerves.

Besides the drugstore owner, two priests from St. Dunstan's University were regular buyers, two kegs at a go, I'm assuming for an especially high mass. Oliver mentioned the Eucharistic Congress at the Roman Catholic church in St. Andrews. Another time when being hounded by the RCMP, father and son took advantage of Sunday services at the Presbyterian church in Mt. Stewart, and hastily hid the kegs in the cellar of the manse. They retrieved it later and no one was the wiser.

Bachelor brothers Donald and George MacIntosh tell a similar story about rumrunners in New Glasgow, NS, who used a hearse to transport the kegs of rum, which they later hid in the graveyard of a church in Blue Mountain. And no one was the wiser.

Church and rum, odd mix, unlike church and food: teas, fairs, box socials, wakes, pancake suppers, and of course, Sunday dinner. After Sunday school, I'd bee-line it for Nanny's just as she was putting the finishing touches on Sunday dinner: roast beef, over-cooked peas and carrots, and Yorkshire pudding. My father married my mother only after she learned how to make his English mother's Yorkshire pudding. All the beef drippings – and I mean ALL – were poured two inches deep into the bottom of a bread pan, and the sticky dough dumped on top. The finished pudding was spongy, saturated, and never enough.

Blanche Bennett was born in 1923 in Summerside, and her mother had ancestral Acadian recipes as well as variations on Sunday dinner:

> Fricot, that's good with the dumplings on the top. Yup. Maman made meat pies at Christmas. And boiled dinner with cabbage, potatoes, turnip, and carrots. We always had turnips. And the pies. Apple pie and raisin squares. Pop and the boys used to go up to Erne Walker's; he was a big farmer and our milkman. Horse and wagon – put the milk on the doorstep, and if it was cold, the cream would rise to the top and pop the cork.

Did people keep animals on Ottawa Street?

> My gosh, yes. Joe Dolphie Arsenault had a cow and horses and pigs. Maman kept chickens in our yard. Of course. Yes. Maman'd go out on Saturday and

chop. Cut the head off of one and that was Sunday dinner. She could cook anything. Make something out of nothing. And Mulligan stew. Did you ever hear of Mulligan stew? OK, we lived on that. We lived on rabbits in the '30s when food was really scarce and so was money. The boys go out and snare rabbits. We had them roasted, fried, cooked, boiled. We lived on rabbits. Hey – to people today it's a delicacy, but it wasn't then. It was the essential food.

Relax, Bugs, it wasn't all bunnies:

And for some reason, things must have gotten a little better as I got a little older because we had a meatman who used to come from New Annan, Allie McNeil was his name. He'd bring in great roasts of beef. We always had the biggest roast of beef on Sunday. Cooked in this great big black pan. There'd be half a dozen of our relatives from the country, and we'd all have dinner. It was a wonderful time, yeah. We never went hungry.

Mrs. Landry was quite a woman:

Maman was a beautiful woman, God love her. Kind of short and chunky. Barbara, my daughter, is the image of her. Maman was always well-dressed. If the priest came to visit, we would all be shooed out of the house. She'd go, 'The priest is coming!' and put on a big white apron. The priest was a special person. Priests were special; doctors were special. There's no respect today like there was then.

There was an Indian lady, Mrs. Knockwood, who used to come from Lennox Island with Mayflowers in the spring. Maman would buy a bouquet of Mayflowers, and we were shooed out of the house because she was making dinner for Mrs. Knockwood. Yeah, God love her. Every spring, she would come because Maman's nephew taught school on Lennox Island. His name was Willie Overbeck, and he used to come to see his Aunt Tillie. He called Maman, Tillie. Matilda was her name but almost everybody called her Tillie. But we had to call her Maman.

Like her mum, Blanche is a remarkable woman. She's a veteran of the Second World War, and survived the V-E Day riot in Halifax when officials foolishly shuttered all the bars and liquor stores fearing anarchy. Instead, it sparked a riot. Halifax was a barracks town, and the thousands of soldiers, sailors, and civilians wanted booze to celebrate, and, one presumes, to calm their nerves. They went wild and wrecked the city. Oliver Smith and his dad – or a script doctor – could have made a fortune that day.

When she was young, Blanche performed on Summerside's radio station *CHGS*, which was located in Holman's huge department store. Little Blanche not only sang but clogged on live radio as well. Dancing on the radio. Blanche's brothers picked the potatoes in her family.

And so back to where we started: I first interviewed Margaret Shaw when she 101 years old. When Margaret was 103, I showed up one Sunday afternoon to pick her brain again after being warned "Don't show up until after church." I brought along my tape recorder and a list of questions, and eventually asked Margaret if she was allowed to play on Sunday when she was a girl. *Never*! She was allowed to read two books – the *Bible* and *Anne of Green Gables*, co-incidentally first published the year Margaret was born. So, no play and no work.

"Never," she replied. "By rights, we shouldn't be doing this."

"Doing what?" I asked.

"Well, you're working."

I laughed, "Not really – I'm having fun"

Quick as a flash she shot back, "Shouldn't be doing that either."

103 years old. I'll take her word for it.

Frozen Eels and Molasses

Lloyd Gates with painting of
Mayflower Grist and Flour Mill

If there's one thing I've learned over the years it's that people would rather hear a happy story than a sad one. It took me a while to twig, even though it's just horse sense. When I started interviewing folks, events like the First World War, the Spanish Flu epidemic of 1918-19, and later the Great Depression of the 1930s were part of the collective memory. Maybe I was easily led into asking questions about those topics. Like one old lad said to me, "a nod's as good as a wink to a blind horse." So, here's a few stories about horses, eels, men's suits, and ladies' pants that I hope bring a smile to your face.

The next time you drive under the overpass on the Lower Malpeque Road just west of Charlottetown, look closely and you might just make out the remains of the mill-pond for the Mayflower Grist and Flour Mill of West Royalty. For years, it was run by the Gates family. The last miller was Second World War veteran Lloyd Gates' father Fred.

> I can remember skating even up around midnight, beautiful moonlight, full moon, bright as day, skating with your girl around the millpond. I hope my wife Mary's not listening to this – different girl. Might

have been one of the Curley girls up the hill. That's when I didn't know what girls were like.

If Mary reads this, he's going to find out.

And I think everybody in Charlottetown came out to fish there at one time or another. Gates' Pond. Below the dam, the salt water fish would come up, and above the dam, we had the freshwater ones. Dad would say, 'Go down and get some fish for supper,' so we'd go down and nail a couple. The smelts used to come up every spring just below the waterwheel. And eels. They'd get into the waterwheel, and I'd have to go down and get the eels out of the waterwheel. They'd plug it up. Slimy old waterwheel. Scared to death somebody'd open up the flume and let the water in when I was down there. There was a lot of eels in freshwater ponds. I never ate them, but Dad loved them. Fry them up. I couldn't stand them. I think they were still wriggling in the pan.

Across the fields from the Gates' farm and the Mayflower mill was the Rhynes farm where Alexander "Slick" Rhynes was born in 1926:

Gates mill pond – I grew up on it. Great old place and a great man – Fred Gates run it. That bypass runs right through the centre of the mill pond. Skated on it, and we used to have an old 1930 Plymouth car, Junior Jones and I [Jones was one the pilots at nearby Upton Airfield], and we'd be going like the devil, spinning around on the ice having a helluva time. Lots of good trout in it too and we used to fish eels in the wintertime. The men would be cutting ice and we'd be pulling big eels out of the mud. Big buggers – here to the door there.

Five feet long?

Yes. Bodies on them six-seven inches around. Oh, that was great fun – but you know what? I don't know where you go to get an eel now. We used to go there in the wintertime just for fun. Half the time we'd just leave them on the ice. The buggers would freeze and then come back to life again. You ask Agnes [Slick's wife]. Agnes – tell this man the experience you had with eels.

Years ago, Elliott Jones said to me, 'Aggie, you like eels.' And I said, 'Yes – I love them.' Elliott and his son Rollie were going catching eels one winter. So, they dropped off two eels for me and they were frozen solid. I had a great big enamel basin and I set them in that and filled it full of cold water. So, I was working around the kitchen and I could hear 'splish splish splish' and I thought, where in the name of God is the water splashing? The eels had come back to life and were swimming around – I was petrified. So, I started screaming in the kitchen, and Slick and his father were in the barn. They heard me so they came running over to see what in the name of God had happened. I put newspapers on the table, and took a pair of pliers and caught the eels and set them on the table. I waited a long time and thought, well, they must be dead now so I could cut the head off and skin them. And they wiggled off the table and onto the floor right at my feet. Well, I started screaming again. That's the story of the eels.

The eels wound up in a big pot, and after the wiggling and screaming was over, eaten for supper. Husband and wife Leonard and Lucy LeClair from Rustico told me eels were an important part of their diet when they were kids – they even had eel-skin bootlaces. Their feet never stopped dancing.

Not sure if the Clark family who ran general stores in Mt. Stewart, St. Peters and Montague bought eels – they bought just about everything else including potatoes, blueberries, and wool. Keir Clark was born in Mt. Stewart in 1910, and remembers his father Russell selling everything, including funerals:

> Two horses for the hearse. He was the undertaker for the community. A MacIntyre fella put on the top hat. After the funeral, he'd drop off the horses down near the shore where the hearse was kept, and the horses would travel themselves right up to the farm and go into their own stalls. They were lovely horses. My mother used to have a favourite horse. She had a horse and buggy. I remember when I started driving a car my father would say 'gee' and 'haw.' This was horse talk. To him, 'gee' meant go left and 'haw' meant go right, and he'd say to me, 'Now gee here,' to turn left.

A case of putting the horse before the car. Keir was driving a car when he was twelve years old. No such thing as driving licences when he started behind the wheel. If you owned a car, you drove. Sort of the way it is with impaired drivers nowadays. In winter when the Hillsborough River froze solid, Keir would drive the river into Charlottetown, going as fast as he wanted – no cops to worry about. Maybe the odd frozen eel. Keir witnessed many changes in Mt. Stewart over the years. When he was a young man working in the store, schooners back from the Caribbean sailed right up the river:

> Barbados, two trips a year, spring and fall. Molasses – I remember one year I bought a hundred puncheons. A hundred gallons in a puncheon. The moonshiners were great molasses people. I knew all the moonshiners. I remember them bringing in those five-

gallon cream cans, getting two cans of molasses. Ten gallons. Well, you knew of course they weren't making cookies.

Molasses cookies? Never heard of them.

~~~~~

Let's tag along with Jumpin' Jack Proud and his teen-aged buddies as they tour downtown Charlottetown:

There was the Queen Hotel. And the Russ Hotel-that was on Prince Street across from Johnston and Johnston the drugstore. And the Revere Hotel.

Where was the New England Cafe?

Queen Street. And Tom White had a restaurant on Queen Street.

During the Second World War, there was still Prohibition on PEI and Tom White, feeling sorry for the Royal Air Force trainee pilots and navigators who were accustomed to going to their local pub every night, would send out rum in a tea pot if a man in uniform asked for "cold tea."

And another thing – Prowse Brothers, Moore and MacLeod, and S.A. MacDonalds – every Saturday we'd go and get three suits to take home to try on over the week-end. You'd take then back on Monday morning. Then you'd go back to S.A.'s and Prowse Brothers' and get three more.

What were you doing with the suits?

Just to try them on. You had a new suit all winter – but you never wore them, you just tried them on and took them back. And LePages had a shoe store and Wrights had a shoe store. You'd get three pairs of shoes, take them home, try them on. Take them back Monday morning.

Closet fashion models. Actually, if anyone could have afforded three suits a week, it was Jumpin' Jack. From the time he was 10 years old, Jack was collecting overdue bills for his father, the esteemed P.J. Proud of Proud and Moreside Blacksmiths. Jack's commission was ten cents for every dollar he collected. Jack's strategy was to start knocking on doors at 7:00 on Sunday mornings. People paid up just to get rid of the little pest.

My wife, who is quite a bit older than me, tells about going to school on cold winter days in the 1960s, and being sent home to change because she was wearing pants. Not allowed, dresses and skirts only for girls, regardless of the weather. So, hats off to Madeline Roberts, born in 1921, whose first job – besides pickin' potatoes – was as a clerk in Callaghan's store in Kinkora. Every day, Madeline arrived early to light the pot-bellied stove. She walked to work and to keep warm she had sent away to the Simpsons Sears catalogue for a pair of long pants. Slacks. Well, Father Smith was the parish priest, and early that frosty morning, and Madeline wore her brand-new pants, he landed at Callaghan's store with the horse and sleigh:

> So, I had these on this morning; imagine walking in snow up to your knees.

There probably weren't many women wearing pants back then.

> Oh, there was nobody wearing them then. No way. But I was going to wear them regardless. I wasn't going to freeze. And I went in and started the fire in the stove, getting warmed up and Father came in. And he took a look at me. I said, 'It's cold this morning, Father.' He said, 'What are you wearing those pants for?' I said, 'To keep warm-what else?' He said, 'Women don't wear pants!' 'Well,' I said,

'I'm wearing them.' He said, 'Get them pants off!' 'I'm not taking them off,' I said. He said, 'The Blessed Virgin never wore pants.' I said, 'How do you know? She never worked in a place as cold as this. She needed them!'

I said, 'Now what would you want this morning, Father?' He said, 'I'd like a jar of molasses.' I said, 'Well it's pretty damn cold for molasses to run this morning, so you're going to have to wait until it thaws out a bit.' So, he never bothered me again – I wore the pants after that.

Quite a woman. Madeline was known as "the Quilt Lady." She wore out six sewing machines making quilts to give away to people in need. Her house looked like the bargain basement at Moore and MacLeods had exploded – bolts and bits of colourful fabric everywhere. I was visiting one day and a young couple with a new baby knocked on the door. They'd had a house fire. Madeline gave them three quilts. It brought a smile to everyone's face, even the baby's.

General Stores

Henrietta Mackinnon Morrison

The Mall. I missed hanging out at the mall. Stores weren't joined at the hip when I was a teenager. I did catch the last of the general store era though, the shopping mall's prototype. The general store was one-stop shopping before the term was invented. Henrietta Morrison worked in Clark's big general store in St. Peters, PEI, for thirteen years:

> They had everything. You didn't have to leave. It was like going into Zellers or one of those stores today. There was a counter all the way around, and up above there, were all these little shelves. And, no matter what they needed for the cattle, you could go to one of those shelves. Veterinary supplies. Everything was there; you never had to go further than Clark's.

Horseshoes and horseshoe nails?

> Oh yes, all that. He was well-set up there. Leather — if you wanted a piece of leather you went up to

the third floor. They had shoes: men's, women's, children's. They had overalls and underwear; the all-wool underwear so many people bought. Stanfield's underwear, they wore in the summertime as well as in the winter. Caps, hats – we used to laugh at one fella from up Fortune Road who come and say he wanted to get a cap. We loved to say to him, 'What size?' '6-7-8,' he'd say, '6-7-8,'[meaning six and seven eighths] he'd say two or three times.

Down in the basement were the puncheons of molasses. And vinegar and oil and kerosene. We sold a lot of molasses. They liked the moonshine back then. We'd know by the size of the can they'd have. It was up in the back porch, and we'd have to stand there and pump. It was a busy store. We'd go in at eight o'clock, and were supposed to go home at six, but it'd be twelve before we got home.

Sounds like the staff needed a shot of caffeine. Actually, caffeine was available thanks to a clever innovation the Clarks – Russell and his sons Stirling and Keir – initiated, and much appreciated by their customers. This, of course, was long before shopping excursions to Moncton or Bangor, Maine, came along. The train came through St. Peters twice a day, so:

We knew what time the train was coming. Ten o'clock in the morning, it came from the east and all the seniors from up east came down to Clark's store to shop. They'd spend the day, and at three o'clock, they had to be back at the station to go back east with their groceries. We'd make tea and a lunch for them when they came to the store. Once a week, sometimes twice. It was an outing for them. We'd look out and see them coming down the road – old ladies, we called them at the time. We took them to what used to be the bank. The Bank of Nova Scotia that Clark's had re-opened and made it a place for dry goods. That's where we had our stove. We'd get the teapot going and make some sandwiches, and greet the old ladies who thought it was great. It was all free.

Henrietta went to work at Clark's store in 1941 when she was 17 years old, making $4.00 a week. Her mother, Katie MacEwen MacKinnon bought flour from Clark's in 98-pound bags. Ninety-eight pounds because the quantities were based on the 14-pound "stone" old English system. Hence, 98 pounds equaled seven stones and a barrel of flour weighed 196 pounds or 14 stones times 14 pounds. Confused? One more twist – it was called the American system. Go figure.

Most shopkeepers saved the sugar and the flour bags, which were highly prized by homemakers. They would recycle the bags into bloomers or tea towels or the backing for quilts. Back to Katie, who was going through a 98-lb bag of flour every week, baking bread, biscuits, and bannock for 10 children and a hungry husband. Like most women of her generation, Katie recycled the cotton flour bags. Some were boiled in lye to remove the printing and became curtains or pillow cases, others became patches for the family's home-made quilts:

> She'd wash them in the spring in a big tub, with another alongside for rinsing, and she'd throw them over her back, and they would drip all the way over to a fence. Not a clothes line, a line wouldn't hold them. She'd put them on the fence and they'd be there probably for a week to dry. She made aprons and the apron had a bib on it. And backing for the quilts. They were never thrown out. They were always used for something. It was good cotton.

They made bloomers of the bags. A couple of old ladies with a big horse and wagon came in [to the store] to get their few things. We'd tell them how much it was, and they'd pull this layer of skirts up, black skirts, and get their hands into their bloomers made out of the flour bags, and they'd get their money out to pay for their groceries. It'd be a joke when we'd see them coming in.

Your mother probably didn't have a wringer washer, did she?

No, but she lived long enough to have a bathroom, and that was quite a thing. I bought a fridge, a second-hand one, it wasn't a very good one, made quite a noise, but anyway I bought it. And that was something. Put your stuff in the fridge even if it was an old one.

In Glenwood up at the western end of PEI, Everett MacDougall's father ran a store as well as serving as the village blacksmith as his father had before him. Everett said the store was bigger than a grocery store and smaller than a general store. Regardless of size, the store was the hangout for the locals, often called "loafers," because they loafed around chewing Hickey and Nicholson Black Twist tobacco, continuously spitting into the pot-bellied stove. Well, the men anyway. The news of the day was discussed and debated, and everyone loved when the various peddlers and salesmen making their rounds blew in, bringing gossip from other parts of the Island.

One travelling salesman was known from East Point to West Cape: James Montgomery from Charlottetown, better known as "The Candyman." Jim wholesaled a wide assortment of candy: licorice all-sorts, haystacks, fireballs, chicken bones:

Jim was a nice man. I knew Jim quite well. He used to travel by train. Carvell Brothers and DeBlois' would have a salesman and they'd all get on a train, head west and stop off in Coleman or Portage or Richmond. When they arrived in O'Leary in the winter, they had to have somebody to drive them with sleighs and horses. They'd take them out to my father's store and get the orders. They always had big fur coats. There was more than one person driving these salesmen – there used to be quite a fight to see who was going to get them. There'd be two or three rigs waiting at the train when they got off. Arguments and fights sometimes. They'd have fur coats for the salesmen to put on.

Would you call that a buffalo?

No, a buffalo is different. A buffalo went over your knees. A fur coat you just put on like a coat.

Buffalos evolved over the years, starting out as actual buffalo hides shipped in from the Prairies, and by the end of the horse-and-sleigh era in the 1950s or 1960s, they were usually heavy wool or cotton rugs used to ward off winter's chill, but still called a buffalo. Everyone packed a footwarmer of some kind as well, sometimes simply hot bricks, but also metal containers with the glowing embers from wood or coal stoves.

Jim Montgomery told me the sleeping arrangements at the homes and boarding houses he stayed at varied widely. He said some nights it was warmer in the sleigh than in the drafty bedroom. Food was also an issue. Some nights, Jim said, he pushed his untouched plate aside and went to bed with a mound of samples from his candy case. He had a sweet-tooth – coconut haystacks were his weakness – and often by mid-week, he rarely had a full sample case to show shopkeepers.

Jim was also the rep for the Macdonald Tobacco of Montreal. When I smoked, my preferred brand was *Export A*, a Macdonald's best-seller. The Macdonald brothers were originally from PEI, starting out in business back in the 1850s. They got a leg up in the 1860s during the American Civil War when the Union soldiers couldn't buy Confederate tobacco.

~~~~~

Everett MacDougall got into the store business himself after taking an egg-grading course in O'Leary in 1934. He landed a job at a big general store grading eggs:

> Everybody had eggs. We used gas lanterns. A nice light-yellow yolk – now that's a good fresh egg. Dark getting on to red – now that's an old egg. You could grade a case of eggs, which was thirty dozen at that time, in fifteen or twenty minutes. You always had two eggs in your hand. Two in each hand. You got so you just flipped them and graded for size. You got so you would know whether it was grade A or whatever. Extra large is twenty-four ounces per dozen. The small ones are eighteen ounces. I've done as many as four hundred cases in a week. Thirty dozen to a case.

If you're not beat figuring out the flour system, do the arithmetic: 400 cases, times 30 dozen times 12 eggs = 144,000 eggs. That's a lot of hen fruit! Other egg-graders confirm Everett's amazing ability. Everett was paid $12.00 for a six-day week. Late fall before the hens stopped laying was a busy time for the egg-graders. Egg money bought Christmas presents, and one old farmer told me if it hadn't been for eggs, in the lean years of the Great Depression of the 1930s, people would have had no income at all. A cow sold for $10.00, and a 100-pound bag of potatoes fetched only a few cents. General store proprietors like Keith Pratt, who ran the store in Bloomfield Station with his uncle A.J. Pratt, where the egg-grading station is still standing, was forced to branch out in the 1930s, and bought everything from hay to rabbits to Irish moss. No money changed hands: it was all barter, and, as Henrietta noted, there was always a run on molasses. Keith told me that in early December, they'd order in an extra boxcar load of molasses – dozens of 1,200-pound puncheons – because people were running off extra batches of moonshine for the Christmas and New Year's festivities. Moonshine helped take the sting out of hard times.

Everett eventually took over a big general store in Coleman. He built the egg-grading station that's still there next to the old railway line. Eggs shipped by train were packed in square wooden crates called Humpty Dumptys, manufactured in Cadillac, Michigan, by the Humpty Dumpty Manufacturing Company.

In 1938, Everett moved down east and bought the Federal Creamery in Vernon Bridge, and converted it to a feed mill for grinding oats and barley. He also bought and sold potatoes and turnips. The turnips were sorted and waxed for shipment on schooners to faraway places like Halifax, Sydney, and Newfoundland. At the time, there were three general stores in Vernon: Frasers, Jenkins, and Cummings. Now there are none.

Bobby Clow and his sister Arlene took over a bustling general store from their parents in Hampshire in the rolling hills west of Charlottetown.

Bobby: Can you remember the first two loaves of bread that Dad put on the shelf? Mum said we'd never sell them.

Arlene: I remember the story, that he brought home store bread from town, Mrs. Kenny's Home Bakery. We called it 'bought bread.'

Bobby: Mum said, 'You'll never sell it, Everett.' because everyone made their own bread. Oh, the changes. Everything came bulk: vinegar, bulk rice, bulk peanut butter in twenty-five-pound pails, and when someone came in for peanut butter, you put it in a wax bag or they brought a little jug to put it in.

Molasses, my that was an awful thing to get in the wintertime. Molasses came in in these great big puncheons and Dad would roll them down outside onto a big rack. You had this big crank and you held a milk bottle underneath and filled the milk bottle first. And you'd wait and wait, and every time anything runs, you know what you have to do? You have to run too. So, you'd have to set the molasses down and off you'd go. And then, you had to put the molasses into this narrow jug, the molasses dish we always called them. It would take you an hour to get a gallon.

In many villages, the general store was the community centre. Bobby remembers the local men running competitions in his father's general store in Hampshire. A favourite was setting mouse traps throughout the store just as it closed to see who could catch the most mice overnight. The prize was a bag of oranges. They also had orange-eating contests to see who could eat the most oranges. Not sure if the prize was a bag of mice.

The days of the general store are long gone. One of the last to close was C. R. Wallace's in Coleman near O'Leary. Rankin Wallace's niece and her daughter were the last to run the store. One day in 2002, a big car with Massachusetts plates rolled into the yard. An older lady and what turned out to be her daughter came into the store and asked if they kept the books back to the 1930s. In fact, they did, in a little room off the stairs leading up to the attic where wallpaper and shoes dating back to the 1930s were stored on dusty shelves. The older lady who appeared to be in her eighties asked to look for a bill for so-and-so Murphy. No one recognized the name but after a quick check, an order book was found dating back to 1930.

The bill owing was $43.86. The old lady explained that in 1929 her father lost his job and had no money. He had five kids and wife to feed and was desperate.

> He went to your uncle and asked if he could charge some groceries even though he had no way of paying him back. Your uncle said to take what he needed and not to worry. A week later, my father got a letter from his brother in Boston. If my father came right away, his brother could get him a job delivering ice door-to-door. So, we packed up and left immediately, the whole family. I promised my father I'd repay this bill if I ever got the chance. So here I am. How much do I owe you?

The Wallaces were dumbfounded. "$43.86," they replied. The old lady dug in her purse and paid accordingly. The Wallaces marked the bill "paid"; mother and daughter got back in their car and headed back to Boston.

The general store: more than a building; a state of mind.

Words Not Found in the Oxford English Dictionary

Murray Harbour North Clow's Wharf

The English language is a wonderful thing. I don't just say that because I'm unilingual. OK, partly, but the English language is alive and evolving. New words are accepted after wide-spread usage and become not only part of our vocabulary but also are added to our dictionaries, while words no longer in common use become obsolete and eventually fade from dictionaries.

I'm not sure if all of the words or phrases that my older friends have enlightened me with are in the Oxford English Dictionary (OED) but they were new to me. People like fisherman Gus Gregory, born in 1917 in Chepstow, who introduced me to the phrase "squirrel hake." Gus fished all his life and landed tons of cod and hake off PEI's North Side.

> Back in the '30s, there was any amount of codfish in the water, all kinds of codfish. The big school of hake came here about the middle of July and lasted for

about six weeks. They came right in shore chasing the bait. About fifty hooks on a line, a thousand hooks, and you'd get anywhere from twelve to fifteen up to two thousand pounds if you had good bait. But you didn't always have good bait. The hake would be anywhere from a foot to three feet long. The little fellas, squirrels they called them, about so long, they were the fellas you cut up for bait. A small hake was called squirrel hake.

So, a squirrel hake is like a tinker mackerel: the small fella. Gus sold a lot of fish to Matthew and McLean's General Store who had their own wharf in Souris.

I split hake on McLean's wharf, I think it was in '37 or '38, for twenty-five cents a hundred pounds. Twenty-five cents for a hundred pounds of split hake. You had to go out and catch it, and take the head and guts out of it, take it in and split it down the back, and take part of the backbone out ready for salt, and you got twenty-five cents a hundred pounds for it.

Most fishermen preferred evaporated salt called "solar salt" brought up from the Caribbean. Prices for cod were slightly better than for hake, and just as much work. The only advantage was it took fewer cod to fill the boat because they were bigger.

Years ago, I fished four and a half miles off Campbells Cove; there's a little bank there and I accidentally found it by jigging and handlining, and I used to set on that. Every day when you'd come in, you'd have what they called a 'gaff cod,' a big codfish about the length of the table here. It was called a gaff fish because you took your gaff and you hooked it in the lower jaw, and a fella pulled it up on the wharf. You normally forked the fish up, stick the fork in the head, and fork them up onto the wharf, but those were

too heavy to fork up. Some days, you got a dozen
of them. In 1960 or'61, you could see the codfish
going down on the North Side, getting scarce. They
began going down, down, down, and the last of it,
you wouldn't see a gaff cod at all.

The gaff cod weighed over 75 pounds, head off and guts
out. Gus fished alongside two other Northeastern Kings
County fishermen I got to know: Robbie Robertson and
Clive Bruce. Between the three of them, they spent 200
years fishing, from sail to diesel, from gaff cod to no
cod. Robbie and Clive confirmed Gus' story, and said
sometimes the gaff cod weighed as much as 85 or 90
pounds gutted.

Roy Clow was another fisherman I got to know. When
Roy built his house in Montague, he put up three sides,
roofed it watertight, and then built three fishing boats,
which he sold to finish the rest of the house and pay off
the mortgage. He was still living in it 60 years later the
first time I dropped in to interview him. Things got off to
a rocky start. His wife threw us out of the house because
we were making too much noise, and she couldn't hear
Coronation Street. One thing Roy knew was: don't get
in the way of Corrie, so we finished the interview, one
of many as it turned out, out in the driveway sitting
in Roy's car.

Roy grew up on a farm in Murray Harbour North. While
explaining how to de-worm a horse – feed it Hickey and
Nicholson Black Twist chewing tobacco – and how to
make moonshine – don't go to sleep while the mash is
cooking like he did once – he mentioned they sometimes
used "mud shoes" on their horses.

They were mud shoes Charlie Moreside in West
Devon made. He had a lot of marsh on his land,
boggy marsh, and the marsh hay used to grow

about four or five feet high, tall coarse hay. You've probably seen it in swamps. It was good horse or cattle feed, but you couldn't get on the ground with horses because they'd go down in the soft mud. So, Charlie made a pair of mud shoes for his horses, and he give me a pair of them. They're down in the Montague Museum now.

They're made out of wood and rounded on the nose and straight back on the sides and square across the end. Like big duck feet. They'd be eight inches wide anyway, and about twelve inches long. You put them on the front feet of the horses. They're awfully awkward and the horse would trip, step one foot on top of the other. But, finally, they'd walk with their front feet wide apart so they wouldn't trip themselves.

Snow shoes for horses. And I learned something else that day: I always thought we stopped harvesting marsh hay years ago. Marsh hay was highly valued by the early settlers since the Maritimes was covered in forest; trees that had to be cut down, and the land stumped before hay or oats could be planted. Marsh hay meant you could have a cow or horse.

Speaking of trees, Paul Jenkins asked in passing one day if I knew what a "pine float" was. Ah, no. Paul grew up in Charlottetown in the days before the mall was invented, so he and his teenage pals used to hang out at the Rendezvous restaurant, a hop and skip from Prince of Wales College.

We used to go to the Rendezvous a lot and get what we called a pine float. It was a glass of water with a toothpick in it. Pine float. And the waitresses would look at us and say, 'Are you serious? You fellas are going to be put out of here.' We'd sit there for two hours and drink the water. There were times when they did put the run to us when they were busy, sure, but we have great memories of those two lads.

The "two lads" were the Rendezvous' owners, Doug Hill and Pud Beer. The Rendezvous was on Kent Street. I remember it as The Jolly Knight, nicknamed The Foggy Dew by the legendary Cheverie brothers; later, it morphed into The Tradewinds Club and then Piazza Joes. One building with a lot of memories for a lot of people, and always a place to rendezvous.

A pine float would have been handy to wash down a Digby. Digbys were ubiquitous on store counters across the Maritimes at one time, alongside the punch board and figs of Hickey and Nicholson chewing tobacco.

Remember Bobby Clow and his sister Arlene who took over their parents' general store in Hampshire?

> Bobby: We bought the store in 1963 from Mum and Dad, and we used to have a box of Digbys on the counter. Smoked herring. Very salty. We called them pickled fish or Digbys. Digbys were about twenty-five cents a pound. We'd have the open wooden box on the counter and if any of the fellas came in, they'd take one and break it in two and chew it up. But there was one fella, he never shopped here much, but he always made a point every time of getting something for nothing. Even today, he'll take matches.
>
> Verna [Bobby's wife] used to get so cross with him, coming in and taking the Digby before he left. So, one time he came in and he said, 'You still have the Digbys?' 'Yes,' Verna said, 'We have them. Do you want one?' 'Yes.' So, she waited and waited. And didn't offer him one, and he never took another Digby. That fixed him.

I couldn't find Digby in the OED, but a Canadian dictionary lists it as "Digby chicken," a smoked herring named for Digby, NS, and first used in 1915.

"Gansey" is also listed in the Canadian dictionary as a "sweater or pullover," derived from the English Channel island of Guernsey. My grandfather Joe wore a torn, filthy gansey to do the barn work. It hung on a nail next to the woodstove in the kitchen. Like the Clows, Ella Willis, RN, was from Hampshire, and she used to have to wear her father's gansey to milk a cow he'd bought from two bachelors.

When Ella was born in 1910, her grandmother Janet MacLeod Watts was the midwife. Janet was married to a crusty old Scot by the name of John Watts who had an unusual insult for his wife when he was cranky. He called her a "cowhorse."

> My grandfather was a lowland Scot and my grandmother was a highland Scot. Grandfather was a bit of a peppery gentleman and, of course, families do have their little squabbles, and when he'd get cross at Grandma, he would call her a cowhorse. Now I don't know if you've ever heard this story or not, but it was an old old Scottish story. The Highland Scots were very very poor. The Lowland Scots were better off and, apparently, there was a horse that drifted onto the shore in the Highlands. They needed food so badly, they brought it onshore and they ate it. They said they thought it was a cow. So, the Lowlanders called the Highlanders cowhorses and he called her a cowhorse.

What would she call him in return?

> I never saw my grandmother lose her temper. She was a wonderful old lady.

Which explains the words of that classic Scottish tune, "Oh, ye'll tak' the low road, and I'll tak' the high road."

~~~~~

> Your room cost you a dollar a day. With a five-dollar meal ticket you would eat good plus get a few meals from the hockey club.

The phrase "meal ticket" has been around since the 1800s, and has always had a sport or a food connotation. Edwin Tiger Mackie, one of the best Island hockey players to ever don a pair of skates. lived off five-dollar meal tickets for 20 years, playing one step below the NHL back in the days when there were only six teams. He played in cities across North America: Baltimore, Springfield, Detroit, Pittsburgh – not bad for a kid who started his career playing with the Southport Mohawks.

Tiger was born in 1914 and, by 1935, he was making $40.00 a week playing with the Pittsburgh Hornets. Every summer, Tiger came home to work on the family farm in Southport, where he milked cows and forked hay, so he knew how to make a dollar last.

> Your five-dollar meal ticket in Pittsburgh would do you for a week. Buy it in the restaurants, go for three meals a day, and they'd punch out your ticket. On the average, in a month twenty dollars would feed you. And, by God, it was good. I believe we were fed better back in the 1920s and '30s than what we're getting fed now going to the supermarket.

The first time I met Tiger, he was sporting a black eye. He had been knocked into the boards playing in a non-contact league in Port Hawkesbury, Cape Breton. 'So, how'd you get the shiner', I asked. 'Dirty player,' he replied, 'No problem. You should see the other guy.' Tiger was 80 at the time, which I guess explains his nickname.

Sticking with food, Clarisse Gallant was born in Oyster Bed Bridge in 1913. She grew up in a French-speaking house with ten brothers and sisters where the old home remedies and Acadian recipes had been passed down through the generations.

> Patie is, well, people call it meat pie but it wasn't in the shape of a pie. It was more like a turnover, and you sliced it. It's still a tradition in Acadian families, but a lot of them are making it in the shape of pies and I deplore it. I say, 'That's English; that's not Acadian.'

Akin to making that most English of side dishes, Yorkshire pudding, in the shape of a pizza.

> And fricot was very common at my home because we always had chickens. Now I remember having house parties, the young people, and if we could have a chicken, it was great. Sometimes the chicken was stolen from somebody's henhouse. So, that added to the fun. It shouldn't have, but it did. But if we didn't have a chicken, we made a fricot of onions, butter- there was always butter- and potatoes, water, and salt and pepper. That was it. We called that by another name: fricot à la bazette. That meant it was like a chicken fricot but there was no chicken. I don't know where the word bazette came from.

One translation for *fricot à la bazette* is "stupid cook's stew," meaning the chef had forgotten to add the meat. Regardless, in my Anglo-opinion, the best part of fricot is the dumplings, anyway.

Clarisse's father and brother Ed ran a water-powered flour, grist, and saw mill in Oyster Bed Bridge. When she was a girl, Clarisse worked in the sawmill bundling shingles, dangerous with all the machinery, but she knew the workings of the mill inside and out.

The water has to come from a brook, and it's dammed at the mill to form a pond. Then the water went through a flume. When the gate was open, the water would release into the flume and fall into a cylinder that had the waterwheel at the bottom, that activated the gears to power the flour mill or the saw or the grist mill. In the spring, if there had been a winter of a lot of snow and then a sudden freshet, my father would always be anxious about the dam: would it stand the pressure of the water? The pond would fill very high with water, and there was immense pressure on the dam.

I heard it break one spring. In the middle of the night, we heard a loud 'whoosh.' The next year, people moved to Brackley Beach who had worked in the States for years with cement; cement was a new thing in our area in those years. And they were called the 'Concrete Neils.'

Problem solved. Bring on the Concrete Neils with their American technology.

They persuaded my father that what he needed was a concrete dam for his mill. So, during the spring months, they came and built what was supposed to be a real Titanic.

Why do you call it a Titanic?

Because it couldn't break. Nothing could happen to it because it was invincible. The next spring, it broke. It broke, and what a disappointment it was to my father. He thought he'd have it for years, but it didn't last.

So, it was well-named.

The Titanic sank too. Anyway, those people had built a house in the Brackley Beach area out of concrete.

And it didn't last.

The Concrete Neils personified the definition of irony. Maybe their house fell down because they were drinking bug beer. Bug beer was new to me until one night, while enjoying the fiddle-playing of the MacIntosh brothers, Donald and George, they mentioned playing at house parties where cheap bug beer flowed. For years, Donald played the fiddle at bootleggers, house parties, houses of ill-repute, and at outdoor dances all over eastern N.S.

> I got thirty dollars. There were other ones there playing a few hours, and they got nothing.

> George: Now you shouldn't say they got nothing, Don. You're not sure. Don't make that statement.

> I don't think they did. I played six hours steady, and had a few drinks of rum in between. And then I played, years ago at an open-air dance at Moose River — you know where Moose River is, out towards Garden of Eden — and the moonshine used to come over from Barneys River, and I used to get into a little of that. Mac Ross was making shine in Barneys River — that's where our mother was born.

Not sure she'd appreciate being lumped in the same sentence as Mac Ross' moonshine. The year my family lived in New Glasgow's North End, the MacIntosh brothers were our next-door neighbours. Donald drove an ancient half ton truck to and from Stellarton every day where he ran a shoemaking shop. Like his father, Donald was buoyant and breezy, and called himself a cobbler; between them, they re-heeled and re-soled thousands of coal miners' boots.

George, the quieter, more cautious of the two, was a milk man, starting out in the horse and wagon days, a familiar sight with his steaming cigar. Everybody knew the two brothers who, after they retired, sat in the Aberdeen Mall chatting up everyone passing through for the next twenty years. They were inseparable, and confirmed bachelors.

> Donald Sutherland, my cousin in Laggan, got married twice. He wouldn't take no for an answer the second time he got married. He said to me, 'I want you to play the violin and nobody else, and there'll be a bunch of drunks there who'll chord on the guitar with you.'

> George: I hope those fellas don't hear that.

> Donald: I didn't mention any names. Now, do you know where Glengarry is? I've played open air dances when I had that 1929 Model-A Ford. You saw it out there when you were a little boy. I played out there and that stage was packed every night. And lots of liquor. A long time ago. It wasn't all shine. They'd take a bottle with them, a lot of fellas. Then there was bug beer you used to get years ago, two quarts for a quarter. Bug beer, that's a way beyond your time.

What did they make bug beer out of? Not bugs.

> Donald: No. A seed.

> George: It seemed if you put water in the bottle, it would start again. That's why it was so cheap.

Never a dull moment with the MacIntosh brothers. They swapped the fiddle back and forth all night, playing old tunes like "Red Wing," "Over the Waves," and my mother's favorite, "Maple Sugar." I checked out bug beer and it was one of several types of beer described as bug or seed beer, beers fermented with wild yeasts. Wild yeast and bacteria beer are still being brewed, only the two-quarts-for-a-quarter price has escalated to $10 to $25 for a 12-ounce bottle. Not exactly a loss leader.

Keir Clark knew all about loss leaders. In fact, he may have introduced the concept to PEI. Keir and his brother

Sterling and their father Russell Clark ran big general stores in St. Peters and Mt. Stewart, buying and selling everything from blueberries to potato baskets made by the Indigenous peoples in Scotchfort. In 1934, Keir opened his own store on Main Street in Montague.

> It was a real general store, biggest store east of Charlottetown. Most of the general stores at that time bought their flour at the wholesalers, and it cost them a couple of dollars more. So, I bought a boxcar load of flour, a thousand bags and decided I'd sell it a dollar under my cost. I advertised it at this price, and so, the first day the store opened, people came in swarms, and they also bought their groceries. So, I lost a thousand dollars on the flour but I made about three thousand on the groceries on the same day. So, I got off to a good start. That was a loss leader to me that time.

Keir bought the lumber for the store at Fitzpatrick's sawmill in Woodville Mills. A two by four by eight-foot stud cost eight cents in 1934.

Keir was born 1910 and lived to be 100, immaculate in his suit and tie every day right to the end. He and his father Russell were both elected several times to the provincial government, and Keir was also a cabinet minister in the 1960s. Two very successful and well-liked entrepreneurs.

Equally successful in the 1920s and '30s were both the men's and women's hockey teams from Victoria-by-the-Sea whose home rink was one of the few covered rinks on PEI at the time. The rink, with natural ice, was run by husband and wife H.B. and Kathryn Wood, and was where both the Victoria Unions and the Union Sisters dominated for years. Cora Ferguson was born in 1917, and played goalie and occasionally left wing for the Union Sisters.

I played hockey and I loved it. Boy, I loved it. I always used the Unions' goalie pads, so I was rigged out fine. But, gor, I used to love to play out. I was very good at scoring goals, but I was stuck in the nets.

Were the games rough?

Oh yes. They'd trip them and give them the elbow and everything. Oh, we had that down pat, boy. Before I was put in the nets, I could get that elbow going. They said I was another Gordie Howe because he always used the elbow.

How many people still remember the Gordie Howe hat-trick? That would be a goal, an assist, and a fight in the same game.

Did you watch the Union men play?

Oh, always, heavens, I wouldn't miss that for anything. The big rivals were the Borden Nationals and Summerside Crystals, and then they'd go up to Alberton, and the Alberton team would come down here. They'd hire horses and sleighs in Albany and come down to Victoria. They'd stay at Herb Profitt's hotel and put the horses in the barn there.

While telling me about Victoria's hockey exploits, Cora asked if I knew what a chamber pot was. Indeed, I did, but I wondered what a portable toilet, that wide china pot that lived under the bed in the days before indoor plumbing, and a much warmer alternative to a mad dash to the outhouse, had to do with hockey.

So. Anyway. Alberton came down with intentions they were going to win the championship, but they didn't win the game. They were determined they were going to take home the cup. So, what did they do the next morning, but go down to Wright's store and buy a couple of big chamber pots and some ribbon. And they had them tied to the back of the sleighs and when they were going up town and past the school, they were singing out. 'We won the cup! We won the cup!' And those chamber pots were flopping along behind them.

My guess is the Alberton players drank bug beer, went fricot, and spent their meal ticket money on chamber pots. What a bunch of loss leaders.

Ghost Stories

Ralph Gallant

Let's get likkered up and go ghost-bustin'! Booze and boos... Ralph Gallant had to be the most colourful person to come out of Duvar up in western PEI. Ralph was a Second World War veteran, a coal miner, a horse-whisperer, and when he got sentenced to the Prince County jail for making moonshine, he put his skills to good use:

I done a year in Summerside jail. The Queen come over that year. That was the last time the Queen come over. So, I got an extra month off. I was working with the sheriff at the racetrack. Every day. Sheriff [Robert] Dewar. Did you know him?

What were you doing at the racetrack?

Looking after his trotting horses. He used to come to the jail every morning to take me to the racetrack. He'd leave me there all day. He used to take me home to sleep at home some nights-and me supposed to be doing time in jail. So anyway, my father came down and said, 'Ralph, I'm going to bail you out of jail.' I said, 'You're not. Don't do that.' The jail wasn't hard — old Hughie Daly was the jailer. We used to make beer in there and everything.

Where were you making beer?

> Behind the furnace in gallon jars. We had three- or four-gallon jars going all the time. We used to pick nightcrawlers for the lawyers. We'd send out to the bootleggers to get a quart.

You mean you prisoners were outside on the lawn?

> Yeah, with flashlights. Nightcrawlers. Sell them to the lawyers. We wouldn't run away, eh. We would never think of running away.

Ralph got caught a time for making 'shine. His car and 15 gallons of shine were confiscated. To make a few dollars – he had 13 children – Ralph set up a still in the jail's furnace room to make moonshine. His wife Amelia – a coal-miner's daughter from Minto, NB – told me she went to the judge who'd sentenced Ralph and pleaded for his release. She told the judge she was afraid Ralph would turn into an alcoholic if he stayed in jail.

If you think you need a drink after that, you'll need one for sure after you hear Estelle Soloman Bolger's story about a sick cow and the psychic powers of prayer. Estelle was born in 1909 to Lebanese parents who had immigrated to PEI in the 1890s. The Solomans ran a bakery, a barbershop, and a hotel, where you could also get a ten-cent bath, in Georgetown:

> We had a great big barn and a barn loft, with a chicken coop, and a stall for the cows, and an out-house. One time, the cow was having a calf and there was something wrong with it. Papa was in Montague, on horseback. Mama was terrified. She got us all in the dining room on our knees praying. And Papa came home like somebody at the races. The horse landed in the yard rearing up and frothing. And Papa said, 'What's the matter! What's the matter!'

Mama said, 'How did you know?' He said, 'I heard you calling me.' He was in Montague. Mama said, 'I think the cow is dying.' So, he got the vet and the two of them saved the cow. But he heard her calling him. We were all on our knees, all the children. Oh, there was an awful lot of funny things, you know.

Is that a forerunner? Or telepathy? A husband and wife in Corraville showed me an old clock that had been given to them by his uncle who was moving to Ontario. The clock didn't work but it looked good on their dresser. One night. they both woke up to an odd sound in the bedroom. The clock had started ticking. They went back to sleep, and in the morning the telephone rang. Their uncle had died during the night, you guessed it, at the exact time the clock started ticking. How do you explain things like that? The couple had no reason to lie to me.

Who better to trust than a sea captain, like Captain Ernest "Ben" Pike who captained PEI's best-loved ferry the old *Abby*. Ben was a Second World War veteran, and came from a Newfoundland family of sailors and fishermen. His father was a Grand Banks fisherman, one of 180 men who drowned in 1927 in one of the worst hurricanes to ever hit the eastern seaboard. Ben was a young lad, at home in Burin Bay Arm with his mother and siblings:

We were over in the back field of our place taking up hay, it was late. And a crow flew by. One crow. And Mother said, 'There you go. Something happened to your poor dear father. One crow, sorrow. We'll go home.' Soon as we got home, we looked way out in the narrows about four or five miles out, and we saw a little boat coming. And Mother said, 'There it is. The minister's coming in to break the news to us.' I remember that. And Mother was pregnant with Charlie. Mother said to our oldest sister, 'Go over to the wharf and meet the minister, and take him up.' Even at my young age I was wondering how Mother knew all of this. But the minister came and went upstairs — Mother was in bed — and he had prayer with us and told us what happened. Father was drowned. Charlie was born two months after Father was drowned.

Captain Pike's oldest brother Douglas was also caught in that hurricane. He survived. Two years later, Captain Pike himself survived the 1929 earthquake and tidal wave – tsunami – that rocked southern Newfoundland and parts of Cape Breton. The tidal wave claimed 29 lives in the Burin Peninsula. The earthquake was felt here on PEI, washing out roads and smashing boats at the eastern end of the Island. At one time, so-called marine hospitals dotted coastlines here in the Maritimes. Vessels bringing immigrants or flying a yellow flag indicating a disease on board would off-load the sick to these quarantined hospitals. Some were simply abandoned houses known as "pest houses" as was the case in Summerside. In Georgetown, there was a rocky speck of an island in the harbour labelled Thrumcap Spit on maps but known locally as Poxy Island, "pox" being shorthand for smallpox.

Keith Mutch was born in 1923 on a farm in Keppoch, next to the Marine Hospital, which for years was run by the Henry family. In 1951, Evelyn Henry was the first to swim the Northumberland Strait, and in 1989 her daughter Andrea Brown repeated the feat. The Marine Hospital was built of locally made bricks: there were once eight bricks kilns in the Keppoch /Crossroads area. It was surrounded by the graves of sailors and immigrants, marked by plain white crosses. Over time, the trees and bushes reclaimed the fields, the white crosses rotted away, slight depressions in the ground the only sign of the graves, the big brick building abandoned:

> It was supposed to be haunted. I've been down in the old hospital many times. A buddy of mine and I would go down and walk through the place. Great big rooms. We were in one particular time, and we heard this clamping and banging so we got out of there in a hurry. It turned out a couple of young cattle had gotten in and were making all the noise. We saw them coming out after a while.

After the Marine Hospital was abandoned in the 1930s, rumrunners used the cellar to store kegs of rum. The rum boats were leery about going right in to Charlottetown harbour with its narrow entrance and exit. Too easy for the prohibition officers to set a trap. The rumrunners knew people wouldn't snoop around because of the hospital's reputation for being haunted. Reverend Bryer Jones grew up not far away in Tea Hill, and he remembered when, as a boy in the 1930s, he watched a man dig up the bones of the smallpox and diphtheria victims buried at the Marine Hospital. He loaded the bones into a horse-drawn wagon and reburied them up the hill at the Crossroads Christian Church.

When Newfoundlander Elsie Bowdridge Collier moved to PEI, she didn't have to worry about haunted Marine Hospitals. Elsie was born in 1912 in a small village called Messieurs at the west end of Grandy's Island, connected to Burgeo an outport on Newfoundland's south coast. Her mother Matilda, known to one and all as Aunt Tillie, was a midwife and country nurse who brought people into the world; and Elsie's father was a carpenter who made the coffins to take people out of this world. Elsie and her husband came to Murray Harbour after the Second World War. She missed her seal flippers and cod tongues, and her best memories were from back home in Messieurs:

> I was telling my friend the other day – she said she didn't believe it. It is true. I was a big girl. Now, maybe I shouldn't tell you anyway... No, no. Now this woman, she died. They picked her up, and the doctor came in and pronounced her dead. She was in her casket. That was all right. They had the service in the house – well they didn't take them to the church. And they were taking her wedding rings off, and she moved. Came back to life. She came back alive, and she said, 'I've been to a beautiful place. It was just beautiful. But I've only got six months to live.' And from that day, it was six months when she died. Dr. Keane couldn't understand why he made a mistake. Because she was really dead. There was no pulse or nothing. And that was really true. That was really true.

An early glimpse of heaven's "streets of gold," a forerunner? A memory of something before it actually happens. Elsie lived to be 94, the same age as her grandmother. When the grandmother died, Elsie's parents dressed and buried her. At the wake, the family shared memories. Elsie's memory was of her Granny "dancing like a cricket" on her 90th birthday. We should all be so lucky.

~~~~~~

> He was an air gunner and was killed near Aachen between Germany and Belgium in 1942. He had a dog at home on PEI, and the night he was killed, the dog cried all night. Some things of his were sent home after the war, and the dog would never leave the room where they were.

Second World War veteran Donald MacKay's experience with a barking dog. Donald served in the Air Force with that airman also from the Kensington area. There are many stories about dogs mourning their masters, sleeping on the grave. Funny, you never hear similar stories about cats. Just saying, cat people.

Pull up a log, I'll throw a few sticks on the bonfire, and let's spend some quality time scaring ourselves with ghost stories. Harry Heffell and his sister Marjorie grew up in Travellers Rest; with that name, perhaps not a place you'd expect to elicit bad dreams; however, let's hear what Harry has to say:

> I was in the room there, laying down on the lounge, and when I woke up, there was a young woman standing alongside looking down at me. I opened up my eyes and I thought perhaps I was in the hospital. And then just like that there was nothing there. She was gone.

Are you sure it wasn't a dream?

> Oh, I was awake.

At the same time, Marjorie was in Charlottetown visiting her stepdaughter.

> She was on her way out with cancer. And she thought a lot of Harry, always asking how he was, a very jolly woman, and when I came home that day, I said that was the last day I'd see her because she was dying. So, Harry told me what he saw and I said,' I guess that was her little angel.' The same day, the same time just as she died, Harry saw this lady looking over him.

Harry's "little angel" did her job. Harry lived to be 100. Marjorie has another story:

> And another thing: our sister Mary Ellen who just lived up the road, Mary Ellen thought a lot of Aunt Aggie, Mother's sister. The morning Aunt Aggie died,

Mary Ellen was lying awake, and before she got up, she heard three raps on her bedroom door loud and clear. That morning at the nursing home, the nurse was getting Aunt Aggie ready, talking to her, getting her washed and dressed, and the nurse turned around, and Aunt Aggie was dead. She went out just that quick. Mary Ellen heard the three knocks on her bedroom door at the same time.

Some people have other-worldly experiences all the time, other people scoff because they've never encountered a ghost or forerunner. Take husband and wife Russell and Elsie Quigley in Cape Traverse. While Russell slept soundly, Elsie had a supernatural encounter one cold and windy winter night.

It was a gale of wind but it wasn't stormy, and I woke up and thought, 'Oh my gracious, the house is awfully cold.' So, I got out of bed and ran downstairs, and the front door was open and the furnace was blood red. We had a floor furnace. So, I shut the outside door and I had to tie it, tie it into the inside door knob. I sat down in the big chair alongside the furnace and thought, 'Oh my goodness, the house is going to burn down. There's no way I can get this furnace to calm down.'

All of a sudden, I heard running on the stairs, thump thump thump, down the stairs, out the hall behind me, and then down cellar. And I thought, 'Oh, it's not before time that man's getting out of bed.' I thought it was Russell. And a few minutes later, I heard the tap in the kitchen running, and then I heard the taps in the bathroom running. After a while, this tall handsome blond man came in, and he stood right over me, and he took my hand and said, 'Everything's all right here tonight.' He had beautiful white teeth and blond curls, and I looked at him and couldn't believe my eyes what I was seeing. And he disappeared. That's as true as I'm sitting here.

Did you ever find out if he belonged to the house before?

No, he didn't. He said, 'Everything will be alright here tonight.' And then he just disappeared. I wasn't scared. I was relieved. I was so relieved I just sat back in the chair and went sound to sleep.

You're sure it wasn't a dream?

It wasn't a dream. There was no dream!

Elsie's son Wayne lived down the road and he woke up at the same time, at three in the morning, because he'd had a dream that something was wrong at home. He looked across at his parents' house and a feeling came over him that everything was OK, so he went back to bed. Russell slept through it all.

A different family lives in the Quigley house now, and they've not seen the tall, handsome, blond man with the good choppers. Yet.

There's an old saying that a rooster will crow before a death. Some believe it harkens back to the New Testament when Jesus predicted Peter would deny Him three times before the rooster crowed. Peter did deny knowledge of Christ three times, and the rooster crowed. Back in Travellers Rest, both Heffells heard not a rooster but a hen, yes, a hen, crow twice before sudden deaths. Harry kept a mix of chickens, ducks and geese, so he knew hens weren't supposed to crow. But one night, one of his hens did crow: just before a car crashed into a train at the level crossing just down the road. Three people were killed. Harry was perplexed about the hen crowing, but he always believed that dogs had supernatural powers.

Dogs, they know. Archie MacLeod in Stanley Bridge was an undertaker. He said he knew when he'd be called because his dogs would whinge and cry all night. Sure enough, he'd get word that such and such a person had died. Well, then over here, across the road, they got a big black dog and usually kept him in the house but one night he barked and cried, and they had to get up and let him out. So, the dog went up on a snowbank, and he looked away across that way and – you saw him, Marjorie – and he barked and cried there all night.

Marjorie: I could see him outlined on the white snowbank. It was a moonlight night and he sat with his head back and he just went 'wooooooooo,' howled a mournful dismal howl there by the hour. The next morning at ten o'clock a neighbour came in and said, 'Jim MacDonald died last night.' Now, Jim MacDonald lived in that house, he and his mother, where the black dog was living at the time. It was the MacDonald house originally. And the dog howled all night.

But the dog wouldn't have even known the MacDonalds.

Oh no no no no.

The dog never howled before nor after. Go figure. Many cultures believe the devil takes the shape of a black dog. But that's not the case here. I've several versions where a black dog that no one recognizes suddenly appears at a dance, and everyone leaves in a hurry thinking the black dog is a portent of death. In rural communities, strangers were sometimes suspected of being in league with the devil especially when they showed up at card parties or frolics, and accidentally revealed a cloven hoof. Young women were especially thought to be targets of the mysterious stranger asking them to dance, always cloyingly polite, and whose cloven hoof is somehow let slip.

In 1933, pretty and petite Estelle Soloman from George-town married tall and handsome Lenie Bolger, a fiddle player from Foxely River at the other end of the Island. They moved to a rented apartment in a house in Tyne Valley, run by a Mrs. Phillips. Estelle ran a barber shop – in fact, she was the first female barber on PEI – and Lenie set up a shoemaking and harness shop. One night just after moving in, they were sleeping soundly when Estelle:

I woke up and standing by the bed was a man with a crewcut, white shirt with the sleeves rolled up, black necktie, black pants with white lace shoes. He was passing me a square thing like a brick only it was rolled up in paper and tied. I started to cry, and Lenie said, 'What's the matter?' I said, 'There's a man standing by the bed.' And Lenie said, 'Don't be so foolish. Where is he?' The man had disappeared.

Lenie got up and he lit the lamp – there were no lights – and he looked under the bed and he looked all around and he opened the hall door and looked outside and there wasn't a sign of him anywhere. That night I shivered and shivered all night. I had the pillow on top of my head and Lenie put one leg over me and one arm around me to protect me.

When we got up the next morning, Mrs. Phillips said, 'Estelle, you're awfully pale this morning,' and Lenie said, 'Is it any wonder? She was awake all night.' And I told her what I saw. Mrs. Phillips looked at her daughter and her daughter looked at her, and the two of them went into the pantry and talked. They came out and decided to tell me: the banker had died a month earlier in that room, and that was the way he dressed. The banker from the bank in Tyne Valley.

Neither Lenie nor Estelle had ever met the banker.

There's a follow-up to Estelle's eerie encounter. Many years later, long after Lenie and Estelle moved to Summerside, Estelle was getting a large sum of money out of their bank. The money came wrapped as a large package, shaped like a brick, wrapped in paper, and tied. The man who handed it to her had a crewcut and was dressed like the Tyne Valley banker, everything exactly the way she'd described seventy years before.

Estelle was not one given to flights of fancy. She came from a hard-working family in Georgetown where her mum and dad ran a bakery, a hotel, a restaurant, a barber shop, as well as a public bathhouse and smoking room. The Solomans were a close-knit family, and when Estelle's beloved grandmother suffered a heart attack, Estelle and her mother sat in vigil at her bedside in the old Charlottetown Hospital.

> 'Oh,' Grandma says, 'Oh I'm dying.' And her head went back and I grabbed her hand, and said, 'I'm here, dear.' Now, over the bed was, what would you call it, a heatwave. And it started to rise. I saw it. I'm telling you the truth. I told the nuns [the nursing Sisters] about it and they said it was the soul leaving the body. Some people are given to see that and some people are not. The heat went like this over the bed, shimmered, and it rose. It went up and up.

You could see this?

> I saw it. She was dying then. So, I grabbed her hand and said, 'I'm here dear,' and she just went 'Ahh,' and she was gone.

Belief in ghosts and forerunners and the supernatural is very personal. But one thing is for certain: Estelle Bolger and Donald MacKay, and the Heffells, and the Quigleys, one of them anyway, knew what they saw and heard. And they believed.

Stranger than Fiction – Canadian Girls Are Good to the Last Minute

Frances Lavers Llewellyn

Sometimes truth is stranger than fiction. Frances Llewellyn was born in 1913, and grew up in Georgetown. Her mother, Mable Stewart Llewellyn, was a midwife and brought dozens of babies into the world, including former Georgetown mayor and present artisan Peter Llewellyn. Times were tough and adding a new mouth to feed at the table meant everyone else had to do with even less on their plates. As a result, sometimes the easy way out was to send the newborn to the orphanage, or find a willing family with the money to raise the child. This story begins one day when Frances was shopping in Montague and met an old friend named Victor:

> I said, 'You know, there was a woman in Georgetown who traded her little girl for a goose.' Victor said, 'I know that little girl.' I said, 'Do you, Victor?' He said, 'Yes. I went to the house one time – I don't know

why – and I could hear that child upstairs, calling. And I thought that child is going to die. So, I took the bull by the horns and I went up to see Dr. Preston MacIntyre. 'Will you do something for a child?' I asked, and he came down and he looked after her, and gave her medicine. And to this day, I visit that girl. She got married, and I still visit her.

Was she really traded for a goose?

Yes. She was traded for a goose. She was a little beautiful blonde girl. And her mother traded her for a goose. They had a big family. Can you imagine?

It sounds like a fairy tale, a cow for a handful of magic beans. Frances insisted I go visit the woman who then was in her eighties to find out for myself. I was tempted. But didn't. Like Frances said, it was a different back then. Children were often sent to the orphanage during rough spells at home, and the parents would retrieve them when things improved. Or not. Earl Gay and his brother were two of those children who spent time in and out of the orphanage, several times over Christmas, always a bad time for families with no money. I asked what Christmas was like, and he said the children were all given a lovely toy as a present on Christmas day, and the toy was taken away from them a week later, to be recycled the next year.

I went to high school with several teens who were living at the old Protestant orphanage in Mt. Herbert. Years later, after I moved to Bunbury, I noticed one of those classmates driving past my house on a regular basis. I happened to meet him in town, and he told me he was still living at the orphanage even though it had shut down years earlier. He was allowed to stay, he said, because it was the only home he'd known. I went home to my drafty old house and counted my blessings.

Annie Callaghan knew poverty when she was a girl, but since everyone was in the same boat, no one thought anything of it. Annie was a "century baby," born in 1900 in Lake Verde. Family meant everything to Annie. She had three older brothers who fought in the First World War. All three were "returned men," and they settled into a casual life: three bachelor brothers running a small general store. Annie didn't marry either, although she had plenty of opportunities from suitors she'd met in Maine where she went to work when she was 22.

Annie borrowed the $9.00 train fare to the States from her uncle. It was her first time off the Island. She arrived in Fairfield, Maine, late Saturday night, and had landed a job in the paper mill by Monday morning.

> They always liked the Canadian girls. If you were a Canadian girl you could get work anywhere. Housework too. Very dependable, they said, compared to the American girls. We'd never leave our bench until it was time to go, but a lot of the girls wanted to go to a dance or to shop, and they'd punch out fifteen minutes early. But Canadian girls were good to the last minute.

> I worked there ten years, eight hours a day in shifts, packing paper plates. I had to work Sunday and all. And then I got a chance to work at housework.

Annie took a big hit in wages, from $25-$30 a week at the mill doing piecework to $8 a month housekeeping, cooking, and babysitting for the Holmes family, the wealthy town banker and his wife. Annie worked for over 40 years in Maine, and initially only went to the Holmes' to fill in for six weeks. She wound up staying 31 years, helping raise their children from diapers to university degrees. She retired back home to PEI at the age of 65, and, even after 31 years with the Holmes' family, Annie never made more than $15 a month. A month.

Obviously, money wasn't Annie's prime motivation. She liked the Holmes family, was satisfied with her room and board, and didn't miss the graveyard shifts at the paper mill. She had grown up on a self-sufficient farm, churning butter, and trading eggs and blueberries at the store for tea ands molasses. She sheared sheep, spun the wool, and wove the blankets. Rather than go to the doctor, her mother practiced the old home remedies passed down through generations: the sulphur and molasses spring tonic; kerosene dripped onto a spoonful of sugar to cure a cough, and goose grease for practically everything. However, her chronic eczema finally required a visit to a doctor:

> I lost my fingernails, and I'd squeeze and the pus would come out of my hands. I tried all kinds of medications the doctor gave me, ointment and stuff. So, after two years the doctor told my mother that if I'd cross water I'd get cured. So, after I went up to Maine, the eczema was pretty well gone. Then the next June, I came home and I stayed all summer. Coming on the fall, the eczema started up again and I went back to the States, and I had to cross water again, and it healed over. Strange. I tried all sorts of medicines, but like the doctor said, water must have something to do with it.

Annie worked for over 40 years in Maine, and most of it as housekeeper and nanny for a banker. She came home every summer bringing underwear and shirts for her brothers. The banker, Mr. Holmes, was curious about this mystical island that had such a hold on Annie, and so he drove her home one year to see what all the fuss was about. Her family immediately adopted him, and he pitched in pumping water and picking blueberries along with the rest of the gang, all the while underwhelmed by the absence of electricity and the necessity of visiting the wooden outhouse behind the barn.

> He came down with me to my niece's wedding. He never had such a time in all his life. He had the grandest time. We went to Vernon River church and Mr. Holmes, when he got out of the car, pulled the buttons off his coat. He was all dressed up. So, my brother Owen said, 'Oh, my Lord. You're doing that early. We don't start with the ruckus until midnight. He never heard such things in all his life. He took to the laughing. So, he waited on tables all night long at the reception. A few of them got pretty well loaded, in one door and out the other.

Mr. Holmes stayed in Lake Verde for two weeks, helping with the farm chores, chopping firewood in his white shirt, vest, and tie. He squired most of Lake Verde around in his car, and came back several more summers to "reconvene with nature," as he put it. Before he died, sick in bed, he told Annie, "One thing I wish before I die, just one more trip back to PEI." He never made it.

Annie came home one last time when she turned 65, and moved in to look after her brothers.

> I had an uncle who was deaf and dumb. When he was thirteen years old, he took the measles and his eardrums burst. He lived with my mother and father. Neighbours and I went to a dance in Vernon River in January, and when we were coming home from the dance, we met a hearse and seven sleighs on the road. We thought somebody must have passed away in town and they were taking them out to Vernon River to wake. My uncle died the next week, and that's what we had for the funeral – a hearse

and seven sleighs. They said that was a forerunner
of my uncle's passing.

Some people believe in forerunners and ghosts, the world of another dimension. In this world, I found it hard to believe that Annie had started off 40 years earlier working for the banker and his wife for $10.00 a month. When she retired in 1965, she was making the grand sum of $40.00 a month, a raise of $1.00 a year.

A few miles down the road lived a good friend of Annie Callaghan's, Jimmy Doyle. Like Annie, Jimmy and his brother and cousins left the Island to find work. For years, Jimmy worked in a New Brunswick lumber camp, thirty miles deep in the woods from the nearest town, St. Martins, east of Saint John on the Bay of Fundy. Card playing was discouraged, but unlike many camps, music was allowed so on the long winter's nights mouth organs and step-dancing flourished. Sawing lumber and step-dancing naturally led to hearty appetites, and the mainstays in the cookhouse were beans, meat, and lots of prunes:

> Not moose-deer meat. Sides of pork. The camp I worked in, the mill camp, had twenty-five men in it and the woods camp had fifty or sixty. For dessert, raisin pie and mince pie, and plum pudding, prunes. I'll tell you a story, now you won't believe it. One fella over there, he worked with my first cousin, and one evening they had prunes for supper. The cook noticed how this man had eaten an awful lot of prunes. The cook told the young fella – the cookee – to count the prune stones. And do you know how many prunes he'd eaten? He ate a hundred and four prunes. The cook told the cookee to go get a hundred and four prunes and weigh them. He did what he was told and they weighed very close to four pounds.

The next day, the same man ate 15 donuts. But who wouldn't have a big appetite after working 12-hour days, six days a week in the freezing cold? The lumber camps were part of an annual work-cycle followed by many Island men: plant their crops on the farm in the spring, head west on the harvest excursion train in August, come home from the prairies after the grain was harvested, take in the crops at home, and after Christmas head to the lumber woods in New Brunswick, Nova Scotia, or Maine. Then start the cycle all over again in the spring after coming home with hard-earned cash from the woods. Jimmy was making $30 a month, with teamsters, sawyers, and the cook making more.

It wasn't just Islanders in the lumber camps: I was once astonished to have my accent recognized while sitting in a bar in Little Rock, Arkansas, by a man who had worked in New Brunswick lumber camps in the 1930s. It seems Islanders weren't the only ones going out of their way to find work. Herb Schurman never worked in the lumber camps, but he would have been right at home, singing and playing pranks to kill the long dark nights. Herb was born in Summerside in 1911, and went to work as a clerk at Brace, MacKay Limited when he was 16 years old. He landed a better-paying job at the post office, heading down to meet the early train from Borden and winding the big clock in what's now City Hall. In 1933, Herb felt secure enough in his job to join in the April Fool's Day antics of his co-workers at the post office:

> We had more fun there in a week than most people have in a year. Ha. I could write a book on the post office. Pretty near everybody sent an order to Eaton's or Simpsons, and the husbands or the boyfriends would know their wives were sending for a new dress or a hat or a coat. So, the husbands would

come up to me or to Blick Smith — we were the two bad buggers in the post office — and say, 'Look my wife has an order coming in from Eaton's, so when it comes in, call me.' So, we'd call them, let them in the back door, nobody around, and he'd take the parcel and open it, take out the dress or whatever. He'd get an old potato bag, put in the parcel, tie it all up again nice and neat. They'd never know it was ever opened, and then he'd take the dress home and hide it.

He wouldn't take the parcel home until the next day, and his wife would open it, see. And put out the potato bag — there was hell to pay then. She knew he'd played a joke on her. He'd produce whatever she'd ordered. That happened two or three times a year. But there wasn't much more to do but to have fun like that.

Try having fun like that over the internet. It seemed everyone in Summerside tried to put one over on their friends on Aprils Fool's Day.

April Fool's jokes were quite the thing. When I worked at the post office, there were three mail carriers. Jim and Annie Hunter ran a little book store down on Water Street — the Bank of Nova Scotia is there now. Annie made her own chocolates and she could make good chocolates. On April Fool's day, she took soap, turnips, carrots, and covered them up with chocolate. The worst to eat was the soap, so if you could get to one with soap in your bag, you had it made for April Fool's joke. So, Cal Lear, a mail carrier, went down to Annie Hunter's and he got a bag of chocolates and he asked for mostly soap ones. He came up to the post office, and he had some good chocolates on the top. He passed them around and I ate one, and he passed them to a few others, and by the time he got down to the bad chocolates he'd pass them to his fellow mail carriers Elton Robertson and Caul Craswell. And Caul was the one this time that got the soap in it, and he was too stubborn to let on he'd been April fooled. He ate it all up, and his face was getting red but he ate it all up and he swallowed it. The whole damn works. It was a good-sized chocolate. I don't know what happened to him after that.

Isn't soap a laxative? Better than eating a hundred and four prunes to get the same result. Maybe. The creme de turnip is the perfect food: chocolate plus roughage. The fear of getting a gag chocolate was overwhelmed by the love of chocolate. Herb was quite a guy. He knew everything and everyone there was to know in Summerside, and I always looked forward to visiting him and having a few laughs. I once took a friend from eastern PEI up to visit Herb to see if he could help her find her birth father. He took one look at her and knew the answer immediately. They drove around in his car for an hour while he filled her in on her and her dad. Believe it.

Help is on its Way

Lenie and Estelle

A recurring theme with folks who lived 100 years ago is helping: neighbours helping neighbours, helping cut wood, helping pick potatoes, helping bring babies into the world, and helping to bury the dead. When interviewing my three Henderson cousins from Freeland Lot 11, they mentioned the Bolger family from Foxley River several times. Their mum, Annie Cody Henderson had been a midwife for several of the Bolger children. The Bolgers were a colourful bunch – I'd love to have had a chance to interview Earring Johnny Bolger – but I did get to meet one of the best fiddle players PEI ever produced, the late Lenie Bolger.

In 1933, Lenie married PEI's first female barber, Estelle Soloman who had moved to Summerside from her home in Georgetown. It was a match made in heaven and they celebrated 73 years of marriage. For years, Lenie played fiddle with the famous Joe Bun's Oldtime Orchestra in Summerside. Here's a story about a musician helping out a fellow musician as told by Estelle:

> Joe Bun – Joe Gaudet – he owned the theatre here, and when I came to Summerside and met my husband, he was playing in the band.

Would you go to the dances?

Oh yeah, and if nobody would dance with me, Lenie would put the fiddle in the case and go home. No one dancing with the wife. I remember one time we were at a party at a farmhouse and there were three or four women in the corner talking, and every now and then they looked over and looked at me and they'd say something. I was talking to some little boys, having a good time in the rocking chair. Rocking away and talking to them. So anyway, the guy playing the piano said to Lenie, 'I'm going to dance with your wife.' And he came over – a real good piano player, his name was Peter Perry and he looked exactly like Sammy Davis Junior. You couldn't tell them apart. Curly hair and everything. He was very talented – he could sing and he could just rip that piano. Anyway, one woman came over and said, 'Is that your husband you were dancing with?' And I thought, 'Oh, boy!' 'No', I said, 'You see that nice-looking man there with the violin? That's my husband. He asked the other guy to dance with me.' 'Ohhh,' she said. Sometimes I had a little trouble like that. I don't know what they thought.

Estelle was a fearless, five-foot-tall firecracker. Lenie taught her to play the fiddle when they were in their seventies. He lived to be 98, Estelle to 105. She was one of the smartest people I ever met, as was Ray Brooks. Ray was born in 1911 in Murray Harbour. He used to help his mother, who cooked for the crew running the starch factory next door. One year, an epidemic – diarrhea, peeling skin, the sweats – swept through eastern PEI:

We had the scarlet fever one time. They used to flag you in. You couldn't go anywhere for six weeks. We took it one after another. I don't know how many weeks we were flagged in. Quarantined. Red flag on the gate post. It was right at potato diggin' and my father didn't take the scarlet fever – he had young people come in and help him with the potatoes. They never came to the house. I remember a young fella came in with some fresh fish. My mother put some quarters – fifty cents – in some boiling water and poured it out on the doorstep for him.

There was an awful lot of people had it at that time. I was the first one who took it. You started in with diarrhea and high fever, terrible high fever. Your skin peeled all over with the fever. Then you had to fumigate the house. The doctor brought a whole pile of stuff in cans and had to fumigate the house. Oh, they don't do anything like that now, I don't think, for scarlet fever. Dr. Brehaut had to find somebody to take care of us, get the groceries. The starch factory was running, and Sam Prowse was the head man there, the weighman. The doctor went down to the factory and told Sam to take care of us. He came every evening before he went home. Six weeks – well, if you took it first and then I took it two weeks afterward – that's eight weeks.

I bet you were a little stir-crazy, were you?

I think we were all crazy.

No doubt Sam Prowse got extra helpings when Ray's Mum was back cooking for the starch factory again.

Murray Harbour is known its sea captains and fishermen. Ask any sailor 70-80 years ago who they depended on the most and nine times out of ten the answer would be the lighthouse keeper. The one and only Clive Bruce was born in 1910 in East Baltic. His home port was Basin Head, but he chased fish all over the Maritimes:

Do you know the lighthouse keeper in Cape North [Cape Breton]? One of the nicest men you'd ever talk to. He talked to me from about eight o'clock one

201

night until five or six the next morning. He knew I was nervous. Nor'easter. I came around Cape North, she went down in two seas, the sea washed over top of her and the third sea come and I thought I was gone. Two fellas with me were so sick; never had a bite to eat from six o'clock that day until nine o'clock the next morning when we got in to Cheticamp. I stood in the door and I stood on the roof – I stood everywhere you could stand. There was a boat lost that night right handy me. She swamped, smashed to pieces. But that lighthouse keeper talked to me all night long. He said, 'You'll make it all right.' I just had to hang on.

I guess that fella saved your life in a way.

Yes, he did. He gave me courage. He said, 'Don't worry, just take your time, you'll make it alright.' Two of them drowned, the boat was gone – she went on the rocks and smashed to pieces.

One of the best days ever was the time Robbie Robertson took me on a "tour" to visit his old fishing pal, Clive. They had over 120 years at sea between them, starting back when they fished cod out of Basin Head, before there was a wharf, hand-hauling their boats up onshore every night. On the surface, Robbie and Clive were polar opposites: Clive short and so excited the words stumbled out of his mouth; Robbie tall and thoughtful, weighing each word as if he was paying for them. But underneath the skin – two amigos, who, like Robbie said to me one day, caught a lot of fish, split a lot of fish, and ate a lot of fish.

After Clive's testimonial to that Cape North lighthouse keeper, it's time we heard from one: Maisie Adams was Canada's first female lighthouse keeper. She took over the New London light in 1939 when her Claude husband became ill. Three years later, she was on her own, raising three young children, cleaning the lamp, trimming the wicks, and hauling five-gallon cans of kerosene to both the light and the range light down the shore:

> At that time, I was getting sixteen dollars a month. Now imagine.

Was the government buying your food or anything like that?

> No, they weren't buying my food for me. Hmmph. I could never have got along in any other community – only in French River. Everybody – and my family – in French River was awfully good to me, awfully good to me. Most everybody was farmers or fishermen, and I never had to buy milk, for example. Now clothes – well, I was a dressmaker – and my husband's two sisters were in the States, and they used to send me boxes and boxes of clothing, nice clothing because I could sit down and make them over for the kids. Hand-me-downs.

One neighbour gave Maisie a piglet to raise in the dunes next to the lighthouse. The Adams children loved their new pet but one day he got loose and made a dash for the water. He swam half way across the opening to New London Bay, making for the Cavendish sand spit before he ran out of steam and floated back to shore where he'd started, exhausted. He grew up to be a tasty winter's worth of pork chops and ham.

Big white schooners from northern New Brunswick known as the Caraquets anchored off the lighthouse every fall, digging quahogs and clams to bait their cod lines. The fishermen only spoke French but they visited Maisie and the kids, playing their mouth organs, singing songs in the lighthouse, keeping one another from being lonely as Maisie used to say. People helping people. Eventually Maisie did get a raise – from $16.00 to $22.00 a month.

Across the Northumberland Strait in eastern Pictou County in the old Highland Scottish settlement of Baily's Brook, perched high in the hills overlooking the Strait and across to PEI, Dougald Dunkie MacDonald was born on the family farm in 1918. Like most of his neighbours, he spoke Gaelic and was steeped in the myths and folklore of his ancestors. Here's a story about how a friend helped pay off a debt for the ghost of Johnny Robert MacDonald:

> Johnny Robert went over to Pleasant Valley, Antigonish County, and he bought a horse from a widow woman. Forty dollars, and he paid the woman twenty dollars, and told her he'd pay the twenty dollars later on. And he dropped dead, the guy who bought the horse. This other fella was coming up from the shore, from the wharf, just at sundown, but it was still light, and he met Johnny Robert. Now he knew Johnny Robert was dead and he pretty near fainted when he saw him. Now you have to address them – ghosts – in the name of God so he called him in the name of God, and asked 'John, what do you want.'
>
> Johnny Robert said, 'I want you to go over to Pleasant Valley, and give the widow woman there the twenty dollars that I owe her for the horse. If you do that, I won't bother anybody again.' And he disappeared. So, the guy jumped on horseback the next morning and went over the mountain, went to the woman, the woman said, 'Yes, he owes me twenty dollars.' So, he paid it to her. And that ended that. Now my father told me that story years ago.

So, you have to address a ghost in the name of God?

Yes. It's not an evil thing, no no no. It's just a spirit looking for help.

Back in the 1920s, Dougald served as an altar boy and several times went along with the parish priest to perform exorcisms, and witnessed Bibles flying across rooms, and the contorted faces of people possessed by the devil. He saw dance halls clear in a flash when the devil in the shape of a black dog wandered onto the dance floor. Like many folks in eastern PEI and Pictou County, Dougald saw the Phantom Ship, the burning ghost ship of the Northumberland Strait, sails ablaze. But his favorite stories were the ones where a troubled ghost, looking for closure comes back to ask for help, and always got it.

Now my father told me that story years ago. I was telling this story to Archie MacLean, and Archie said he'd had the same experience during the First World War. 'A young fella from Cloverville where I lived,' he said, 'bought a suit in Antigonish. He owed fourteen dollars on the suit and he went into the army and he was killed overseas.'

Archie said he was going to Antigonish one day in an old car and he had a flat tire in broad daylight in the afternoon. He was fixing the tire when he felt somebody around him. He turned around and here was the soldier, his neighbour. So, Archie said, 'In the name of God, what do you want?' And the soldier told him, 'If you are going into Antigonish, can you pay fourteen for my suit? If you do, I will never bother you again.' Archie said, 'I will.' And he said he wasn't long fixing that tire. He got to Antigonish and went into the store, and they looked up in the books and they found the bill. Fourteen dollars for the suit. So, he paid it. They say there's a big reward it that. God will give you a big reward for that.

At the very least give him $14.00 credit. In the first story, Johnny Robert was undoubtedly a MacDonald, Robert being his father in the Scottish way of nicknaming people, just as Dougald Dunkie's father was Duncan MacDonald. The horse had no name.

> We had a motor-driven fire engine that came here in 1917. It was a truck with firehoses on it and axes and crowbars and stuff like that. After the Explosion, they sent it to Halifax to help in the cleanup.

Gordon Stewart was born in 1913 into a fire fighting family. One hundred and forty-seven years worth, in fact. His grandfather Albert Large was Charlottetown fire chief as was Gordon, and Gordon's brother Lou was a fireman for 60 years. Many acts of kindness, including sending a fire engine to Nova Scotia immediately after the December 6, 1917 Halifax Explosion.

The explosion was heard and even felt as far away as Pictou County, as well as in eastern Prince Edward Island where dishes rattled in cupboards. A blind woman in Marshfield told me the rumble sounded like a big dog running down the stairs. Eleanor Lowe was born and raised in Charlottetown, the daughter of a prominent builder and contractor. On December the sixth at 9:05 in the morning, she was heading for class.

> I was at Prince of Wales College, and myself and some other students were standing down at the south end, and the ground rippled. We all felt it in the ground. And we said, Oh, there must have been an earthquake somewhere. And we found out it was the Halifax Explosion, felt here.

A painter, Eleanor came back to teach art at Prince of Wales College (PWC) for over 40 years; she was an avid photographer, knew the Group of Seven, and she lived to 107.

Thirty-five miles west of Charlottetown in Cape Traverse, Helen Herring also felt the explosion. Helen was born in 1909, was an exceptional student, and also attended PWC. Helen's father, Montague Campbell, was captain of one of the Cape Traverse-Cape Tormentine ice boats, those study wooden boats that were powered by sail over water, and by the crew over ice. Up until 1917, ice boats were the only winter connection to the mainland, and for the Campbell family, December the sixth was memorable for another reason.

> I was eight years old when the Halifax Explosion occurred, and that was the day that Sir Robert Borden was in Borden to name the town. It became Borden that day. There was snow, and my parents went by sleigh. I was at home and had another girl with me, and we were playing around the yard and we heard what we thought was a clap of thunder. We looked but we couldn't see a cloud but we didn't think anything of it.
>
> But when my parents came home, the word had come over the wire at the telegraph office, and so they had heard about the explosion. I remember thinking it was a clap of thunder.

Forgotten in the excitement was Prime Minister Borden's christening speech for the town named in his honour. The railway track was diverted from Cape Traverse to Borden by First World War German prisoners of war, an ice-breaking ferry docked, and the ice boats and crews were all washed up.

Every year, Nova Scotia ships a huge Christmas tree to Boston as thanks for the train-load of medicine, blankets, and food the Bostonians sent up after the Explosion. Acts of kindness take many forms. A kiss, a hug, a kind word.

A hundred years ago, neighbours helped neighbours at haying time, potato pickin', and when a horse or cow or pig had to be bred.

Ginger Mackay's grandfather had a young sow and his neighbour Mr. Rose had a big registered boar noted for its, let's say, productivity:

> She had to be bred for the first time so my father and I were trying to get her into the cart to take her next door. But ahhh, no, she'd lay down, cranky as old hell. She wasn't very heavy and my father said, 'You'll have to run her down in the wheelbarrow.' We rolled her into the wheelbarrow and rolled her down to the neighbour's. There was no need of staying so I took the wheelbarrow back home and left the sow at Rose's. I put the wheelbarrow behind the house, and went in and had my supper. Later, we went out to do the barn work and my father asked, 'Is that young sow home yet?' I said I didn't see her in the barn. We looked out the back window and here she was lying in the wheelbarrow, wanting to go again. That's a true story, and that's the fun you have on a farm.

Ginger MacKay and his boyhood pal John W. MacEachern remembered their grandparents talking about a mysterious spring with healing powers. Seventy years later, the two old lads spent hours walking the woods around Mt. Stewart and finally found the Healing Spring, and built a road to it through fields and forest, an act of kindness for the thousands of people from around the world who have since made a pilgrimage to bath in its reputed healing waters. The spring dates back to at least the 1750s when Acadians lived in the area. In the 1880 *Meacham's Atlas of PEI* a corduroy road leads through the woods to a "Medical Spring."

The Great Depression of the 1930s is the benchmark for hard times and lean living. Tommy Duncan, a century baby, born in 1900 in Mill River, remembers the lean years starting much earlier, when the days of "iron men and wooden ships" were petering out:

> I'm telling you boy – listen, I knew all about hard times. When I was a little boy, I remember how little we had. My God, a small little house with knots on the floor that you'd trip over. My mother would send me down to the swamp to get white sand. That's what she used for scrubbing the floor. We were brought up on fish and potatoes, lots of molasses. Go to school with a couple of slices of bread with molasses on them tied up with brown paper. That was it.

The days when apocryphal stories about trading a molasses sandwich for a lobster one with an embarrassed classmate circulated.

> Ah dear God, and yet people were just as happy as they are today. People helped one another and no money. If a fella wanted an acre of land cleared, they'd come for miles. If you lost your barn or were building a house, they'd be there, boy, helping. And have a dance at night. The women would go and do the cooking, have a big meal, and then dance at night.

A house party where, like thousands across the Maritimes, the fiddle and piano players weren't paid a cent because there were no cents:

> I'm telling you and I'm not lying, if you drove with a horse and wagon to Summerside and asked everybody that you met if he could change five dollars, he couldn't do it. No. There was no money. I mind one time we ran out of flour and my father said to me,

'Now, I want you to go into O'Leary to H.W. Turner's store and ask him for fifty pounds of flour on credit.' Well, I went but I didn't get my flour. No, sir. Ha! You either had to have the money or do without.

Tommy Duncan lived to be 100 years old. He was 16 before he made it to Summerside, less than 30 miles away. He had, as he put it, "poor cousins" in West Devon, "so poor they couldn't afford sugar," so when Tommy's relatively well-off family visited, they always brought sugar for everyone's tea.

Tea and molasses were among the few store-bought items in the pantry. Greta Grigg, born in 1921 in the ship-building community of Port Hill, made molasses toffee and watched her father pour molasses on top of everything he ate, including boiled potatoes. Her mother also scrubbed the wooden floors with white swamp sand. Greta was one of the legions of unpaid musicians, and her first job was house cleaning:

> I'd often say to the kids I think I cleaned every house in Port Hill. A dollar-a-day. A dollar a day, and I'd come home somebody'd call and say, 'There's a dance at such and such a place. Would you come accompany the fiddler?' So, I'd play the organ for the rest of the evening. I did that night after night. I often said the worst thing that ever happened was I learned to play the organ, because you couldn't dance. So many times, I'd like to up having a dance too, but I'd be sitting there.

Who were the fiddlers?

> Lenie Bolger. Les MacAusland. Lenie was a great player. One of the best. I remember one night there was a dance down at Art Millar's. They used to have splitting frolics. People would have a big pile of fire-

Big cod in North Rustico

Borden Mooney

Noup Head

Maisie Adams and Dutch on set of Emily of New Moon

Adelaide Hamm

Babs Fitzgerald

Captain Ernest "Ben" Pike, Merchant Navy

Charles Gallant

Mac Dixon and Mum's piano

"Rich Uncle Tim and Aunt Bee" (Tim and Bernice Donaghue)

Mary Malone MacPhee at Vincent Macphee farm in Big Pond

Upton Field, PEI, 1938: (L-R) Gordie Gray, Junior Jones, Joe Anderson (later killed), Leo Power, Garnet Godfre

Minnie Down and Syd Clay, ex-RAF
War Groom from Nottinghamshire

Edith Whitlock Pryce

WWII veterans Les and Bill Price at the old tavern pub in Kington, Herefordshire

John Rendall of Holland House farm, Westray, Orkney Island

Mae Ames

Hilda (Henderson) Cunningham

Union Road School, 1946: Mildred Hardy Smith (2nd row), Miss Gillis, teacher

Don MacNeil, pilot 4th from right

Flight Lieutenant Donald MacNeil

Evening Patriot advert, Upton Field, 1932

Ivan Kennedy at Kennedy's Store, Breadalbane

Donald Macintosh, fiddler

Harold Dunphy

Emily of New Moon set, South Granville

Leo Farrell on Emily of New Moon set

Dorothy and Walter Maclure

Charlie Scranton, Order of Canada

Blanche Landry Bennett

Nicholson farm, Hartsville, 2006

Jumpin Jack, his brother Ralph
and their mother Winnie Proud

Jumpin Jack Proud in the Gold Cup Parade

Receipt from C. R. Wallace's
general store in Coleman

Eggs shipped by train were packed in square
wooden crates called Humpty Dumptys

Robbie Robertson and Clive Bruce with the dory Clive built

Tiger MacKie

Roy Clow

Estelle Soloman Bolger

Elsie Collier

Sheriff Bob Dewar and daughter Katherine at his Studebaker dealership, Reads Corner, 1947

Jimmy Doyle

Annie Callaghan on vacation at Buffalo Park, 1986

Tommy and Pearl Duncan

Mae Ames on set of Emily of New Moon

Maisie Adams with hooked rug of her lighthouse

Keith Pratt and Chris Smith
at Bloomfield Station, 1926

Captain William and Tom Trenholm on
Raeburn schooner at Pickards wharf, 1920

Billy Wilkinson's maple sugar bush
in Broadway, N.S.

CN Conductor Andrew Leslie with his 40 years
of service plaque and railway watch

Jill and Dutch's wedding with his family
smirking and her father crying

Dave Mills and his model railway

Herb Schurman holding Summeride's pioneer
and founder Joseph Green's tea caddies

Medius Wedge, the Summerside
policeman who arrested an elephant

Bert Paquet with Engine 1130 at
Bloomfield Station, 1930s

Charlie and Rose Deighan

Summerside Crystals hockey team

Lorne Stevenson, R.N. on minesweeper HMT
Goshawk WWI (photo: Mark Stevenson)

WWI veteran Lorne Stevenson

Bernice Henderson (on right) in USA.
Note the shoes

Hilda Henderson Cunningham
with presents from the States

Mary Jane, the car from Boston (from the Joyce MacLeod collection)

Louis Cantelo, RCAF

Hickey & Nicholson Bright Cut sign

Mary (Wood) MacDonald with her Mum, brother Melvin and sister Lucille in Boston, 1929

Ray Brooks

Sam Kennedy with Hugh and Martha Walker
in their "jaunting sleighs" in Charlottetown

Captain Thomas Trenholm and wife (and 1st Mate) Mary
with their family aboard the schooner Nellie Dixon

22 horsepower Massey Harris (third from left)

Deep snow, 1947

Horse and tractor in Dundas, PEI

John and Lois Campbell

Sandy Fraser, Halifax Explosion survivor

wood, get it sawed, and if they wanted to get it split in a hurry, they'd invite anybody who wanted to go. Men would split wood all afternoon, and then that night they'd have a dance for them. And this night, I was playing the organ, and Lenie was sitting right next to me, right beside a big window. I don't know who it was, but somebody outside had a big jar of homemade beer or moonshine, and nudged Lenie. He stuck his head out the window, never stopped playing the violin, and they poured it into him. He took a big swig. Beer or shine... likely shine.

Likely. Most beer mashes wound up being distilled into moonshine, yet another practical use for molasses besides a topping for boiled spuds. Greta said she was never paid for playing at house parties, not even the odd swig, but the hat was passed at Milligan and Morrison's dance hall, and she'd get two or three dollars, big money. Edgar Milligan and George Morrison had made a lot of money in the 1920s breeding silver foxes on PEI and across North America. In 1925, they shipped $770,000 worth of silver foxes from Summerside on one train. Milligan and Morrison's enormous silver fox ranch in Northam had a horse-racing track with a unique feature: lights for night-racing. In 1933, both men were tragically killed in a car accident in Hamburg, a town near Buffalo in upstate New York. They were en route to one of their fur-farming schools in Illinois.

Mae Ames, RN, took a Nova Scotian soldier's name when they married in England during the Second World War. After a particularly devastating blitz on Manchester, Mae went to work at the hospital and met Private Frank Ames who was guarding German Luftwaffe airmen who'd been shot down. The drone of German bombers was part of everyday life in the industrial Midlands during the war, as was rationing:

Well, the rationing. Everybody got sufficient. It was just boring. It was a little of everything for everybody, and was very well organized. If you ate all your rations, or like my mother did, drank your tea rations, then you were in trouble. My mother lived on tea – so do I – so she used to barter. She'd come to my house with a cup of sugar and say, 'If you have a bit of tea to give me, I'll give you some sugar.'

Everyone got a little butter, and we had three eggs a month, I think. It all depended whether the convoys got through from Canada or Australia, then we were given an extra egg. And it was headlines: "Extra Eggs in Rations This Week!" My goodness me. But we all survived and they do say that the bonniest babies – the healthiest – were born during the war.

What was Christmas like?

I lined up for three hours one Christmas to get a piece of a rabbit. They cut the rabbit up into threes, one rabbit between three people. If you were lucky, you got a meaty bit when your turn came, a leg or something, and if you weren't, you got the back which was very bony, no meat on it. Three hours I remember I lined up for that and it was our Christmas dinner. It was only supposed to be rations for two, but if you were having guests, well, just too bad. They brought what they could, everyone chipped in.

Really and truly, everyone pulled together, it was a wonderful time. I've always said that if it hadn't been for the bloodshed and heartache of the war, it was the best six years I ever spent really. Really and truly. Meeting people and making myself feel needed. That's the word: needed.

Mae bought her white wedding dress on the black market: irony or oxymoron? Debate. The neighbours all showed up with flour and eggs and sugar, bits and pieces to bake the wedding cake. Mae was a well-known actor, a five-foot tall ball of fire who for years mentored many young aspiring actors on PEI.

Slick Rhynes knew at least one man who was kind-hearted to children. Slick was born in 1925, and grew up in the tough 1930s on a farm just west of Charlottetown. His father Alex was a milkman who bottled and delivered milk door-to-door, nine cents for a quart for milk:

> There was no money. I'll just tell you what now, boss: we had no electric lights here and my Auntie lived in town – Mrs. Joe Duncan – and they'd take us kids in for Christmas night to see Santie Claus coming. They had a Christmas tree all lit up, and we just had an old tree stuck in the corner, no lights or nothing on it. I remember the first Christmas in there, I got a little car, a little black car I bet didn't cost twenty-five cents. That was my Christmas present and I thought more of that. And we used to get a stocking and there'd be an apple and an orange in it, and that was your Christmas.

I bet you didn't see many bananas

> No, never did. Now you're talking about bananas, Earl Thompson – you wouldn't have known him – he used to work at Paul Murray's in town, the whole-salers, sold fruit and stuff. He'd come out here with the big three-ton truck on a Sunday and he'd have a drink or two with my father. And he'd put some bananas in the back of the truck in the straw, and us kids would get up there looking for them. We'd think this was great, finding those bananas, and

he just put them there so we would find them, by jeez. I often laugh when I think of it. Poor fella was thoughtful enough to put apples and bananas, and the odd orange or two in the truck, and we'd think this was great because we were finding them. The second he stopped in the yard, we were in the back of that three-ton truck. Makes you laugh when you think of it, doesn't it?

Bananas are now the most-consumed fruit in the world. I guess people figure ten million monkeys can't be wrong.

If You Can't Stand the Heat

Bertha Ross

Wood doesn't heat you twice – it heats you five times: you saw down the tree, you buck it up, you split it, then you haul it to the wood stove. And finally, you burn it.

Bertha Ross was born not far from Spry Point in Durrell, now just a few foundation depressions in the ground. Her father died young, in 1923, when Bertha was twelve years old. Her mother carried on with the farm and the raising of four children – Bertha was the oldest – and the children all learned valuable lessons about hard work. Firewood was an ongoing occupation.

Norbert Corcoran was born in 1909 in Piusville, and grew up sharing chores with 15 brothers and sisters, probably as many hands needed to keep the wood box full.

> There were six bedrooms, five upstairs and one down below. We burned I suppose between twenty-five and twenty-eight cords a year. We cut half here and went to Bloomfield to get softwood for the summer. That fire in the kitchen never went out even in the summertime and it'd be so hot upstairs at night. My mother was baking all the time. Sometimes, we burnt more wood in the summer than we did in the winter. Longer days, eh.

Pratt's General Store in Bloomfield Station, run by A.J. and his nephew Keith, sold hundreds of cords of softwood a year even though the Pratts themselves preferred imported fuel that came up by rail.

> We burned mostly coal. We'd get about five carloads of coal a year. A lot of people burned coal. And we had a great big pile of softwood and had to get it sawed up. But the old outhouse was near the field where the wood was piled and the women wouldn't go out while the men were in the field. They wouldn't go out at all to the outhouse for fear of being seen. But when the men came in to dinner, there was a mad rush to the outhouse. And they'd be cutting wood for three days.

I know the feeling. Nothing works for me if there's a lumberjack nearby. No one burns coal anymore, the smell of many childhoods. PEI coal was shipped in by schooners returning from the Pictou County and Cape Breton coal towns after their loads of potatoes and turnips and cabbages had been sold. Captain Thomas Trenholm captained the former Grand Banks schooner *Nellie Dixon*. Captain Tom was born in East Wallace, NS, and was literally raised on schooners. At one time, his father Captain William Trenholm owned seven schooners, one bought in 1917 with the very modern name *Telephone*. By the age of seventeen, Tom had his captain's papers and was hauling coal to PEI.

> Bringing up coal from Cape Breton, Sydney. This is what brought me to the Island from Louisbourg. Louisbourg is out on a very rough coast, very open to the Atlantic, and hard, bad sailing going or coming from it. So, I used to load at Sydney and come up through the Bras d'Or Lakes most of the time, then on to Charlottetown or Georgetown. Then potatoes back again, or sometimes you'd take a load of lumber from the lake ports down to Sydney. There's nothing like that going on now – they do it all by truck.

In the Second World War, the prices were low. I mean wages were down too but there was no way to get anybody who was any good. Anybody who was any good at all wouldn't be deckhand aboard a coal schooner like that unless they were starving to death. They'd be in the navy or army or somewhere like that. Wages were twenty dollars a month. Sixty-six cents a day, so you can't blame anybody.

The cook and first mate were paid a little more, $25.00 a month. Captain Tom's schooner *Nellie Dixon* was fast on the water, built in 1889 in East Boston, and designed by Edward Burgess, famous for designing several America's Cup racing yachts. That came in handy during the war when Captain Tom, First Mate, and wife Mary hauled coal to Newfoundland where German submarines prowled.

One night while Mary was standing watch, a U-boat surfaced, shone a light on the *Nellie Dixon*, and then slowly sank below again. Tom figured the U-boat captain didn't want to waste a torpedo on a fifty-seven-year-old schooner with a hundred tons of number two soft coal on deck. In the hold though was another two hundred tons of "Old Sydney Screen, the very best coal." Tom was making a $1.65 a ton at the wharf in Charlottetown, and $4.00 a ton in Newfoundland, the extra $2.35 explains chancing the Gulf of St Lawrence and German U-boats. After years of procrastination by the Canadian government, Tom and Mary, along with thousands of other Merchant Mariners, were finally officially recognized for their services in the Second World War. One in seven merchant mariners was killed during the war, the highest fatality rate of any of the Canadian armed services.

Ethel MacKenzie Park was born in 1913 and remembered PEI schooners docked for weeks in the fall of the year at the bridge in New Glasgow, selling Island potatoes and turnips. She was born and raised in the coal town of Stellarton, NS.

> We burned coal in the furnace and in the kitchen range both. And in the fireplace. I remember the miners being on strike one summer. They had to take the horses out of the mines, and they were blind because being down in the dark so long they couldn't see. They put the horses in a field handy the mine. There was fighting, so my father sent us away down in the country. He was scared something would happen to us.

That was in 1925 when after no income for five months, the miners were forced back to work at reduced wages. The Pictou County miners were always threatened by notoriously high levels of dangerous methane gas, which caused explosions. The United Mine Workers represented the miners, and the strike divided the community down the middle. Ethel's father Howard MacKenzie delivered freight with a horse and wagon for the railway even though as a boy working in a mill, he'd lost an arm. Ethel said her father could tie his boot laces with one hand.

> He was in and out of the miners' houses, and the women would curse the men, and the men curse the women. We were never allowed to associate too much with the miners' children, only in school. We weren't allowed to go to birthday parties or any-thing. My sister didn't think that was right and let her sons go with the miners' kids, but I said you don't know what Father knew. On Saturdays, they all went together, so many miners, and got a barrel of rum. They'd congregate in one house so you can imagine what they'd be like when they drank all that rum, 'cause it's a terrible thing to swear. Gorsh, one time

I said, gosh darnit, and my father gave me a bawling out. He said, 'You might as well say the words.'

Taking into consideration the history of coal mining disasters in Pictou County, in my humble opinion even if Ethel's story is accurate, the miners' drinking and swearing should have been the least of anyone's worries. In 1992, the explosion at the Westray mine killed 26 more miners, the final nail in the coffin for underground coal mining in Pictou. Over the decades, it took a lot of nails.

Ethel's exile to the country that summer was 20 miles east to her mother's family homestead, a rare trip for Ethel and her sisters. It was a long journey for horse and wagon, no one in the family owned a car, and trains cost money. Such was also the case with the Easter family in Indian River, PEI, where Eddie Easter was born in 1905 within sight of the magnificent W.C. Harris-designed St. Mary's Roman Catholic Church. Trips to exotic and far-away places like Summerside were few and far between.

> That was a big trip. You'd go only when it was neces-sary, and it might be quite a long time in between. Father would go in in the fall, and after we got a bit older, Harry and I would go in with him, but not in the winter. We'd play around, poke into places and the stores, and we always ate at a Chinese restaurant. We'd have dinner, and we always had ham.

Were the streets paved in Summerside back then?

> No, no, no. Some wooden sidewalks. Back of Holman's [Holman's department store on Water Street], that was a bog. We'd have to buy coal because Father was no good to keep wood ahead. I don't know why. He didn't like going to the woods, I guess. We had the wood but he wouldn't cut enough to do a year, and we'd usually run out in January.

Well, there was a lot of winter ahead of us and they were real winters back then, I can tell you. So, we'd have to go to Summerside and get coal, soft coal, pretty dirty, and Mother didn't want anything to do with it, but she had to burn coal or go without a fire. Anybody who had a baseburner would buy hard coal, the soft coal didn't work in the baseburners, and that was the people who were a little better off, you know. They could afford to buy the expensive coal.

The Easters hauled their sleigh-loads of coal across the frozen Malpeque Bay, the shortcut over the ice. All the bays and rivers across the Island were bushed with spruce trees to mark the route. The trees were stuck upright in the ice after the first big freeze by either the bravest or stupidest man in the community. One man told me he was paid $5.00 to bush Hillsboro Bay, the ice heaving and cracking under his and the horse's weight. And he supplied the trees.

~~~~~

Coal or wood, nothing tastes better than homemade biscuits or cookies cooked in the oven of a woodstove. Hilda Hilchey was born in Flat River in 1917. Her mother Annie MacLean was from nearby Culloden. Annie raised sheep, sheared them, spun the wool, and made woolen suits and dresses for the entire family. Hilda's father was Alec Beaton, better known as Sandy's Alec, and both parents spoke Gaelic. Hilda's mum did all her cooking on a woodstove and Dad kept the wood box filled.

My mother put biscuits in the oven one day. My father came in with the kindling, and he didn't know the biscuits were there, and he opened the oven door and threw the kindlings on top of the biscuits. That didn't make my mother too happy.

Bruised biscuits. Good with shredded marmalade and clap shot. The kitchen is a violent place. Hilda Hilchey's grandmother Christine MacLeod MacLean was famous for her hermit cookies.

> I loved going there, and I was called after my two grandmothers: Hilda Christine. I loved going there because they had yellow transparent apples, and great big red strawberries. I would get a little letter in the mail asking, 'Are you going to come and sing for us?' So, I would have to appear and sing for them, which was no problem. I'd sing mostly hymns for my grandparents, but I could sing anything I wanted. I was the apple of their eye.

I bet she wasn't called Grammie's Little Sugar Pop like someone I know. OK, me.

> And cook. Could she ever cook. Make great big cookies called hermits. It was kind of a spicy cookie, soft, and there were raisins in it. Ohhh, they were so good. It's making my mouth water now.

Bannock was another baked weapon in Grammie Christine's floury arsenal. There are two schools of cooking when it comes to bannock: with or without buttermilk. But with shorts?

> She used to make a bannock with what she called shorts [middlings is a coarse flour consisting mainly of wheat germ and bran and usually fed to livestock]. This bannock was for the hens. There was a little room off the kitchen, which they called the dining room. She put the bannock in there to feed to the hens later. The minister came to visit after dark, and he decided he'd break a piece off this bannock and eat it. My grandmother laughed about that because he was having a fine time eating the hen's bannock.

Like most farm women, my grammie was in charge of the chickens. Every day, she boiled up potato culls, leftover porridge, and other scraps from the previous day's supper, mixed with a couple of scoops of shorts. This was fed to the hens along with their usual rations of corn and grit and crushed eggshells.

One day, while talking to a well-named man from Queens County – who shall just go by Mr. Pidgeon – he mentioned mixing up a similar concoction for his hens. Pidgeon was a fisherman whose family for generations made their own cod liver oil. Throw the livers in an open barrel, leave it out in the elements all summer and fall, the oil floats to the top, drain off the dregs of the rotted livers, and voila. Cod liver oil, of which, he read in *The Family Herald*, a tablespoon every day was a good supplement in the hens' food.

Pidgeon figured if one tablespoon was good, two must be better. He kept increasing the dose until one day, the man from the egg circle showed up at his door, with news there had been complaints about Pidgeon's eggs: they tasted like fish.

If You Go Down to the Woods Today[4]

Robbie Robertson with the dory he built from his father's design

PEI has had various critters lurking in the woods and streets. Here's Robbie Robertson was born in 1904 and grew up on the Snake road in Kingsboro east of Souris:

> Speaking of bears, you know my father cleaned up all the bears on the Island. He was christened Johnny Jim, the Bear-Killer. You see in those days, bears — the main thing is they killed sheep. A bear could strip the hide off a sheep, you know, take it into the woods — they wouldn't eat it all, but when they'd find the carcass, they'd get my father. And he'd go, and he'd climb a tree at night, and wait for the bear to come. Shoot the bear. I remember he used to load the old muzzle-loader, put in the wadding, and put the powder in. He used to make the balls of lead for the bear.

4   John W Bratton and Jimmy Kennedy, Teddy Bear's Picnic, © Sony/ATV Music Publishing LLC, Warner/Chappell Music, Inc.

He killed 14 anyway. People didn't think there were bears for years and years, and this other fella showed up. That was 1927.

The other fella refers to the last bear on PEI. In 1927, Geordie Leslie, a young boxer from the eastern end of the Island, was out checking his traps in the woods when he came across an unusual sight on the Souris Line Road. His nephew Andrew Leslie, a retired railwayman, remembers the day the family's name went into the PEI history books:

> My uncles, there was two of them, George and Bernard, they were young fellas, I guess seventeen years old, perhaps, they left early in the morning, and they tracked the bear across the Souris Line Road. He went east for quite a piece, the bear, and then he headed north going towards the North Side. Could be around noon time perhaps or maybe a bit later when they found him under a tree. They shot him there. They said there was some old marks on him. He was big male, a big black bear. I think they skinned that day too and took the skin home. But then after that they got quite a bit of money for the oil. Word got around, and somebody wrote them from England looking for bear oil or grease. I don't really know what it was for at that time, but anyway they got quite a bit of money. I think they got near a gallon of grease off him after they boiled him down.

Bear grease has been and still is used as a rheumatism and arthritis cure because it's supposed to be easily absorbed into the muscles. For the same reason in recent years, emu oil was the rage, mixed with oil of wintergreen and guaranteed to lubricate our old worn shoulders and knees.

This was recorded as the last bear on PEI. But was it? Louis Cantelo didn't think so. Louis was born in 1904 in Seven Mile Road near Cardigan.

> The last bear it would be in the '20s. There was two bears killed one winter near Dingwells Mills. For a while, they were on display there and, shortly after that, there was a man by the name of Geordie Leslie, he was champion boxer of the Maritimes for a while. He chased the bear, and he finally got to him and shot him, and he rendered all the grease and sold the grease in England.

> But there was one bear after that. One night, my mother heard the dog barking, and she went to the bedroom window, and looked and she seen the bear walking down through the grain field. That was about 1935. That was the last bear on Prince Edward Island. We expect he died of old age.

I like to think the last bear died of old age rather than a bullet. Heavens knows our ancestors and people like Johnny Jim the Bear Killer killed bears for their own survival. Just like Billy Wilkinson from Pictou County where bears still harass livestock. And maple sugar men like Billy who ran a sugar shack for years out behind his farm in Broadway, Pictou County. Billy was born in 1910, and started making maple syrup the old way, the hard way:

> When we started out, we just had a little wee camp, and we tapped and carried the sap with buckets. Ah my gee, we were right up to there in snow. Couldn't use a horse — too steep. And then there was a bear here in the camp. Clawed the door open. And he went in and he carried all the sap bottles out and took the tops off of some of them. And when we started tapping, there was teeth marks where he grabbed it. I can show you a tobacco can down there. He took

225

that out but he didn't get the lid off it. They're bad things. I don't like them.

One fella chased me. A mother bear and her cub. They stopped right there looking at me and if I'd kept my mouth shut, everything would have been all right. But I hollered. That big one just jumped sideways up on the bank up through the field after me. I made for the old house and went upstairs, and I thought she'd come up after me, right up to the house. I went upstairs. I went in a bedroom. I looked out the window, and here she was with her cub. Right through the window. So, I waited for a while, about dark, no sound, and I thought I better get going. My truck was a way down at the pavement. I jumped out the window and I run down to the truck. My tongue was out like that, I had to sit in the truck. Ah my gee. My brother was living and I went over and he said, 'What happened to you tonight?' And I told him. He said 'No way.' I said that's a fact.

Billy hollered so loud the bear jumped sideways. I don't blame either one of them. Let's switch gears and talk about another animal that once roamed PEI but is now extinct. Elephants. Just kidding but elephants were regular visitors to the Island when circuses travelled by train, and sometimes by schooners in a circuit around eastern Canada and the USA including the Atlantic provinces. In fact, they still tell the story about the time Sparks Circus came to Summerside, an elephant got loose, and was arrested. Don't believe me – the late great Herb Schurman, born in Summerside in 1911. Herb was pal of mine – in fact, Herb was a pal of everyone:

I remember one time, there was a circus in town and the big tent was set up where the Amalgamated Dairy is now. They came to Summerside pretty near every year; every second year anyway. There were several elephants, but this one was named Nell, I think, and Nell [actually it was Lindy] knew pretty well everything that was going on in Summerside. So, she broke loose this night, and she went right up to Joseph Read's storage, broke the door down, and ate all night. She knew exactly where to go. And they knew exactly where to find her. Elephants never forget. It's a wonder she didn't go through the floor.

Joseph Read had a big warehouse on Summerside's waterfront where he shipped potatoes and grain and brought back coal in his schooners. She headed straight for the grain. The Summerside police officer who tracked Lindy to her late-night snack was Constable Medeus Wedge. His daughter is Sally Wynn:

He was a police officer when I was a small child, and I remember hearing the "elephant story" as we referred to it all of our lives. And as a little girl I believed it, but then as I grew up, I began to think it was just something else that my Dad told me that was just one of his funny stories. He had many of them. But then, not many years ago I received a [newspaper] clipping from an old aunt of ours – she had found it when she was cleaning, and we had to then believe the elephant story was true.

The clipping reads "Local police officer Wedge makes large arrest last night."

There was a circus in town. It used to be quite a big event, and apparently one of the elephants got loose and my Dad was sent off to find him. Dad figured the elephant was probably hungry, so he checked out different places, and sure enough he went into one place, found the elephant, and arrested him. He led him up Water Street back to the circus.

As Herb noted, Lindy the elephant certainly knew her way around Summerside. Lindy weighed three tons, and that takes a pile of carbs to maintain. She first broke into The Pure Milk Company and ate five bags of pig feed, then headed to the waterfront and Joseph Read's warehouse where she went through a wall to get to the grain. And Lindy got her name because she came to North America on the same boat that brought the famous American aviator Charles Lindbergh back home after his historical solo flight from New York to Paris in 1927. And another coincidence – Lindy the elephant marched in the parade down Broadway in New York City to celebrate Lucky Lindy's flight.

Adding to PEI's elephant lore, according to my old pal Roy Clow from Murray Harbour North, one of the Chapman boys from Murray Harbour South, Captain Milton Chapman, once had the contract to ship the circus to Newfoundland. It was the fall of the year, the seas were rough, the elephants got seasick. Normally, Captain Chapman hauled potatoes and turnips to the coal towns of Cape Breton and Pictou County. Roy said after that shipping the circus, Captain Milton could only use that schooner to haul coal.

Nostalgia Ain't What it Used to Be

Vivian White and Austin Graham

Nostalgia is tricky. Author Adele Parks wrote "The past is for learning from and letting go. You can't revisit it. It vanishes."[5] Maybe. Marcel Proust built his legacy on a book about nostalgia but cautioned: "Remembrance of things past is not necessarily the remembrance of things as they were."[6] Agreed. After all, nostalgia is the domain of the old, not the young, and the older we get... I forget the rest but you know what I mean. So, let's indulge in a bit of nostalgia because as Vladimir Nabokov observed, "one is always at home in one's past."[7]

One thing we can all agree on is as the world turns, it changes. Our wedding cost about a hundred dollars – we were married in our living room. Nanny made the cake. Jill wore her best dress. We danced in our parlour, and after paying the fiddler thirty-five dollars, we drove him and his brother home because my five brothers were all too drunk on moonshine.

Austin Graham and Vivian White grew up at different ends of PEI, but somehow, they managed to meet, court and spark, and eventually get married. It all started with

5   Adele Parks, *Young Wives' Tales*, UK: Michael Joseph Limited, 2007.

6   Marcel Proust, *In Search of Lost Time / À la recherche du temps perdu*, trans. C.K. Scott Montcrieff, France: Grasset and Gallimard, 1913-1927.

7   Vladimir Nabokov, *Speak, Memory: A Memoir*, UK: Penguin Reissue, 2000.

Vivian landing a job in Cavendish:

> Sunny Acres Tourist Home. I worked there one summer, and Austin was taking out my first cousin. He went to Halifax to work and she went to Toronto and so they split ways. I came to Charlottetown and in the spring. another friend and I were taking a walk around Dizzy Block [the four-block square of Grafton, Queen, Kent and University Avenue].

Why was it called Dizzy Block?

> Because people walked around and around the block. There was nowhere else to go so you went around and around the block, meet the same ones and then turn around, and go the other way. Anyway, I met Austin on one of my trips coming around the Block. I guess he asked to go to the show the next night and that's how it happened. We'd go to White's Restaurant and have a hot hamburger. It was twenty-five cents with the chips and everything. We got married in '43 in Murray Harbour down at my home.

Where did you go on your honeymoon?

> We came all the way to Charlottetown. It happened to be a Wednesday – you had to get married on a Wednesday. That was the only day anyone got married in those times. We hitched a drive to Montague with the minister because the bus didn't come to Murray Harbour on a Wednesday, and Austin didn't have a car. Then we came all the way to Charlottetown. Austin took one day off from work, so we went out shopping. We bought a broom and a dustpan, a few things to start housekeeping.

Talk about simpler times. Austin's first job when he came to Charlottetown from Bayfield near Stanley Bridge was driving a team of white horses and the milk wagon for

The Pure Milk Company. The day he happened to meet Vivian, he was probably heading for the bowling alley in the old market square, which bordered the Grafton Street segment of Dizzy Block, still wearing his rubber boots from delivering milk. Being new to town, the horses taught him the milk route, stopping at the right houses on their own. Austin takes up the story:

> Like Vivian said, we hitched a ride in from Murray Harbour with the minister. It was raining cats and dogs. The poor old fella had a flat tire about half way to Montague. He had a withered arm, and he couldn't do much, so I had to get out with my good suit on and change the tire in the rain. I got soaked.

See? Nostalgia isn't always fun and games, although the Grahams managed to stay married for more than 70 years.

One of the biggest changes over the years has been the decline of the general store not only on PEI but also across the continent. The general store did more than buy and sell goods – it was a hangout for the after-supper loafers, usually men sitting around the stove, chewing Hickey and Nicholson Black Twist tobacco. Since money was scarce and the debit card hadn't been invented, most people bought their supplies on credit, charging their groceries and sometimes not paying for months, until a cow was sold or the lobster season started. Sometimes credit was refused. Keith Pratt was born in 1910 and, with his uncle A.J., ran the general store in Bloomfield Station at the western end of the Island:

> They were good old days but they had their bad spurts just like we have today. A lady up here had a store and her brother George came home from western Canada to settle. Now, he never did any business with us but we were all good friends – we knew it was proper form for him to deal with his

sister. But this morning I noticed him walking up the road with the oil can, kerosene, and he came back. He came into our store and asked, 'Is A.J. around?' I said, 'Yes, he's over at the house, he'll be here in a minute.' So A.J. came over and spoke to George — they were good friends. George said, 'Look – I have to ask you something and I'm ashamed. I went up to my sister's to get some credit and she wouldn't give it me. She put the run to me.' A.J. said, 'Alright, George, what do you want?' And George got what he wanted. Oh, she was a flamer.

I've known a few "flamers" in my time, but I'm not going to mention any names because I'd like to stay married as long as Austin and Vivian. George paid back the Pratts in full and became a good customer. Keith Pratt loved the railway and the trainmen who steamed through Bloomfield Station. He bought a camera when he was a young lad and photographed the engines and crews, and I know he'd agree with Harold Gaudet's memories of the demise of the railway on PEI

Harold was born into a railway family and lived in the east end of Charlottetown near the station. Harold went to work in the railway shops in 1937, a scared rookie among the veteran boilermakers and blacksmiths and section men. Years later, long after the last train left PEI, Harold met an old friend, a steam engine driver, at Zakem's store. Neither Harold nor his old pal thought much of diesel engines:

'Diesels. Hah. Diesels have no personality.' That's what he thought about diesels. I was heading home and I started thinking about it and I thought, you know, that's true. Diesel engine, you turn it on and that was it. Steam engine, you put a fire in it and you could feel her moving and the steam coming...

she come alive. But a diesel engine was like starting a car, just a motor going, and that's it. So, I got
thinking about the first morning I ever went to work
down there, used to be a little gate coming through
a board fence. So, I went down and peeked through
the windows – all broke. Looked in the machine shop
where I had spent so many hours working around
steam engines as a machinist's helper. Broken glass
on the floor, dust everywhere. Ah, it was heart-
breaking looking in there and seeing that. Make
you feel sick to the stomach.

A big strong railwayman, getting all weepy. Who can
blame him for that heart-felt lament? The CNR went out
of its way to erase any remnants of the railway not only
here but across the Maritimes. Stations were torn down
and the tracks lifted before the last smoke had cleared.
The railway was a family, once the biggest employer on
PEI, and the divorce, like most divorces, left a cauldron
of mixed emotions. Incidentally, Harold Gaudet wrote
a lovely little book called *Remembering Railroading*,
and we are all indebted to Allan and Mary Graham who
researched and wrote *A Photo History of the PEI Railway*.
Both books are rare treats.

One of my favorite stories was passed on to me by Dave
Mills whose Dad was the B&B superintendent – in charge
of maintaining the railway bridges and buildings across
the Island. Dave grew up just a couple of blocks from
the Gaudets, and was in the crowd the day the big water
tank that serviced the steam engines was torn down.
This would be in the mid-1960s, about ten years after the
dreaded diesels, which came early to PEI, had replaced
the last of the beloved steam engines. The east enders
thought the water in the tall steel tank was especially
pure and tasty. Folks filled buckets for their drinking
water, and so were watching more than the end of an

era come crashing down that day. When the last support was pulled out and the tank landed on the ground, kids like Dave ran over for a look inside. To their surprise, the inside was a graveyard with the remains of dozens of dead pigeons and other vermin. Maybe that's what gave the water its unique taste. Nostalgia ain't what it used to be.

And neither is Sunday. It used to be a day of rest. The trains, when we had them, didn't run on Sunday. Working on Sunday was frowned upon, as was playing of any kind. One woman told me the only "play" she was allowed was reading a book, as long as it was either *Anne of Green Gables* or the *Bible*. Period. Donald MacKay was born in 1917 to strict Scotch Presbyterian families: MacKay on one side, MacDonald on the other:

> My old aunts who came from Scotland, they never did learn English well you know. My great-grand-father MacDonald in Hopedale — his house is still there — but ah, there was a Presbyterian church in Hartsville, and Rose Valley and Granville [South]. On Sacrament Sunday in summer and the week before they'd have services every night. People would come to Hartsville from Granville and Rose Valley. The service in Hartsville would run for hours. I can remember Presbyterian ministers preaching for two hours. They'd preach, and we'd sing the Psalms without music.
>
> A crowd of people came to my great-grandfather Kenneth MacDonald's in Hopedale for dinner. The springs were running down below the barn where he used to get all the drinking water from. They brought in a bucket of water Saturday evening and set it on a bench in the porch, a dipper above it and if you wanted a drink of water you drank it. So, when they

walked from Hartsville to Hopedale – it would be about three miles – they soon drank all the water. And nobody could go for water on Sunday. The religious people wouldn't carry a bucket of water to the house on Sunday. You wouldn't carry a stick of firewood on Sunday – no fire on Sunday. But my great grandfather Kenneth wasn't a church member so he could get them a bucket of water, so he went down and got a bucket and they all drank it.

Where there's a well, there's a way. Sacrament Sunday was a big occasion, folks catching up on the news since they probably only saw one another twice a year. Strangers were a rare commodity in rural PEI, and were regarded with a fair amount of suspicion. One of Donald's Gaelic-speaking aunts learned enough English to briefly speak to a stranger who came to the door one day, asking directions to Breadalbane. She put the boots to him, exclaiming, "Get out of here – everyone knows the way to Breadalbane."

Speaking of Presbyterians, my distant-but-no-less-loved cousin Kathleen Henderson Jelley was born in the front parlour of the family home in Freeland, Lot 11, in 1913. Kay was the youngest of 10 children born to Annie and Cummings Henderson:

> There was twelve of us, but the first two died. Daddy raised ten children and looked after his mother and father. We had lots to eat and lots to wear, such as it was. I mean we had a good dress for Sunday and we had school clothes but we didn't have money to waste.

> I never was able to smell from the time I was born and the first money I spent on myself, I went to Charlottetown to Dr. Lantz [father of Dr. Brodie Lantz, and grandfather of Dr. Chris Lantz] to see if there

was anything he could do. He said I must have fallen when I was little.

You'd be a good one to do the chamber pots.

> Oh, don't worry I did them all. We'd line them up in the hall upstairs and soak them in some lye. One time, my brother Lloyd came home on Saturday, and a fellow teacher came to visit him and to spend the night. He taught up in Foxely River. He ended up being a doctor, Dr. Grant [Dr. Tom Grant from Montague whose sons and daughters were all doctors and RNs]. Lloyd took him upstairs to show some certificates he'd gotten framed and when they got up to the head of the stairs, there were all these chamber pots lined up. Lloyd was mad at us. I never forgot that. Lloyd thought it was an awful thing but he should have been glad that we were cleaning up and scouring them.

Cousin Kay said she had three things working against her: she was the youngest, she was female, and she couldn't smell; therefore, by default, the chamber pots were her territory.

Does anyone wax nostalgic for the days of chamber pots? Or the two-holer behind the barn? I doubt it. Courtney Maynard from Port Hill told me that when his father built a new house in 1929, he installed a bathroom, complete with toilet, bathtub, and sink. He was anticipating the day when electricity and indoor plumbing would arrive. The neighbours thought he was crazy, but that didn't stop them coming over for a look at the gleaming white porcelain "gadgets." His dad died in 1955, four years before the power lines were run in that end of the Island.

Sic transit gloria mundi, which roughly translated means "worldly things are fleeting," and which I take to mean you can't be nostalgic for something you've never had.

Jill biking on the Confederation Trail near Royalty Junction

The first train rolled across PEI in 1875. The last train left in 1989. The rails in the Borden-Cape Tormentine ferry terminals weren't lifted immediately, faint hope however remote. The old rail lines are now the Confederation Trail, hikers and bikers puffing up the "wet jacket runs" that once sweated up the locomotive firemen heaving Springhill coal into the firebox right through to their jackets. Blueberries and blackberries still thrive along the cuttings, as do apple trees sprung from the cores thrown from passing trains.

Charlottetown is one of several mile-zero stations. Heading west, the first stop is St. Dunstan's, now the UPEI campus. Eighty years ago, and you'd have seen a funeral train gliding past, a "special," heading for the second stop on the line, Cemetery Station.

Who better to describe Cemetery Station but Allan Graham, the son of a railwayman, and the man who wrote

A Photo History of the PEI Railway. And where else but on PEI could you rent a special train for a funeral. And in happier times, a hockey special to take the teams and fans from Charlottetown to Summerside and vice versa. It cost under a hundred dollars to hire the train and crew.

> The original station [was] on the Sherwood Road out by what is now the Charlottetown airport. The reason it was called that is because people went out by the train all draped in black, with the casket in the baggage car and the mourners and friends a passenger car. The train would stop very dignified at the Cemetery Station. All the mourners would get off, the pallbearers would get the casket from the baggage car, and then the whole procession would proceed up the hill to the graveyard.

> The train would wait until they were a respectable distance away and then would start up very slowly and as noiselessly as possible and proceed to Royalty Junction where it would turn very quietly on the wye. Come back in twenty minutes time to pick up the mourners at the Cemetery Station.

Charlie Deighan told me he once fired the engine on the western run to Tignish, arrived back in Summerside sweaty and sooty just in time to grab his hockey gear and then fire the hockey special carrying his Crystals' teammates and their fans to Charlottetown. He played the game, managed to avoid the fight in the street after the game was over – obviously the Crystals won – and then climbed in the engine and fired the train back home to Summerside. Not sure where he and Rose found time to have ten children.

Borden Mooney's father Phillip was a railway section foreman, overseeing the repair and maintenance of the tracks in Peakes, east of Mt. Stewart. Phillip had his own pump car to haul men and equipment. The Mooneys lived two miles from St. Cuthbert's Church in St. Teresa but even in the spring mud season when the roads were impassable, the Mooneys and their neighbours always showed up on time.

> We used to go to church at Holy Week in the spring of the year, bad roads, on the old pump car. Dad would park it over there at the crossroad. They had two cars. They had a flat car they used to haul their equipment on, so we'd put that fella on the rails and then put the pump car up behind it, and the most able fellas would do the pumping and the smaller fellas would get on the flatcar. There'd be twelve or fifteen on the flatcar and four on the pump car.

> It wasn't very good going up because it's all upgrade but I'm going to tell you coming down it was worth coming out for. We'd go over thirty-five miles an hour! It's a wonder we weren't killed! My father done away with it at the last of it. He was afraid someone was going to get killed if it jumped off the rails. Oh, it was all good fun but I'm telling you there were places we were going forty miles an hour.

Borden said his mother used to pray fearfully before church, and then thankfully after church when everyone came home safely. Actually, there was no fear of meeting a locomotive head on. Sunday was a day of rest for the steam engines, too.

Eastern PEI stations had evocative names like Village Green, Hermitage, and Roseneath. Paul Jenkins' first job was with the Royal Packing Company, his family's business, which canned chicken and bought furs and snouts. The province had a bounty on skunks, which paid people two dollars for every snout they sent in. Paul's job was checking the mail every day for skunks' snouts. He decided to give his own snout a breather, and took a job as brakeman on the railway.

> We were on the Murray Harbour line one night in the middle of winter and I did what they called 'overcarry' a passenger. I took him five miles down the line to the next station. We didn't find out because he was on the floor. He was drunk. I didn't see him, but you were supposed to know where your passengers were going and to keep an eye out.

> But in any event, I overcarried this individual and the conductor came up and said, 'So-and-so was supposed to get off five miles back.' I said, 'Well, I didn't see him.' So, we both had to go up and have a talk with the driver who was Jim Leightizer, and who later turned out to be a good friend of mine, and a character. But he made a big fuss about it. Then of course he started to smile, and I could tell he was just teasing me.

> We backed that train up five miles and let that man off. Now if you were in New Brunswick or Ontario, the whole train crew would have been sacked within five minutes because you just don't back a train up on the main line. But the main line between Murray Harbour and Charlottetown is not very heavily populated with high-speed trans-continentals.

High-speed never figured in PEI rail travel. A favorite joke was the one about the woman who had a baby on the Murray Harbour train. Not so unusual maybe, except she wasn't pregnant when she got on. Incidentally, Paul Jenkins eventually decided he'd rather work with dead skunks than dead drunks and rejoined the family enterprises. Through his hard work, Jenkins Transfer Ltd. became a thriving business, and maybe not surprisingly, none of their big moving vans carry passengers.

When the Murray Harbour train did finally steam into its home station, a crowd was waiting.

> Waiting to see who got off the train. Sure. And a friend of mine would be crawling under the platform to look for cigarette butts.

Angus Johnston, aka "the Meatman," and his father ran a butcher shop in Murray River and also travelled the back roads of eastern PEI selling beef and pork from the back of a horse-drawn wagon. Thinking the passengers disembarking in Murray River were grand travellers made sense to a young Angus because, "I was sixteen before I was ever on the train."

That trip was also his first time in Charlottetown, a double whammy. And like a typical 16-year-old, he made a bee-line for the downtown car dealerships including Ives' Studebakers, whose listing in the 1935 Telephone directory oddly reads T.G. Ives Automobiles and Oil Burners, 117 Great George Street, later Elm Avenue, then University Avenue, and now, let's see, oh yeah, Great George Street.

Angus loved horses – he had one named Dizzy Dean after the great pitcher, a charter member of the St. Louis Cardinal Gashouse Gang, and, in 1934, he was the last man to win 30 games in one season in the National Baseball League. That same year, Angus and his dad traded in Dizzy Dean the stallion and the meat wagon for a new Ford roadster from one of those Charlottetown car showrooms. They converted the rumble seat into a meat box and carried on with their business.

Murray Harbour was the fishhook, the end of the line, where the ashes and clinkers in the steam engine were swept out, the fire banked, coal and water taken on, and the train rotated 180 degrees for the journey back to Charlottetown the next morning.

Nearing Charlottetown, the train went through the tiny hamlet of Bunbury, where trees were once milled, and schooners built and crewed. Bunbury only warranted a flag station, the size and shape of an outhouse. If you wanted the train to stop, you flagged it down, just like in the old western movies.

The train snaked its way through fertile Bunbury farms to the railway bridge across the harbour into Charlottetown. The Hamm family owned one of those farms, and the train passed through a wide field close to their farm gate.

> I had a cousin, John Livingstone, he was an engineer on the Murray Harbour train. I'd always see him and wave to him. All the trainmen knew me, and if I was on the train, they'd let me off at my own railroad gate. Before that, I had to go past, right up to Bunbury Station, and then walk all the way back. They'd let me off at my railroad gate and the dog would be there to meet me. My own dog, Sport.

Adelaide Hamm was born in Bunbury in 1902 and lived for over one hundred years. When Addie was a girl, she took eggs packed in buckets of oats to keep the eggs from breaking into town to sell. She got ten cents a dozen, the price of a ticket from Bunbury to Charlottetown.

> Ten cents. To save the ten cents sometimes I walked so I could get some ice cream. So that'll show you how plentiful money was. You'd get a saucer of ice cream and two pieces of cake for ten cents. And that was a treat.

Cake and ice cream at White's Ice Cream Parlour on Kent Street. Livin' the high life.

The high life now is travelling the old railway lines on PEI or anywhere else in the world, steaming along on your bike, imagining the hisses and snorts and the black smoke of a steam engine, barreling along St. Peters Bay awash with pink roses in July, and only one wet jacket run between you and Souris.

Shirts Off Their Backs: Doctors of the Island

Lorne Stevenson

Dr. Stevenson, A.V. Stevenson, my uncle, my father's brother. My wife Louise was the first baby he brought into the world, and my daughter Patsy was the last. What do you think of that now?

First World War veteran and amateur actor Lorne Stevenson from the road to Mt. Thom, New Glasgow. No, not the one in Nova Scotia – the Mt. Thom named for his ancestor in New Glasgow, PEI. The days of the country doctor are long gone. A hundred years ago, every community in the Maritimes had at least one doctor, one blacksmith, and one midwife. In 1967, the doctor came to our house in the middle of the night to see my brother suffering from the croup. Margaret Shaw, born in 1908 and still living in 2018, told me when her sister Phemie contracted rheumatic fever Dr. Murchison from Hunter River made twenty-eight house calls and the bill was $28.

Marguerite Howatt might have known Dr. Murchison. She lived further west on what is now the Trans-Canada Highway in Tryon. Her mum was a midwife who inspired Marguerite's brother Everett to become a doctor and a good one:

She was just the midwife in the community. She was called upon to nurse smallpox cases, confinements, and anyone who was very ill would have her come for a few days to nurse them better. She made all the boys' suits when they went to college. My father made the boots. I used to have to wear them too.

My brother Everett became a doctor and came to Borden. First, he was overseas in the First War and when he came back, he finished going to McGill. He had a call from the Mayo brothers [sons of the founder of the Mayo Clinic in Rochester, Mn] in the United States to go there he was so talented. He won a gold medal at McGill, but he didn't go to the States, he came back to Borden.

With the coming of the ice-breaking ferries in 1917, the port of Borden was fast becoming a thriving centre. Sadly, Dr. Everett Bell only practiced there a short time. He managed to survive the First World War, but died young back home on PEI, a tragic loss for the family and the community.

He wasn't the only Dr. Bell in the area. A few miles further west in Crapaud, Dr. Marvin Bell had gone to the USA to study and was not only a medical doctor but also a dentist. His first cousin once-removed, Charlie Bell, knew his multi-degreed relative:

Actually, he was a first cousin of my Dad's. He studied and got his degree in Baltimore, Maryland. He decided after he got his degree, he wasn't going to practice medicine and go traipsing all over the country, so he went back and took a three-year course in dentistry.

Just imagine what it was like getting teeth pulled back then.

You're telling me! His freezing wasn't very effective. He was rather an individual as they used to say back then. Some of the family would say a little peculiar. For instance, he grew his own cocaine, his own plants, and extracted the cocaine. Today, he would be arrested. Oh yes. By doing this, he didn't have to buy this stuff. I would have preferred that he'd bought the best medicine they had. He made his own teeth too, and actually was a very good dentist. He was meticulous in his work. Today we have electric drills and all that kind of stuff. He used a foot pedal. There was no electricity. The pedal looked like the pedal on a Singer sewing machine. To a nervous patient having a tooth pulled... Oh, dear.

Several of his patients told me Dr. Marvin Bell liked to chat while he worked on your teeth, and as he became engrossed in the story, the pedal that was powering the drill went slower and slower. His patients lived in hope he'd made a strong batch of novocaine.

The false teeth he made were embedded in a recently-invented rubber compound called vulcanite. The patent was held by the Goodyear Tire and Rubber Company. The dentures were held in place by suction cups, which eventually brought a smile to the patient's face. Maybe.

One doctor who didn't mind traipsing all over the country was the legendary Dr. A. A. Gus MacDonald in Souris. Dr. Gus was also a long-time member of the provincial legislature. People have confessed to me that they loved him but voted against him at election time because they said they'd rather have him for a doctor than an MLA. Good reasoning. A doctor might be able to give a stirring speech, but not many politicians could operate on the kitchen table and remove a ruptured appendix.

Brothers Danny and Francis Rose from Lakeville were two of hundreds of people brought into the world by Dr. Gus on what's called the North Side. Danny was the youngest of the family, born in 1931:

> Born in the house. There must have been a midwife, too, because the doctor came later, and he asked my mother what she was going to call me. She said 'Daniel' but she didn't know what else so Dr. Gus said, 'What about Augustus,' so I got my second name from the doctor.

If he was late arriving, by rights you should be called after the midwife.

As well as squiring around his mother, Florence McInnis Rose, a midwife as well as an RN, who trained in the USA, Danny's older brother Francis drove Dr. Gus to and from emergencies in the wintertime:

> He'd always go. He'd go out in any snow storm. You wouldn't get a doctor today to go out. He was a big man. He filled the whole sleigh by the time you got all the fur coats on. There was no room at all. There was a neighbour over here who took appendicitis. They called Dr. Gus, and he put him on the kitchen table and operated on him. Nothing but the old kerosene lamps. You know what that'd be like. He was as good as ever, boy.

That wasn't the first time Dr. Gus operated on a kitchen table by lamplight. In 1908, he famously reattached a young boy's feet after they'd been severed by the cutting blades on a hay mower. It was reportedly the first time that limbs had ever been successfully attached, and fifty years later, the *Boston Globe* ran a feature article as tribute to Dr. Gus, who still had the vase the MacCormacks had given him as payment. The patient,

A. J. MacCormack, had become a schoolteacher walking three miles to school every day. When I asked Pat Hennessey, who had shared a desk with young A.J. at St. Margaret's School on the North Side if he thought Dr. Gus had performed something like a miracle, he thought for a minute and replied, "Yes, but A.J. always walked with a limp."

Like Dr. Gus, other country doctors such as Dr. Lester Brehaut operated on kitchen tables, sometimes by car headlights. And like Dr. Gus, Dr. Brehaut from Guernsey Cove acquired a legendary reputation for his skills and, perhaps as importantly, his empathy. These were country doctors who were country born and bred themselves, so they understood they might get paid with a cord of firewood or the hind quarter of a pig, if at all. Ray Brooks was born in 1911 in Murray Harbour, Kings County, brought into the world by Dr. Brehaut:

> He was quite a tall man. He wasn't a fleshy man. He used a horse and wagon in the summertime, and, in the old days, he had someone drive him around in the horse and sleigh. He done the whole county. My gracious, there were some big families: ten, twelve was a good-sized family, and he brought most of them into the world.
>
> He used to go into the house and give the kids money. I'd like to know how much he was owed in his books. He scratched it all off before he died. No collection.

Apocryphal? Maybe. Often legends are based on fact. Although he wasn't there, Ray was somehow able to quote this story, one of many regarding Dr. Brehaut:

His wife said to him one time, 'Where's your sweater?' He said, 'I don't know.' She said, 'That new sweater I gave you, where is it? You do know where it is.' 'Well,' he said, 'There was a baby born up country and they had no clothes, so I took off the sweater and wrapped up the baby.'

It just happens a lady from Beach Point tells a similar story. Ada Baker MacKenzie was born the day the First World War ended, 11 November 1918. Her first four children were all birthed by Dr. Brehaut:

> When Nellie was born, my third one, he came here with a Mrs. MacDonald, [Edith MacDonald, RN and also a midwife] a nurse from [Murray] River, and they talked politics and things the whole time. He used to be awful to tease people, you know, and get the best of them. But anyhow he was only going to charge me $10, but he wouldn't take it for fear I would need it for myself. Chester [Ada's husband] was away on a boat. It was wartime, Nellie was born in July of '40, and Chester was away, so Dr. Brehaut wouldn't take the $10. No, No.
>
> Dr. Brehaut told me he was at a house one night and this woman had a baby, and there wasn't a thing clean enough he figured he could use, so he took his shirt off to wrap the baby in. And he went out collecting one time, and he had a bit of money on him when he left. And he had no money when he came back. Oh, it was awful, nobody knows.

Dr. Lester Brehaut knew.

Summertime: Boston Visitors and Other Activities

Hendersons of Freeland, PEI

Jim, Jenny, Alice went before she was married. She worked for a minister and his wife, looking after a little girl. Jim, Jenny, Alice, Ken went, Margaret went, Maud went, Daddy went for a while.

Kathleen Henderson Jelley rhyming off members of her family who went to the Boston States to work. Most of her siblings went and as did her father, and Kathleen, born in 1913, went too.

I went away when I was seven, and the only ones who were married there then for us to visit was Jim and Jenny. She lived at Aunt Maud's and Uncle Joe's, Dad's sister. That's where Jenny was brought up. My father's family had Aunt Alice and Aunt Laura and Aunt Abby and Aunt Maud. There was Aunt Lisa and Aunt Maggie and Aunt Mary Jane. That's seven. They had seven and five and we had seven and five. And Mum had ten and six. Ten girls and six boys. The Codys.

With such big families, it was inevitable some would move away. The family farm could only support so many mouths. Kathleen made another trip to Boston a few years later to have an operation, but she came home to PEI, taught school long enough to earn the money to put herself through nursing school, and became an RN. She was following in her mum's footsteps. Annie Cody Henderson was a much-sought-after midwife in western PEI, and had a home remedy for everything, from hives to pneumonia.

My grandmother, Hilda Henderson from Nova Scotia, a distant cousin of the PEI Hendersons, studied to be a Registered Nurse specializing in midwifery in New-buryport near Boston. She had a sister who stayed in the USA, but Grammie came home and nursed briefly in Halifax. As was the custom of the day, marriage ended all chances of her working. When Greta Grigg was born, the midwife was Ethel Maynard, and Greta's grandmother was a midwife in Boston. Greta knew all too well about women carrying the load when those Boston relatives came "home" for the summer visit.

> All Dad's people were in the States, so they'd be one coming every two weeks during July and August. When you didn't have a whole lot, I often think now how hard it must have been for Mum. We only had one spare room and they'd land home with two or three kids and stay for a week. What were you going to feed those people for a week, you know? She would cook and cook and cook the whole summer. No electric or propane stoves, so she'd have the fire on and you know what that'd be like in the summertime trying to cook. Dad was the worst talker in the world. He'd talk you blind. Him and whoever the man would be visiting would sit up, and talk and talk and talk.

I asked if the Boston relatives helped.

Probably wash the dishes. No barn work. No no.

Would they tell you about Boston?

Oh yeah, how good it was. I often said to them, if it was that good, why didn't you stay there?

The cream eaters, as they were so appropriately nick-named, got the cream of the beds and food; their mere presence an honour. Let's honour them with a feed of lobster... aka a hundred years ago as "poor man's fare." Margaret Townsend Crozier, born in 1916 in Grangemount near Summerside, drove both cars and horses, and she knew where to find the cheap lobster.

Oh, I've been driving a car since I was thirteen or fourteen. I can remember taking my mother to Charlottetown long before I had a licence. And one of my jobs when I was a kid at home was on Satur-day. We had an old mare we called Minnie, and Dad would put a box in the manger so I could reach up to put her bridle on. So, I'd harness the horse and wagon, and take two potato baskets and go over to Locke's Shore to the lobster factory.

In those times, they didn't do anything with the bodies. They took off the claws and the tail and the bodies were thrown out into a pen and the men would come with the horse and cart, and take those lobster bodies and spread them on the ground as fertilizer. So, we'd go over there before the men had a chance to get them and I'd fill my two baskets and we'd have lobster every Sunday. In those days, the bodies were worth picking because they were big.

Not sure if they ate lobster in Boston or not. I do know they drank liquor before, during, and after Prohibition. The American prohibition of liquor was enacted with the *18th Amendment* in 1919, and then repealed in 1933. Prohibition started earlier and lasted considerably longer, until 1948, on PEI. In both in the USA and in Canada during prohibition, rumrunning became a golden opportunity to make money, but much of the rum and cheap liquor was consumed at home by people like Roy Clow.

Roy, was born in 1917 in Murray Harbour North, and, when family came to visit, he bought the odd five-gallon keg of rum and bottle of Scotch whisky from one of the many rumrunning schooners anchored out three miles off the eastern end of the Island.

> We had to be terribly careful, leave the shore after dark, no lights and the rumrunner had no lights. You had to find her in the dark. The cutter [the RCMP ship *SS Ulna*] would be there, sailing around, but I never heard of anybody off Murray Harbour being caught by the cutter. Some of them would bury the kegs on the shore; they wouldn't take it away. The odd one would take the liquor in a truck or a big car right to Charlottetown. There was one fella had a great big Dodge car and he'd take five or six kegs. I don't know how many trips he made to Charlottetown and he was never caught.

Some of the rumrunners kept to a regular schedule so you'd know where and when they'd be lurking off shore. A flash of headlights or a lamp in a bedroom window signalled that a convoy of small boats was waiting on shore, powered by five horsepower marine engines, that sometimes ran on boat rum. Roy and his pal George Millar sometimes telephoned the RCMP to warn them rum would be landed at such-and-such a beach that night, and then they'd land the rum ten miles away. Playing games with the coppers was half the fun.

> We were never caught once. One fella, he lived down

in Sturgeon and the Provincial Police, [before the RCMP arrived in PEI in the early 1930s], they give him an awful time. In the spring of the year, he dug holes in the ground big enough to put a ten-gallon keg in. Took all the clay away and cleaned it all off perfect and set a car tire on top of the hole with a board covering the middle of the car tire. Then he put clay on that and his wife planted flowers on it.

One time, the police came and spent the whole afternoon going through everything they could think of, all around the shore probing with steel bars looking for rum buried in the sand. About four or five o'clock in the evening, this fella asked, 'Did you find any rum, boys?' 'No, we didn't, but we know you've got it somewhere.' 'Who told you I've got rum?' 'Oh, never mind. We know you've got it.' 'Look', he said, 'I never deal in rum. You fellas know better than that. Come on in and have a cup of tea.' So, he gave them a cup of tea and some cookies, and as they're walking out the lane past these car tires. he said, 'Lookit there – that's what I spend my time at. The wife and I planted them lovely flowers. Now isn't that beautiful. You fellas coming around here bugging me about selling rum. I've got no rum, for God's sake.'

And a ten-gallon keg under the tire.

Maybe that's where Four Roses Whiskey got its name.

One man took the back seat out of his car so he could pack in more kegs and drove around with a big vicious German shepherd that snarled when anyone came within ten feet of the car. Which no one did. Another trick when the cutter appeared over the horizon – unfortunately for the prohibition officers the *SS Ulna* was coal-fired, and the black smoke spiralling out of its funnel was a warning to the rumrunners – was to put a half-dozen kegs in an old herring net along with several bags of salt, and throw the whole works overboard. Over time the salt dissolved in the water and the kegs bobbed to the surface. By then, the *Ulna* was back in her home port in Pictou.

Now that the cream eaters are liquored up on cheap rum, let's give them one last treat and an appropriate one at that according to Anne of Green Gables:

> *Ice cream!*
> *Is anything more delectable than ice cream?*
> *Why even the most respectable eat ice cream!*
> *It's wonderful on a summer's afternoon in June*
> *Ice Cream!*[8]

Kathleen Wood lived in Victoria-by-the-Sea, loved ice cream, and her dad drove a Model-T Ford.

> Getting up the Strathgartney Hill was tough. It didn't want to go up. Didn't want to go to Charlottetown. I can remember getting out and putting stones behind the wheels until it got enough power up to get to the top of that hill. I stayed with a friend in Charlottetown, an older friend of my parents, and their daughter asked me if I would like to go to Woolworths, and I said yes, I would. She bought me an ice cream cone. I had never had an ice cream cone before. So, I licked all the ice cream off the top of it and after a while she said to me, 'Don't you like the cone?' It wasn't until then I realized one could eat the cone. That was a very exciting time.

Kathleen was born in 1907, four years after Italo Marchiony, an ice cream salesman filed for the patent of a machine to make an "ice cream container," aka the ice cream cone. Marchiony was from New England, so the cream-eaters weren't all bad.

---

8   Herron Campbell, "Ice Cream" *Anne of Green Gables: The Musical,* mojim.com/usy207368x1x4.htm

"They Were Everywhere": Leaving PEI

Louis, Isobel and Bill Cantelo

I had a third cousin twice removed who moved to Boston from PEI. She landed a job working as a telephone switchboard operator. She'd never used a phone before. She and several other women who went "up to Boston" told me all they had to do was say they were from PEI and they were guaranteed a job because of the Islanders' reputation for being hard-working and temperance-abiding.

Over 120 years ago, Arthur Edward Peach observed: "The best and smartest are drawn to the United States. Very soon, there will be more Canadians in the USA than in the Dominion." Unlike his surname, Peach was a crusty, opinionated, and prosperous clothing manufacturer in Ontario. But he was right to worry about outmigration, then, and now, and in between.

> Well, I just wanted to get away. I had a travelling notion on me and so I did a lot of travelling during my time.

Louis Cantelo from Seven Mile Road in south-eastern PEI was born in 1904, and was one hundred years old when he reminisced about the "travelling notion" that took him to Boston.

> There was a lot of work there then and I worked in a woolen mill, working on the cloth, bunching the cloth.

Did you like it?

> No, not exactly. No. I'd sooner a job outside. We got forty cents an hour there and here you'd get a dollar a day with a farmer but you'd only get a day .once in a while.

A 54-hour week meant a pay packet of over $21.00. Steady work meant steady wages, money that was often sent back to help out at home.

I suppose you sent money home, too, did you?

> Ohhh. Not too much.

Louis had a sister and a brother already living in Boston, and where Maritimers congregated, there was sure to be a fiddle and a dance.

> Oh yes, there a dance hall there, just outside of Boston, run by an Islander. There used to be a dance quite often and all the Islanders would meet there. Another place the Islanders used to meet was at the Columbus Avenue Presbyterian Church, met there on Sunday night. That's where my brother got his wife. She was a Nova Scotia girl.

Louis wasn't kidding about his travelling notion. In the 1920s, he went west on the harvest excursion train to the wheat fields of the prairies, and for several winters, he snigged logs with a team of horses in New Brunswick lumber camps. Money was always the motivating factor especially when free spirits like Louis were confined ten miles deep in the woods in no-drinking, no-music and no-card-playing lumber camps.

In 1971, Atlantic Canada's population was 25 percent larger than Alberta's. In 2017, Atlantic Canada's population was 47 percent smaller than Alberta's. Obviously, many situations and issues happened in those 46 years for Alberta's population to become double that of New Brunswick, Nova Scotia, Prince Edward Island, and Newfoundland combined. Oil for one, but outmigration, a scenario that's been played out here in Atlantic Canada for generations, also contributed. Combined. It makes my head hurt. And we're not shipping off the dummies. The brightest and most ambitious leave. It's a wonder we survivors can tie our own shoelaces. OK, I use Velcro, but you get my point.

Heading west to look for a job didn't always mean you had to be Alberta bound. Johnny Reid is best-known for operating JR's Lounge and the Davy Jones Locker restaurant in Charlottetown, and for promoting musicians like Anne Murray and Stompin' Tom Connors at his establishments. But before that he tried a couple of other jobs, including one off-Island.

> I worked in a grocery store after school, at nights and on week-ends. They really didn't need me but they took me on. I was paid a dozen eggs a week. They were just helping me out, I think. Then I got fifty cents a week, then a dollar, then I got two, and I was up to five dollars when the Second World War was on.

> I went over to work in an airplane factory in Amherst, N.S., the Canada Car and Foundry. I went to work there as a riveter and a fitter. I was there about three months and I got fired. Now you're going to ask me why I got fired. I set the factory on fire. By accident, of course.

> Actually, I didn't set the factory on fire — I set a Mosquito bomber on fire. What happened was, my

brother was a news agent on the train and he came from Charlottetown to Sackville, and I went down to see him. I met this sailor when I was coming back to Amherst, and he said he had nothing to eat and no money and he wanted to know if I'd buy this cigarette lighter off him. I didn't smoke nor drink, but it was a brand-new bullet lighter [made out of the shell casing of a bullet]. I can remember as if it was yesterday. I really didn't want it, but he said he was hungry, so I gave him fifty cents for the lighter.

So, I was sitting under this wing that night. I was going to clean the gun turrets out, and they gave me this cleaning fluid, but never told me it was flammable. And I was flicking the wheel on the lighter and the sparks ignited the thinner. The flames were floating around the air, underneath the wing of the plane. Someone came running with a fire extinguisher and got it out, but they didn't know what happened, no one knew, and I didn't say anything.

They had a big meeting in the hangar, five hundred employees, and the superintendent of Canada Car and Foundry was there and he said, 'Who dropped the cigarette in the cleaning thinner?' No one spoke up. And he kept it up, and said he'd fire the whole crew. Well, I was a kid, and everyone was married and had kids, so I couldn't let that happen, so I said, 'No one dropped a cigarette in the thinner. It was me.' And I told them what happened. They suspended me with pay for two weeks while they investigated me to see if it was sabotage. Then they let me go. That's when I came home.

He set up Johnny's Fish and Chip restaurant with the motto "Eat here or we'll both starve," which led to the Prince Edward Lounge, and PEI was never the same.

Kathleen Gillis was born in Indian River in 1914. She came from a long line of Gillises; in fact, both parents were named Gillis, and while they were born in PEI, they met and married in Saskatchewan.

> My older sister Beatrice and brother Stephen were born out in Saskatoon because that's where they settled. My father's sister was already there, Aunt Flora. In the meantime, the next brother to me was born in Boston, because my father decided instead of going back to Saskatoon, he thought he'd get carpenter work in Boston. So, he took off to Boston. My aunt, Dad's sister was one of the first I knew about going to the USA, and it seemed we always went where some of our connection were. And yet, there were babies coming until we were nine kids. So, in the early years, he used to leave the family here and go to Boston by himself to make a living, work, and send the money home.

For years the outmigration route was mostly due south to the "Boston States," which usually meant somewhere in Boston itself or nearby towns like Medford, Waltham, and Lynn. Kathleen went to Boston in the late 1920s, for the same reason her father and aunts went "always to look for work, to bring in a little something to keep the thing going."

Kathleen's father Joseph eventually returned home and tried farming, but in the 1930s, farm commodity prices went through the floor. Like many farmers, he wound up dumping his turnips and potatoes over the bank. He tried raising silver foxes, just missing out on the early boom years. The cages were opened and the foxes were set free.

Joseph Gillis' generation, born in the 1880s, was the first to head west and south looking for work, a trend that continues today. Now our politicians lament the health care burden of seniors who left in the 1960s and are returning home to retire – and ultimately die – in the Maritimes, which as it turns out, is not a new phenomenon.

> My Aunt Martina, my mother's sister, a lot older than my mum, she came home from Edmonton. She went when she was in her early forties. There were a lot of PEI people there and they got finding a man for her, so poor Aunt Martina did marry, a John MacMillan up in Edmonton. When she came back home here, she was ninety-eight and they bundled her off right quick to get her down here. Mum's sister. So, she would tell us how they lived in the old days back home here. They had an old shed loft where they went up to weave, and they would weave yards of material and cut out suits for their brother Joseph who was Father Joseph. They cut the suit for him to go to college to learn to be a priest.

Like hundreds of other young Island women, Kathleen started her working days making a few dollars a month as cheap, disposable domestic help on PEI.

> My first work was in Summerside making eight dollars a month, and I thought I was lucky. Yeah, eight dollars a month.

But once again the bright lights of Boston beckoned.

> I saved money enough and two girlfriends, one from Tignish and the other from around Summerside, wanted a trip for a vacation to Boston, and they asked me would I have some money I could lend them. Oh sure, yeah. They came back and told me that you could make eight dollars a week up there [in Boston]. I said, 'There's where I'm going to go.' And that's what got me thinking about it. And when

they went back to Boston, that's where I stayed, with them, until I got a job.

It was Kathleen's first time off the Island, and to her surprise, the pay was in fact four times what she had been making back home, plus a uniform and two half days off a week.

> It was eight dollars a week and then afterward one of the daughters of Johnny-at-the-Shore [McLellan] came up to Boston, and she got a job right across the street. And she was making ten dollars a week. I wasn't putting up with that. So, I spoke to my lady and told her I wanted ten dollars a week. Well, she thought I was lucky being trained by her. But she came across, and she gave the ten or I wasn't going to stay.

What a woman. All 90 pounds of her, standing up to "my lady," like a scene out of a Dickens novel. Kathleen didn't marry, and after 50 years in the States, she came home to Indian River where she helped preserve local history, the family homestead, and her car. I dropped by to visit one day and all I could see were two feet sticking out from beneath her car. She was tying up the muffler with a piece of wire. She was 95 at the time.

Another smart, independent woman who lived a long productive life was Mary Morrissey, born in Emyvale in 1904. The choices for women were few when she was growing up: nurse, store clerk, secretary, domestic, telephone operator, or schoolteacher.

> When I was sixteen starting out to teach school, I got thirty-five dollars a month, for ten months. It was about the same wages as anyone who was working at the 5 and 10 or any of the stores in town at that time. That's the reason so many of the young girls,

my sister included, went to Boston to work at house-cleaning. Go up and get into a wealthy family there, and they'd give them a decent wage and dress them for their work. Seemed to be an awful lot of them did that, and they used to have their Island parties and dances in Boston. It wasn't unusual to go to a party and it'd be mostly Islanders.

There were dances and fiddling competitions between the Islanders and the Nova Scotians. The Webster boys from Cardigan area were regular fiddle champions. And are still terrific musicians to this day. The story may be mythical but I'm told when former students from Colonel Gray High School in Charlottetown had their reunion a few years ago, so many lived in Alberta, it was more convenient to hold the reunion in Calgary.

Mary Morrissey lived every one of her 110 years on PEI. In her lifetime, she saw huge changes in the way women were treated. In the 1930s when she asked the bank for a loan to buy a Charlottetown store, the bank wouldn't lend her the money unless her husband co-signed even though he had nothing to do with the business. That certainly rankled Mary, but she grinned and bore it, was very successful, and paid off the loan in record time. And never did business with that bank again. Touché.

We started off with Johnny Reid whose various enterprises in the east end of Charlottetown were two streets over from Mary's store. Johnny only went as far as Nova Scotia to find work off-Island. Around the same time, only coming the other way was Sandy Fraser, who left Halifax for a job on PEI.

I was talking to somebody and they said why don't you go to work in the Lord Nelson Hotel as a bellhop. So, I did. I wasn't satisfied there so I went to work at the Nova Scotian when it opened up in 1930. I started as a bellhop, then I got the job as cashier in the office and then clerk, and then night auditor. I worked in the accounting office for a while and, in 1938, they were looking for somebody to come over to Charlottetown as night auditor [at the Charlottetown Hotel, another CNR hotel]. So, I thought this was a chance for me to go over there and perhaps see different things so I came over here and have been here ever since.

When I came over, I didn't know anybody and, at first, I didn't like it, and I was going to go back to Halifax. But anyway, as time went by, I kept improving my likes here. So, I stayed and I don't want to go back to Halifax now because this is home. As they all say on the Island, 'You're from away.' So, I'm not really an Islander even though I've been here a good many years. I'm still from away.

There's lots of Frasers on PEI. Have you ever lied, and said you were an Islander?

Oh no. No no no no!

A pretty honest addition to the Island. Sandy worked his way up the ladder at the Charlottetown Hotel and he retired as the manager. As a young lad, Sandy watched the Bluenose win her first race in Halifax Harbour. He was one of the last survivors of the 1917 Halifax Explosion, and he lived to be 100 years old. And, to take us full circle, his grandchildren all live in Saskatchewan and Alberta.

Where have I heard that before?

Mary MacDonald was also born in eastern PEI, in 1926 near St. Peters, and she had two aunts who were working in Boston.

Aunt Marie and Aunt Marion. A lot of our clothes came from Boston, big barrels and packages from Boston. They taught school, and they sent some beautiful clothes down to PEI. So, we made out not too bad.

The first time you went to visit, was it by train?

Yes. Another girl came with me. I was scared, oh yeah. I had never been off the Island. I missed home all the time.

Mary had a Boston accent that might have been inherited from her father, Carl Wood, who was born in Boston but moved back to the family's PEI homestead when carpentry work dried up during the Great Depression. Or Mary, a school-teacher, might have picked up the accent in the 1940s when she and her husband headed to Boston looking for work. They eventually made it back home to PEI when Mary was offered a job working for a prominent Boston family who had a grand summer home in Keppoch, across the harbour from Charlottetown.

Lester MacLeod's American connection is a bit simpler. Lester was the son of a butcher and cattle-and-produce buyer in Victoria-by-the-Sea. Lester grew up herding cattle and hauling potatoes with a Model-T Ford to schooners and steamers anchored in Victoria's harbour. Lester was also a great hockey player, scoring goals for the Victoria Unions team, and later the Charlottetown Abbies where he was cherry-picked along with Tic Williams in 1933 to go play on a new team over four thousand kilometres away: the Denver Canadians.

Man, dear, Denver's quite a city. Oh my gosh, a beautiful city. At that time, the population was around three hundred thousand. A big city for a young fella.

Lester and Tic boarded the train in Charlottetown, and as the train headed west, players from New Brunswick, Nova

Scotia, Quebec, and Ontario were added along the way. They arrived in Colorado with an all-Canadian hockey team. The red carpet was rolled out, and the players ensconced in plush rooms at the best hotel in Denver.

> A suite of rooms all to myself, right on the ground floor, came out the door right out onto the street. I said, 'Holy Day, this is good.' We got fifty dollars a week and pound.

What's "pound"?

> Room and board. They paid everything. You got fifty dollars for yourself. By jeez we were doing great.

Playing in Charlottetown, Lester had been making ten dollars a week plus all the cigarettes he could smoke. Seriously. The team sponsor was the Hickey and Nicholson Tobacco Company. So, making $50.00 a week with no bills to pay, there was a good chance to salt a few bucks away.

> No. Spent her as she came.

Twenty years old and living the high life in the Mile-High City. Growing up in the middle of Prohibition, Lester was impressed by all the bars and liquor stores in Denver, which was and still is a lumbering/mining/ranching town, only now they now "ranch" marijuana as much as they do beef. The two Prince Edward Islanders settled in, but they weren't alone.

> I met people I hadn't seen for years. I saw them on the Island before they went away and ran into them down there. All kinds of them. God, they were everywhere. One fella was from Albany, a Keough, knew him before and I met him down there.

It gets better. The Denver Canadians moved into a new rink:

The first night we were on the ice to play a game, I was skating around the rink, and first thing I heard was somebody hollering, 'C'mon, MacLeod. You're not peddling meat now!' Gosh, I thought I was hearing things. So, I went around the ice again and I got looking up where this voice came from, and first thing I saw was this fella tumbling down through the crowd – young Muttart from Summerside.

Only an Islander could travel 4,000 kilometres in the middle of the Great Depression and run into "young Muttart from Summerside." Lester broke his leg in that game, wound up in a Denver hospital. He was waiting to get a cast when a nurse stuck her head in the door, asked if he was the Islander. Turned out she was from PEI and she invited him to a party where he met more Islanders, or as Lester put it: "God, they were everywhere."

Maisie Lamont Adams was born PEI in 1913, and she was Canada's first female lighthouse keeper, "manning" the New London lighthouse and raising a family of three on her own after her husband died young in 1943. Maisie lugged buckets of water from a well 200 feet away, and five-gallon cans of kerosene a quarter mile down the beach to the range light. In a pair of Denver cowboy boots, Maisie might have been five-feet tall, but what she lacked in size she made up for in determination and courage. But she wasn't much of a traveller.

I was born right in French River and I lived my lifetime there until I was married and then I lived at the lighthouse. When I put in for the old age pension, they sent me a paper to fill in, where were you this year and that year and some other year, and I missed filling in one little space that I didn't think was necessary. So, they sent it back to me and said I hadn't told them where I was during this lapse of a couple of years.

So, I just turned the paper over and I wrote on the back side of it: 'I was born in French River in 1913, and clear of being on the car ferry once, I have lived in French River the rest of my life.' And they didn't send it back to me.

Louis Cantelo, who in the end came back to PEI, like Lester, Tic, and Mary, told me this story: An Islander was travelling west on the transcontinental express train and got into an argument with an American about the merits of their respective homes. The American bragged, "If we only had a little more rain and a little better society, Kansas would be paradise." The Islander retorted, "Look here Mr. Kansas, I guess that's all hell wants. More rain and a little better society, and it would be paradise too."

Plus, ten dollars a week and all the cigarettes you can smoke.

Times of Milk and Honey

Pure Milk Company Dairy

We had our own produce, our own beef, pork, eggs and vegetables. Potatoes. We had our own wheat and got our flour ground. Otherwise we couldn't have existed. We were well-off people compared to the city people.

Eddie Easter, born near Malpeque in 1905, back in the days when most Canadians lived on a farm and were, for the most, part self-sufficient. They didn't have money but there was always food for the table.

Four meals a day. Supper would be at four o'clock and we'd do a day's work after supper, so we'd be hungry. We'd have a big lunch before going to bed, and what Father wanted for lunch, it never failed: bread and butter, salt herring and buttermilk. He'd eat that three hundred and sixty-five days a year.

Salt herring and buttermilk before going to bed... I toss and turn after eating an Oh Henry! bar. Buttermilk is an acquired taste, like liver and oysters. Greta Griggs told me her father put molasses on everything he ate, even boiled potatoes. Wish I'd thought of that. When I was a kid, I gagged on boiled potatoes and used to sneak them into my pockets. By the time I'd remembered them, the potatoes had dried and seized the pocket shut. Something to cheer my poor mother up on wash day. That is, with six sons, every day.

In my defence, I did love buttermilk, the riper the better. Keith Mutch wasn't a fan of buttermilk, yet ironically growing up on a dairy farm in Keppoch just east of Charlottetown, he was often exposed to it. Twice a week, he and his dad, Hope Mutch, took three, 100-pound milk cans into town to The Pure Milk Company dairy:

> You had to take the milk inside the dairy to dump it. They'd wash the cans with a big steamer and a brush. That was alright, but we used to take buttermilk home again. They made butter there so we used to get hold of the buttermilk to take home for the pigs. Take home about three cans, three hundred pounds, every time we were in.

> Going out to the barn in the morning to milk the Holsteins, first thing my father would do is head for one of these cans of buttermilk. Knock the cover off and tip the can and spill the buttermilk out. Pass it over to me so I could have a nice drink before he had his. Some of that buttermilk was getting fairly old but I wasn't going to be too chicken around him, so down it would go. This was before breakfast, first thing in the morning. We did the barn work and milking, then we'd come in and have breakfast. This was just a little something to keep us going.

In the wintertime, his dad hitched up the team of horses to the box sleigh, hauling hundreds of pounds of milk across the frozen harbour:

We used to take the milk in twice a week, and other people on the route would take it in the other days. You headed down the Wharf Road to the McGarry house. Ralph and Mary McGarry lived there. I went to school with them. Everybody used to go up and down onto the ice there. You had to be careful. Every year, there was a crack in the ice from the railway wharf over to the Southport wharf [still barely visible at low tide]. So, when you'd be going to town with the horse and sleigh, you had to be careful crossing that crack because a piece would break off and you'd fall in. Sometimes the whole team would get into a crack like that, go through and the sleigh would go in, and the load and the two horses. So, you'd have to try to get the horses back out.

How did you get the horses out of the water?

Well, it wasn't easy. They used to choke them – they called it choking or bloating. The horse would swell up with air and that would help float the animal to the surface. Two or three men would grab the horse and heave it out onto the ice. There were a number of livery stables in town [Walkers, Farquarsons, Powers, Larges]. Take them into the livery stable in town to get them rugged-up so they wouldn't get too much of a chill.

Two horses weighed over a ton, plus half a ton of raw milk plus father and son weighing three hundred pounds: about two tons total. Yet, travelling on the ice was common. The roads weren't plowed and shortcuts were welcomed. Every community has a horror story about horses and people going through and drowning. There were currents and springs in every river and bay, so a local man was hired in the late fall when the ice first set to "bush" the safe path across the ice with spruce trees.

It was a dangerous job, and poorly paid. Mac Irving from Cherry Valley told me the man who bushed the ice across Hillsboro Bay was paid five dollars.

In 1945, Roy Dingwell and his wife Jenny bought a one-ton International truck for $1700 to haul milk to the cheese factory in Gowan Brae in north-eastern PEI:

> I paid for it the first year no problem. Today you buy a truck and it'd take you ten years to pay for it. Paid for the truck the first year and had money left over, bought a house and a store and stocked the store. In 1948, you could feed a family of five for $35 to $40 a week. Back when we were running the store, we had two families who dealt with us, and that's what their bill would be for a family of five.

Forty dollars a week wouldn't pay the Lays bill for my wife's chips. There must have been a lot of milk being hauled to the Gowan Brae cheese factory. Jenny was a champion swimmer and used to dive for money off the Souris wharf. Maybe...

Ray Brooks farmed and kept bees in Murray Harbour. The Harbour was the end of the line for the train coming out from Charlottetown. Folks used to go down to the station to meet the train. Ray said some people put on their Sunday best. Murray Harbour boomed in those years. There was Prowse's hotel and several general stores plus lobster factories and a tin can manufacturer.

Up until the 1920s in nearby Cape Bear, the Marconi radio station kept watch over ice and weather conditions in the Northumberland Strait because Murray Harbour was also one of the last schooner ports in the Maritimes. Generations of Whites and Pennys and Harrises all had sea captain's blood in their veins. In the fall, horse-drawn wagons and carts were lined up at the wharf, loading schooners heading to Nova Scotia and Cape Breton. Captain Thomas Trenholm captained the schooner *Nellie Dixon* built in East Boston in 1888:

> Trenholm was a great man to buy honey. I had over two tons of honey one fall. He said, 'If them Whites can sell honey, I can sell honey.' Once they got started, they all wanted it.

How much were you selling it for?

> Twenty cents a pound [in two-pound cans]. Trenholm came and got a lot of honey one day. I said, 'If you can't sell it, bring it back.' He said, 'You mean I can bring the honey back?' I said, 'Yes.' I don't know how much he took but he sold it all. Wally White– that's Hubert's father – would say, 'Boys,' he'd say, 'Boys, I'll give you a can of honey if you buy some of my potatoes. Take two bags and I'll give you a can of honey.'

Sweet deal. Captain Tom told me he hauled the last load of produce out of Murray Harbour by schooner in 1960. Forty tons of potatoes, cabbages, and turnips, and Ray Brooks' honey. He sold the works in Glace Bay and cleared $300. It was the end of an era. Another era came to a sad ending when the famous rumrunning schooner the *Nellie J. Banks* wound up beached on her side on the Murray Harbour shore. To put her out of her misery, someone finally burned what was left of the rotting hull; maybe an empathetic sea captain from the Harbour who couldn't stand it anymore.

One last story about milk. Don't make a face. Not buttermilk. Ella Willis, RN, was born in 1910, and raised on a farm in Hampshire, PEI. Like all farm kids she had chores, and Ella's included doing the morning and evening milking:

We always had cattle, and my father went over to the Green Road and bought this cow from two old gentlemen who lived together. No women around. He brought the cow home and I was supposed to milk the cow. She kicked me and the bucket over, spilled the milk. I just couldn't handle her. I told my father and he said, 'Well, the cow never saw a woman before.' So, the next night before I went to the barn, I put on a pair of my father's trousers. Women didn't wear pants back in those days, it was all long skirts. I tucked my hair up inside a cap, and I went out and milked the cow, and she never moved. It was amazing.

Ella milked by kerosene lantern, and when she started out on her nursing career, she told me she brought babies into the world by the light of kerosene lamps. In the mid-1950s when Hampshire along with most of rural PEI was getting electricity, everyone banded together and held picnics and church socials to raise money to buy the poles.

The end of yet another era... in more ways than one.

Campbell's Soup, Two-Cent Stamps, and Hard Candy: Christmas Traditions

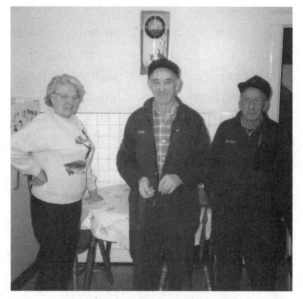

Jenny Dugas, her husband Waldron and
his brother Roy Dingwell, Souris

An apple, an orange and maybe a piece of hard candy.

That was the standard answer when I asked folks from my grandparents' generation what they got for Christmas when they were kids. Several people remembered getting a banana in their stocking, an exotic fruit then, now the most consumed fruit in the world.

Jenny Dugas Dingwell from Souris was what she called a tomboy. She loved to hunt and fish and, in fact, was the first female to land a tuna in PEI waters. Dolls didn't interest her and she made that clear when Santa brought her one:

Christmas I'd get clothes. Boots and shoes. I never wore makeup or jewellery; I hated that kind of stuff. The rest of the girls would get dolls or Teddy bears. I never wanted any of that stuff at all. I remember when I was small, they gave me a doll, the ugliest looking thing you ever saw in your life, and I drowned it. I put it in the rainwater barrel outdoors. They never knew where it went.

Jenny belonged to the generation born between 1890 and 1918 that saw more changes over their lifetime. More than Christmas changed: first cars, first telephones, first radios, first electricity, first airplanes, First World War. Many folks of Scottish heritage didn't have a Christmas tree until they were married and raising a family of their own. So, let's give the reindeer a bucket of oats and head back to the 1920s, to Breadalbane where Donald MacKay's father, Hugh Forbes MacKay, was postmaster:

My father got the job: it was seventy-one dollars a month. He supplied the building, the heat, the lights, and any help. All the family worked in the post office. He couldn't get the mail ready fast enough in the mornings when the express [train] came in. Four mailmen went out from there. One mailman went twenty-six miles every day. He'd leave Breadalbane sometime after nine o'clock after all the mail was sorted off the express. He'd go out through Granville, Millvale, Pleasant Valley, and all around. Twenty-six miles every day, six days a week. I can remember one year that mailman was getting thirty-five dollars a month. Had to have two good horses because you couldn't take the same horse every day on a trip like that. And feed them, six days a week.

When we had the post office, every holiday the post office had to be open four hours. Even on holidays.

Christmas Day and New Years Day somebody had to be in there four hours. At Christmas time, there'd be so much stuff moving, you know. A one-cent stamp went on Christmas cards. Postage for letters had gone up from two cents to three cents. But all the post offices including Breadalbane ran out of one cent stamps, there were so many Christmas cards that year. We had a table at the post office with a pile of hundreds of Christmas cards that had come in to be mailed, and we had no one cent stamps to put on them. You wouldn't put a two cent on because who was going to pay the other cent? But anyway, we had books of two cent stamps left over [when] the postage changed to three cents. There was a hundred to a sheet. Along about nine or ten o'clock, I decided we had to get this stuff out of there. There's more coming in. I took out those sheets of two cent stamps, and I split every one down the centre. And I put half on each card and I mailed all the cards. Everything was paid for. Nobody's cheated. And all winter, we'd get a note every week from Ottawa, the Postmaster General's office, 'Please explain why you cut the King's face in two.' You weren't supposed to cut the King's face in two you know. That's a crime. All winter. My father answered every one of them, the same answer. A short answer: 'Ran out of one cent stamps.'

Eventually the notes stopped and life in the post office went back to normal. Sending Christmas cards is another lost tradition. As is the Christmas catalogue, or any catalogue for that matter. Donald and the rural mailmen and their horses hauled tons of Eaton's, Simpsons Sears, and Holman's catalogues leading up to Christmas. Do people still give a peck of oysters for Christmas like my father and my father-in-law and uncles used to do?

Late every fall, our friend Roy Clow and his pal George Millar worked their way along the Northumberland Strait, digging oysters and fishing capelin to sell in Charlottetown. They lived on the boat, well-stocked with oatmeal and potatoes and turnips. The capelin went to fox ranchers and a pig farmer in Southport. One year, the pig farmer fed his hogs too many capelins and had his pork rejected at the Davis and Fraser meat plant, later Canada Packers, because it tasted like fish. One Christmas around 1930, Roy and George were pretty tired of their diet of oysters and porridge, so they decided to spend some of their cash at a few of the Charlottetown water-front bootleggers:

> There was a bootlegger in there who used to ship rum to Montreal on the train. He put the rum in wooden barrels with a stamp across the top: 1st CLASS OYSTERS. A ten-gallon keg of rum was just the width of an oyster barrel. They'd jam it in tight and he used to put a kind of heavy seaweed, kelp, underneath the keg and on top of the keg and, when they put the cover on the oyster barrels, they nailed them down solid. There was an awful big trade for oysters in Vernon Bridge at that time. I fished oysters there in the fall. He had a stamp that said VERNON BRIDGE OYSTERS or WEST RIVER OYSTERS and he'd ship a whole truckload of rum to Montreal to the wholesalers up there. It all went by train.

Either way, PEI oysters or Demerara rum, you came up trumps. Roy and George always made it back to Murray Harbour North for Christmas. Some people weren't so lucky and, like Postmaster Hugh Forbes MacKay, had work commitments.

Grace Watts Swan was born in Little York in 1920. During the Second World War, she took a job in Charlottetown doing housework:

I had to be in the house at half-past ten at night. Ten times over worse than home. And I wasn't allowed to bring any of my company in there. In the summer, there was daylight savings time in Charlottetown, and in the country, there wasn't. So, my husband was on the farm in York and what would be half past seven out there, was half past eight in town, so he'd be about nine o'clock getting in, you know in haying time and times like that. And I had to be in at half past ten, so... Ahh, dear. And you didn't realize it was such a distance from York to Charlottetown back then. In wartime, there was a bus that went out to the airport on account of the airmen [from the RAF base]. So, we'd get the bus in Charlottetown and go out to Brackley, and then walk the railroad to York. In the spring of the year, it was great: it was all mud roads. The first Christmas that I was in town, the woman I was working for, she was sick, and I couldn't get home for Christmas. I thought I would die. And the train went out every morning so if they had said, 'Well, tomorrow you can go out for the day.' But they never thought of that.

So, you had to stay in town with her? That's a sad Christmas then.

Yeah, yeah. Well, I thought it was, but anyhow.

What kind of money were you making in the 1940s?

Well it's no wonder I'm well-to-do today. Ten dollars a month. But you got your bed and board. No, I got twelve dollars a month there, sorry.

After almost two years of housekeeping, Grace decided to move back home.

So, I said, 'I don't believe you'll get anybody else for the wages you're paying me. And right then, I got two dollars more. I got fourteen dollars a month. 1942, so the Depression was on a long time in my book. It's no wonder you'd want to get married.

Imagine having to lock your spouse out at 10:30. Imagine $10.00 a month. Sorry, $12.00. Imagine trains and buses. Imagine duel time zones within the province. So many changes. The only things the same are airplanes and the airport, where you can still walk the railway line to York. Hard work certainly didn't scare Grace. And she had a great sense of humour. When I asked how getting electricity in the 1960s had affected her life in Covehead where she lived after getting married in 1942, she laughed and said,

> Everything was so lit up. It showed an awful lot of dust on top of the stove. Before that, you couldn't see it, so it didn't matter.

Grace mentioned buses. Gerald Best from Crapaud drove one of the first school buses on PEI: a horse and sleigh in winter and a horse and wagon otherwise. In the spring during mud season, sometimes it was easier to take the sleigh than chance getting stuck with the truck wagon. Gerald was born in 1911, and was 12 years old in the terrible winter of 1923, known by many who lived through it as the Year of the Big Snow. Snow came early and had literally drifted into mountains by Christmas:

> 1923, I remember that quite well. My father went [from Crapaud] to his brother's in Tracadie. The road in them days didn't follow the main road in the winter. It wasn't plowed. Go in this field, across the road, go in another field all the way to Charlottetown. So, he went to Tracadie, and while he was down there the weather moderated. And coming back, he was crossing the telephone line in Bonshaw. The horse broke through the snow and got tangled up in the wires. Fifteen feet off the ground. That's the truth.

He needed reindeer to fly over those wires, and if it had been an elephant instead of a horse maybe it was just trying to make a trunk call.

Let's get back to something we all believe in: Santa Claus and overeating at Christmastime. Every family has their own Christmas traditions, especially when it comes to food. When I was a kid, we always had a big hamper of grapefruit and oranges sent up from Florida where our "rich" Aunt Bee and Uncle Tim spent the winter. We found out many years later that Aunt Bee and Uncle Tim didn't have estates in Boston and Fort Lauderdale. Their rich employers did. Aunt Bee was the cook and maid; Uncle Tim was the butler and chauffeur. But they did send us kids twenty pounds of lovely citrus every Christmas, with a tiny stuffed alligator and a few cotton bolls hidden in the bottom. Exotic beyond belief to us kids.

Anyway, for years, John and Lois Campbell farmed at Graham's Road. Lois had been a Stanley Bridge MacKay before she married Johnny Campbell:

> Big family and oh, we always had all kinds to eat. Mother didn't make big high fluffy white cakes, but she made plum puff and she always made date squares. Nobody could ever beat them. Plain food, but she had a sister who had just one child, and she'd arrive at our place with homemade ice cream and these big mile-high white cakes with lemon filling and fluffy icing. We thought this was great. But my mother could cook like you wouldn't believe, out of nothing. We didn't have any extras like we have today. Her homemade bread was wonderful, and I can remember my brother the minister – he was the oldest in the family and I was the youngest – when he'd come home with his wife, she loved the crust of the new loaves of bread as they came out

of the oven. There'd be four loaves without crusty heels on them.

What's plum puff?

You've never had plum puff? Ohh, I wish I had some here to give to you now. It's somewhat like a raisin pie, made with sticky raisins, the large raisins. It's a layer of cake batter, then a layer of raisin filling, then another layer of dough on top of that. Can't be beat.

What presents would you get?

We didn't get a lot of presents. What you didn't have, you didn't miss. It was rough times. I only had one doll in my whole life. My brother-in-law made a little doll bed. We got that for Christmas one year. We always had a tree and running spruce. My mother would go to the woods and get this running spruce, decorate the house with it, and the smell was just beautiful. We wrote letters to Santa Claus and then put them in the stove and the smoke took the message up to Santa.

Was it the same in your house, Johnny?

At our place, it seemed to be if you liked something. One Christmas, I got half a case of Campbells Tomato Soup, something I was very fond of, I can remember that.

I can't imagine someone named Johnny Campbell eating a soup by any other name. Nowadays, if you gave a kid a Campbell's soup can for Christmas, it had better be one of Andy Warhol's iconic Campbell Tomato Soup can prints. Signed.

John and Lois's son Vern runs the big farm in Grahams Road now, at least the third generation to plow and plant those fields. In 1950, Christmas came early: John traded a horse, five fat cattle plus a $1,000 to buy the family's first tractor, a 22 horsepower Massey Harris. Or, about the same price you'd pay today for a Warhol tomato soup can print. Signed.

It's also a Christmas tradition for sons and daughters to come home for the holidays. Nothing better than Mum's home cooking. Then, let a notch or two out of your belt and put your feet up next to a lovely wood fire to sleep off those calories. Louis MacDonald's mother in Cornwall had their own traditions.

> We had a great big iron pot, half full of boiling fat, and she'd be making donuts. Christmas was roast goose. It was the favourite, goose or duck. And hot mince pie, plum pudding in a bag, and home-made donuts. Fill yourself at dinner, appetite like a horse; the goose would be in the pantry, and I'd go out after dinner and start ripping off more white meat. Eat.

> Well, then, all the holidays, perhaps especially with the Catholics, were a fun time. You had plenty to eat, and you socialized, went playing cards, until New Years.

It wasn't all fun and games. Sometimes Dad had other ideas. Louis was born in 1911 and had four brothers and two sisters. Their Dad always loved to have his boys home for the holidays, and not just to eat:

> There was no insulation in the house, naturally, we didn't have storm windows. Going up the stairs, you could look down right to the cellar. Well in a high wind, the house was like a balloon — she'd rock. So, you imagine the temperature in the house. We used ten cords of wood or more in a winter. Well, one brother George was going to college, and Lee was teaching, so they'd come out for the Christmas

holidays. Well, that was the time to cut the firewood. An axe and a crosscut saw. A great time to get
the winter's wood out.

Even the brother who was a priest pitched in and sawed,
snigged, and chopped the yearly supply of firewood.

~~~~~

Marguerite Cudmore Stewart was born in 1916 in North
Rustico. Her family moved to Charlottetown when she
was a girl, but they always went to her grandparents'
ancestral home for Christmas:

> Going to North Winsloe in the wintertime, I'll never
> forget. One time, we went by train and we landed
> in Milton and Uncle Guy came to meet us with the
> horse and sleigh. The train stopped way up the tracks,
> and we had to wade through this deep snow to get
> to the platform. I'll never forget the hot bricks and
> the straw and the buffalo blankets and everything.
> And the sleigh bells, and the high-back black sleigh,
> going through the pitches in the fields.

You could tell whose horse and sleigh was coming by
the sounds of their sleigh bells.